THE COMPLETE PLAYS OF SEAN O'CASEY

THE COMPLETE PLAYS OF
SEAN O'CASEY

Volume Four

OAK LEAVES AND LAVENDER
COCK-A-DOODLE DANDY
BEDTIME STORY
TIME TO GO

MACMILLAN

ISBN 0 333 37369 3

First published 1951 by
MACMILLAN LONDON LIMITED
London and Basingstoke

Associated companies in Auckland, Dallas, Delhi, Dublin, Hong Kong, Johannesburg, Lagos, Manzini, Melbourne, Nairobi, New York, Singapore, Tokyo, Washington and Zaria

Reprinted 1958, 1964, 1967

Reissued 1984 as *Volume Four* of *The Complete Plays of Sean O'Casey*

Printed in Hong Kong

Contents

OAK LEAVES AND LAVENDER

OR

A WARLD ON WALLPAPER

TO

LITTLE JOHNNY GRAYBURN

WHO, IN HIS SAILOR SUIT, PLAYED FOOTBALL
WITH ME ON A CHALFONT LAWN
AND AFTERWARDS GALLANTLY FELL
IN THE BATTLE OF ARNHEM

CHARACTERS IN ORDER OF APPEARANCE

PRELUDE OF THE SHADOWS

1ST LADY DANCER
1ST GENTLEMAN DANCER
2ND LADY DANCER
2ND GENTLEMAN DANCER
YOUNG SON OF TIME
3RD LADY DANCER
3RD GENTLEMAN DANCER

THE PLAY

FEELIM O'MORRIGUN, *Butler to Dame Hatherleigh*
MONICA PENRHYN, *Abraham Penrhyn's daughter*
MARK, *a Home Guard*
JENNIE⎫ *Land Girls*
JOY ⎰
1ST SPECIAL CONSTABLE SILLERY
2ND SPECIAL CONSTABLE DILLERY
DRISHOGUE, *Feelim's son in the Air Force*
EDGAR, *the Dame's son in the Air Force*
MRS. WATCHIT, *the Dame's Housekeeper*
DAME HATHERLEIGH, *Dame of a manor-house in the West*
MICHAEL, *a Home Guard*
MRS. DEEDA TUTTING, *a Visitor*
3RD HOME GUARD
ABRAHAM PENRHYN, *a Small Farmer*
MR. CONSTANT, *a Resident eager to get his wife to America*
A MAN, *Leader of Deputation demanding shelters*
POBJOY, *a Conscientious Objector*
AN OLD WOMAN OF SEVENTY
FOREMAN IN FACTORY
FELICITY, *a Land Girl*
A SELLER OF LAVENDER

SCENES

———

TIME.—During the Battle of Britain.

Prelude

The room before us shows something like what a central room in a Manorial House of the Long Ago might have been, had we been there to see it. It is gorgeous, but has, architecturally, a chaste and pleasing beauty. Its broad and beaded panelling runs across the walls in simple lines and ovals, so that a dreamy engineer might see in them the rods and motionless shafts of machinery. Two high-up circular pieces of panelling, one on each side of the back wall, have whorling edges on them so that the same engineer might fancy them into germs of revolving cog-wheels. Three great chandeliers, at regular intervals, droop from the ceiling, and the dreamy engineer could see in them the possible beginnings of gigantic gantries. The three semicircular windows at back, the centre one much larger than those at either side, might become, in the far-away future, the head of a great machine, everlastingly turning out fantastic weapons of war. The big bureau might turn into a fine lathe turning out finely-formed tools. The columns round a wide doorway, on the right corner towards the back, might evolve into great ponderous hammers pounding shapes into hard and burnished steel. The wide floor-place below these columns might turn into a mighty coke oven to smelt the steel for the hammers. The end of a grand piano, sticking out on the right — for part only of the great room is visible — might be the beginning of a monster table for the drawing of blue-prints, the skeletons of those things for which the steel melts and the hammers fall. To the side of the window on the right of the back wall, between it and the doorway, stands a tall gold-framed clock that might in the future become a delicate wheel, turning the others, and setting the machinery going with zest and resolution. Above the clock is a circular glass bulb, shaped like the disk of a plain and simple monstrance. All this is hardly seen when the play begins, for the light playing on them seems to come from the ghosts of many candles.

Three couples, dressed mistily in the garb of the eighteenth century, come in dancing, forming a triangle of figures ; they dance to a minuet, the notes played on a piano, a little slowly, and perhaps a little stiffly. The dancers move slowly and stiffly with the melody ; indeed, they dance as if they found it hard to move, and did so as if in a dream ; or as if their thoughts were on things almost forgotten, rather than on the dance. The wide-flowing skirts and high powdered hair of the ladies are dimly grey like the twilight around them, their shapes picked out by narrow lines of black round the flounces and narrower lines following the margins of the bodices. The broad-skirted coats of the men and their wigs are of the same dim colour with lapels and cuffs faintly shown by similar narrow lines of black braid, while from each left hip sticks out a shadow of a sword, slender as a needle, but black like the braid. The music, while faint and low and stiff, strikes a slightly deeper note whenever the couples courtesy to each other.

When the first couple reaches that part of the room close to, and directly in front of, the central window, they all halt and stand motionless, the music becoming even fainter than it had been before. When they speak, they do so in seemingly level tones, scarcely giving any inflexion to, or putting any emphasis on, their words. Their voices, too, are low, a pitch or two above a whisper ; but clearly heard.

Beside the clock, leaning carelessly but gracefully against it, is Young Son of Time, a handsome lad of twenty or twenty-one. He is dressed in a close-fitting suit of vivid emerald green, imagination might think symbolical of youth's earnest and warm vigour ; from his shoulders hangs a deep sable cloak which imagination might think indicative of the *threat of old age bound to come, sooner or later ; and on his head is a conical hat of gleaming silver which imagination again might think symbolic of the remembrance of things past. His voice — when he speaks — is clear and bell-like, and there is a note of authority and finality in what he says.*

1st Lady Dancer [*with a sigh*]. I'm tired ; I shouldn't be, but I am.

1st Gentleman Dancer [*with a sigh*]. So am I ; but we must go on, and hold our own among the shadows.

1st Lady Dancer. I'm cold, too, and I can't see too well. Is the light getting dim ?

1st Gentleman Dancer. Most of the candles give light no longer — look ! their golden glow is gone.

1st Lady Dancer [*echoing*]. Light no longer. Golden glow is gone. Look ! Oh no ; I'm afraid to look. Do not see ; do not hear. Let us move behind.

    [*They all dance slow and stiff again till the first couple is away from the window, and the second couple takes its place. Then the dance stops, though the music, barely heard, still goes on slow and stiff, too.*

2nd Lady Dancer. I am full of loneliness, Nigel. As we came in no crowds pressed against the watchmen and the link-boys to stare at us. The street was empty, and no flame came from the torches the link-boys held, though further on the street was full of sound.

2nd Gentleman Dancer. We need no flame from torches now.

2nd Lady Dancer. But why do our torches burn no longer ?

2nd Gentleman Dancer. Burning torches now are in the hands of others.

2nd Lady Dancer. Hands of others? Whose hands, Nigel?

2nd Gentleman Dancer. The hands of the dull and hangdog crowd.

Young Son of Time [*the clock ticks loudly*]. Time has put them into the itching hand of the people.

2nd Lady Dancer. I'm afraid, Nigel — the guillotine.

2nd Gentleman Dancer. Be at peace, sweet lady : the crowd can never come here ; they cannot harm us now.

2nd Lady Dancer. Hold me closer, Nigel, and let us go. Oh, try to hold me closer.
    [*He takes no notice of what she says, as if he had not heard.*

Young Son of Time [*clock ticks loudly*]. Go ; the clock will never strike again for you. Go, and leave the fair deeds you did to stir faint thoughts of grandeur in fond memory's mind.
    [*These two dancers move away to the stiff tune of the faint music, to give place to the third couple who dance towards the window till they reach its centre.*
    [*From the street, outside, is heard the tender, musical, and low voice of a girl offering lavender for sale in a chant of praise.*

Girl [*singing*] :
        Won't you buy my bonnie lavender,
        Tender-scented tiny flower ;
        Giving honied gardens to the bees,
        Fresh'ning ev'ry passing hour ?
            Lavender, lavender,
        Won't you buy my bonnie laven-lavender ?

3rd Lady Dancer [*in a voice faintly frightened*]. What voice is that ? Something strange touches me from another world. What is it ? Where was it ? Oh, Ned, the deep silences of where we always are force a cry from me that can never come ; and I am frightened. Some sound is hurting me. It is so sad no sign is left to show the strength we had, or the grace and elegance that led it forward.

3rd Gentleman Dancer. The world shall never lose what the world has ever given.

3rd Lady Dancer. Not a single torchlight in the street ; not a glow from a single window ; not a solitary gleam from a welcoming doorway. When we were there, the place was gay with torch and candle. Oh, Ned, it is very dark !

3rd Gentleman Dancer. It is dark to us ; but Goldsmith, Berkeley, Boyle, Addison, Hone, Swift, and Sheridan still bear flaming torches through the streets of life.

3rd Lady Dancer. But the common crew can never see the flame. [*A slow red glare appears in the sky ; a point of deep red in the distance, thinning to a mauvish-red gleam as it shines through the window, touching, with a wan warmth, the dim grey costumes of the dancers. With a faint start.*] I feel the colour change ! What is it ? And afar is anxiety and woe. What sends this sense of danger to us ?

3rd Gentleman Dancer. It comes from those who came from us, for England is at war.

3rd Lady Dancer. No, no, not war ; the flame of war could never light up London.
    [*The two other couples come closer to the window, though*

the three couples stand still in a triangle, the apex formed by the third couple at centre of window.

2nd Gentleman Dancer. Look ! The buildings topple like the town of Troy. The flames get wider. The enemy is striking home to England's inmost heart.

2nd Lady Dancer. Oh, let's go on dancing, and never look again.

1st Gentleman Dancer. Look ! There, in the midst of the red foliage, the dome of St. Paul's stands out like a black and withering lotus blossom !

1st Lady Dancer. Oh, Maurice, is England and the world to lose the glow from a thousand tapers, the colour-shining vestments of the bishops, the jewels in altar and gems in cross, the chorus of sacred song, and the blessed peace of public absolution !

1st Gentleman Dancer. And the gay jest from careless lips of gallants on the pompous steps outside.

2nd Gentleman Dancer [*stiffly putting right hand to his left hip*]. Where are our swords ?

3rd and 1st Gentlemen Dancers [*echoing him*]. Where are our swords ?

Young Son of Time. They lie resting, rusting deep where no man wanders now.

2nd Gentleman Dancer. Where is Marlborough and where is Clive ?

3rd Gentleman Dancer. Where is Wolfe and where is Wellesley ?

Young Son of Time. England's orphan'd of her greatest men. She is alone at last, and she is lost.

1st Gentleman Dancer. The shadows will go forth to fight for England.

Lady Dancers [*together*]. But where are your swords? [*Sadly*] All that's left us is a fainting memory of love.

Young Son of Time. Time has brought a change. The silken things that sheltered rosy bodies are in rags; the rubies, flushing shy on milky bosoms, have gone to dust; and the needle-pointed swords, all hemmed with jewels, that a common man might deem it joy to die on, are blunt and leaden-bladed now.

1st Lady Dancer. Let us dance, let us dance, and never seek a glance at anything.

2nd Lady Dancer. Let us dance, and try to glide to things remembered.

3rd Lady Dancer. Let us dance, always near, but never close together.

> [*They resume the slow dance of the minuet, and gradually pass out of sight. As they dance, the voice of the Lavender Seller is heard again, chanting her wares, her song ending just as the dancers fade from view.*

Lavender Seller [*singing in a low, rather sad voice*] :
Won't you buy my bonnie lavender,
Ladies, for your fine chemises?
Its fragrance rare will make them finer still,
Tempting close the hand that pleases.
Lavender, lavender,
Won't you buy my bonnie laven-lavender?

END OF PRELUDE

ACT I

The dancers are no longer there; and mild lights, that have been shaded slightly to reduce the power of their glow, show us the room plainly. It is as it was when the shades were dancing, though the panelling seems a little stylised away from its normal lines and curving. Feelim O'Morrigun and Monica Penrhyn are busy handling stuff to make a blackout for the window on the left, the central window and the smaller one to the right having been already covered to their satisfaction.

Feelim is a man of forty-five years, wiry, slender, and as cunning as a fox (except when he is in a temper), which he somewhat resembles with his thin protruding nose and reddish hair, now tinged, though very slightly, with grey. He is dressed from the waist up as a second-hand butler might be, creased black swallow-tail coat, black waistcoat, white shirt, and black tie, the bow askew; below these he wears the trousers and leggings of a Home Guard. Monica is a young lass, sweet and twenty; pretty face, well-made body, bright eyes, a little pensive at times. A girl who would be able to concentrate on what was actually before her to do. She is dressed in a neat brown skirt and a bodice of a warmer brown. All are partially concealed by a rough unbleached apron. A gaily-coloured scarf covers her brown hair, and round her arm is a white band with a tiny red cross in its centre.

Monica. I wish you were my dad, instead of my own. I've borne with him since I was ten, when my mother, too tired to go on, left the pair of us to make the worst of it.

Feelim. Strange, isn't it? I miss my own old girl far

more than Drishogue misses his mother. Odd man, your old man. His conscience is a menace to most people. I never could understand men interested in religion.

Monica. We'd better stir ourselves.

Feelim. It wants near a half-hour to blackout yet. How's Mary ?

Monica. Going on fine, though she won't be able to do much for a while.

Feelim. Fool ! Putting a blackout up in th' dark, an' steppin' from th' window-sill on to a chair that wasn't there ! An' how's Tom ?

Monica. Going on fine, though his hand won't let him do much for a week or so.

Feelim [*venomously*]. Another fool ! Not able to drive a nail into wood without shoving his hand through a window and cutting a vein open ! Th' house'll be an hospital before this blackout's finished. [*Something tumbling is heard outside, followed by the crash of breaking glass. With venomous resignation*] Oh ! There's another casualty now !
  [*Mark, of the Home Guard, rushes frantically in through the door faced by the columns. He is in rough civilian dress, wears a khaki forage cap, and has a wide khaki armlet with the words " Home Guard " on it in black. A tall, well-knit man of twenty-seven.*

Mark [*excitedly*]. Miss Monica, quick, come ! One of the men cloakin' a window, top of chair, top of another, top of a table, 'as pitched down, lookin' like 'ee's broken back, or somethin' !

Feelim [*clicking his tongue in exasperated disgust as Monica runs out with Mark*]. Dtch dtch dtch ! The foe'll do less injury to us than we're doin' to ourselves !

> [*Two Land Girls come in by the door with the columns. One is named Jennie and the other Joy. Jennie is a sturdy lass, inclined to be slightly florid, and though she is fairly well educated as things go, having had a secondary schooling, she is at times somewhat rough and strident in her manner. She is enticingly shaped, even a little voluptuous-looking. She has a head of thick, dark, honey-yellow hair which she often tosses aside when she feels it clustering on her forehead. She is twenty-four, full of confidence, and likes to be thought a little Rabelaisian. Her companion is plainer, not so confident, ready to follow Jennie and look up to her. Her brown hair is straighter, but is at present in the grip of a permanent wave. She is slimmer, and, though she enjoys any coarse sally from Jennie, she tries, at times, to appear to be very refined. She has had to be satisfied with an ordinary Council School upbringing, but she is a country lass, and no fool. Both wear brown breeches, high rubber boots, brown smocks, with coloured kerchiefs, fixed peasant-wise, around their heads.*

Jennie [*weariedly*]. Oh, God, I'm tired ! Every bone and nerve in me is aching.

Joy. So's mine. Suppose we'll get used to it in time.

Jennie. Long time, dear. [*To Feelim*] Give two worn-out girls a spot of gin an' apple-juice, will you ?

Feelim [*going to bureau to get the drinks*]. An' then go up to have a rest, an' get outa th' way here where people have to work !

Jennie [*scornfully*]. You don't know what work is. You

should work among cows. [*To Joy*] You'd want to be born with animals like cows, dear. Study their likes and dislikes, says the farmer. If you do, he says, you'll get better results from the feedin' you give them. D'ja know what he told me ? The highly-strung cow always makes a good milker. J'ever know the like ! Film stars aren't in it with cows. Thank God I'm off the job with cows. Too temperamental for me, my dear. I'm not sure yet whether a thousand-gallon cow's one giving a thousand gallons a year, or a thousand a week ! No, I said, take me off cows, and put me on the hay.

Joy. We saved the hay anyhow.

Jennie. We did ; but that'll be forgot, while the failure with cows will live after us.

Joy. Let it, dear.

Jennie. Hear, hear ! [*To Feelim, who hands her a drink*] Thanks. [*As she stands near window, she sniffs gently.*] What scent is that now stealing in through the window ?

Joy. I don't smell anything. Scent of hay from the ricks, maybe.

Jennie [*sniffing again*]. No, not hay, old or new. Lavender — that's what it is — lavender ! Must be a bed of it somewhere. If mother knew what's going on, now, she'd have a fit ! When there's a war on, you can't turn a hot day of it into a holy or a silent night.

Joy. Hard, dear ; but us must do our best.

Jennie. When a girl's beneath trees with a moon flitting in and out of the branches, there's sure to be someone

singing a bar of love's old sweet song somewhere handy.
[*To Feelim*] What d'ye think, old emerald isle ?

Feelim [*coldly*]. I'm not listening, thank you.

Jennie [*mockingly*]. Aha, my boy, I've seen your roving eye
often trying to glimpse what was under the green
jersey. Well, I don't blame you. [*She drinks.*] It's
hard when hand can't follow the eye to start the first
few notes of love's fiddle fantasia. [*She sings :*]

> When we stretch'd ourselves down in a hurry,
> Beneath th' soft shade of a tree,
> Th' moon threw her mantle of silver
> O'er red-headed Johnny and me.
>
> Stars twinkled a welcome, and wonder'd
> How we far'd under Cynthia's shawl ;
> No girl ever suffer'd such pleasure,
> Since Adam gave Eve her first fall !
>
> Ho, then, for young man and maiden —
> Fair jewels of love fiercely aglow —
> Who save life eternal from fadin',
> An' keep a tir'd world on th' go !

Feelim [*disgusted*]. Dtch dtch !

Joy [*pretending to be shocked — but unable to stop a giggle*].
Jennie, you're terrible !

Jennie. Shakespeare, my dear.

Joy [*astonished*]. Is it ? Us always thought he was a
highbrow.

Jennie. Seems he went over the shallow end sometimes.

Joy. Where does that saucy bit occur ? Us ud love t'
read it.

Jennie. Ask me another ! Let's go an' have a rest — we have to meet the boys later on, y'know.

Feelim [*to Jennie as the girls are going out*]. I wouldn't be messin' round after Mr. Edgar — his mother doesn't like it.

Jennie [*savagely — as she goes out*]. She can lump it !
  [*With an expression of hurt disappointment on his face, Feelim goes back to his work with the blackout as Monica returns to help him.*

Feelim. Well ?

Monica. Nothing much ; little shock and sprained arm — that's all.

Feelim. God help me, but wasn't I a fool to come here at all !

Monica. Is the thought of the bombing getting you down ?

Feelim. Bombing ! Not the bombing — the people. Bombing'll never frighten me.

Monica. There's nothing to be ashamed of in a little fear. I've gone through a little of it, so I know.

Feelim. It's the people — not able to do anything without breakin' back, arm, leg, or something. Oh, amn't I sorry I came !

Monica. Why did you come, then ?

Feelim. If I knew why, one of th' world's mysteries would be solved.

Monica. But you must have had a reason for coming ?

Feelim. Of course I had — I wanted a job, and the

owner here wanted a capable man, so the two extremes met.   There's not much to choose from in Knock-nawhishogue.   I happened across an English paper advertising for a butler in a house of six servants ; so, fearing there wasn't too much to be done, I replied, sayin' I was fully qualified, though all my credentials went down in a torpedoed ship.

Monica [*interested*]. You have been through something, then ;   I'd never have guessed it.

Feelim. I felt it worse than me friend who told me about it, for he was all right afther a week of hot blankets an' brandy ;   but I'm not quite th' betther of it yet.

Monica [*astonished and doubtful*]. You weren't, yourself, flung into the sea, then ?

Feelim [*astonished*]. Me ?   No, not actually, for I wasn't in th' ship.

Monica [*disillusioned*]. Then how the hell could you be as bad as the poor man sodden to the soul in sea-water ?

Feelim [*resentful*]. Amn't I afther tellin' you, I was worse than him !   Have you no imagination, girl ?   Hadn't he th' elation of comin' safe out of it all, while I'm stuck strugglin' in it still ?

Monica [*mystified*]. Stuck struggling in what ?

Feelim [*irritated at her want of understanding*]. Aw, th' wather, woman !

Monica [*dubiously*]. I see.

Feelim. Near time you did.   Well, we better get this up. [*He goes to the window with blackout.*]   Hope it'll fit. [*He cocks his nose into the air and sniffs.*]   What's that I smell, now ? [*He sniffs again.*] Lavender. It's here, too ; seems to be all over the house.

Monica [*suddenly and with roughness*]. Oh, shut up, man ! It's not lavender you smell. And if it be, keep it to yourself, keep it to yourself !

Feelim [*astounded*]. What's gone wrong with you, girl ?

Monica. I don't believe it, I don't !

Feelim [*a little frightened — going closer to her*]. Don't believe what, woman ?

Monica. The old wife's tale that whenever death is near, the scent of lavender spreads over the house, and shadows of men in knee-breeches and wigs, with women in out-fanning skirts, dance silently in the bigger rooms of the manor. Dame Hatherleigh's as full of it as she is of her British Israel and the lost Ten Tribes.

Feelim [*startled*]. Here ? Do these ghostly dancers assemble here ?

Monica. Here ; I tell you, I've never seen them ; never !

Feelim [*awestruck*]. Is it tellin' me th' house is haunted y'are ?

Monica [*shaking his arm*]. It's superstition, man. Don't believe it.

Feelim [*in anguished tones*]. Oh, I guessed there was a snag in it ! Come over at once, says Colonel Hatherleigh in his letter to me ; an' quite jovial about it, too. Come along, old boy, says he ; almost anyone'll do me now. You'll do fine, says he, if you can do anything, for the place is destitute since my poor man died so unexpectedly. [*Catching Monica's arm excitedly*] How did th' man die ?

Monica. Blast from a bomb blew the poor man over the highest barn in the county.

Feelim [*angrily*]. An' why wasn't I informed of all this ? Oh, what an innocent, poor gobeen I am, too, to be coaxed into this thrap ! An' I insistin' me son should come, too, without an inklin' that he was itchin' to get into th' Air Force, where he is now. Uncivilised duplicity everywhere ! An' while Colonel Hatherleigh hied himself off to th' ease an' comfort of th' front, here I'm sthranded with his wife, an' women set to talk me into a wild dilerium ! An' all for a job in a house haunted by night, an' a bedlam by day with workers on th' new aerodrome, Home Guard units, air-raid wardens, first-aid post, Land Girl hostel, an' rest camp for th' bombed-out an' evacuees ; with me in th' centre an' on th' fringe to keep harmony an' ordher !

Monica [*impatiently*]. For God's sake, let's forget about this old wife's fable !

Feelim. How ?

Monica. By working to get the blackout up.

Feelim. It's gettin' too dark to see proper. I'll switch th' light on — a second won't matther. Dim twilight makes me feel a trifle queer. [*He turns down switch, and a bright light glows among the chandeliers.*] That's betther.

1st Constable [*outside — with a roar*]. Put out that light !

Feelim [*as he runs and turns up the switch again*]. God Almighty, there's a constable behind every bush here !

Monica. We'll manage all right ; hand it to me when I get on the ladder.

> [*She mounts the ladder, and Feelim hands her the blackout to be put in its place.*

Feelim [*suddenly going tense*]. What's that ? Is that a rustle o' skirts behind me !

> [*Dillery, a constable, appears behind them, and shines a torch to where they work.*

Dillery. You can't be puttin' on lights sudden-like ! I suppose you know it's an offence to show an un-obscured light ? Us'll 'ave to report if it happens again. An' window above 'as a seam of light showin' left side. Better settle she at once. Suppose you know seam can be seen five miles up sky ? Us 'as given a last warnin', mind ! [*He goes out again.*

Feelim. Fuss an' fury. God must ha' had a rare laugh when He made a serious Englishman.

Monica [*bending down from ladder towards Feelim — tensely*]. You didn't really hear it, did you ?

Feelim. Hear what, hear what, girl ?

Monica. The seductive rustle of the skirts ?

Feelim [*upset again*]. Yes ! No ! No, no ! Why d'ye keep puttin' it in me mind ? [*Monica is silent.*] Why, why d'j'ask me, I'm sayin' ?

Monica. Only to sense the perfume isn't so bad as to see or feel the dancers.

Feelim [*very frightened*]. I'm sure I saw them ! Pale figures whirlin' about in gay-coloured skirts — their flounces touched me face !

Monica. You didn't see, you couldn't have seen them ! They don't have bright colours : grey and shadowy they all are. Like young Sir Nigel.

Feelim. What Sir Nigel, which Sir Nigel, whose Sir Nigel ?

Monica. Him whose picture's in the corner there : who kissed his bride, and spurred away to fall on the field of Blenheim.   Less'n a year after, they saw her rise to dance with a young gallant in grey, swooning when the grey shadow faded out of her arms, to die an hour after, murmuring that eternity would open and end for her dancing in the arms of Nigel ; in this room ; in this very room.

Feelim [*awestruck*]. In this very room ! [*He crosses himself.*] Jesus, Mary, an' Joseph between us an' all harm !
   [*They remain silent and still for a few moments ; then Feelim, to conceal his fear, gets angry.*

Feelim [*angrily*]. Why do you keep harpin' on these childish rumours, girl ? You'll be gettin' yourself down if you go on. What's it to us how a damsel died two hundhred year ago ?

Monica. She's still a symbol of a thousand girls kissing a lover farewell, while chafing Death, at his elbow, waits to guide him safely to the battlefield.

Feelim. Ever since you came into the room you've been screeching about death ! It's gettin' a bit monotonous. If what you say's thrue, a house like this shouldn't be left standin'. Thry to be a little livelier, a young one like you. [*As she slowly raises the blackout to cover the window*] Oh, fix it, fix it, till we get a comfortable light in the place ! [*She hangs it up.   The moment it's fixed, he rushes over and switches on the light.*] There's a wee slit of light to the left ; hammer a nail in to keep th' cloth close. [*He hands her hammer and nail. Some moments before, the faint tramp of marching men is heard, becoming louder, till it sounds close to the window.*] Th' Home Guard pit-pattin' about again ! Old men manœuverin' themselves into an early grave. I wonder Dame Hatherleigh lets them make a playground of her grounds. [*Up to Monica*] Go on — why don't you nail it ?

Monica. My hand's trembling !

Feelim [*irritated*]. What's it thremblin' for ? If you go on, I'll soon be as bad as y'are yourself. Get down, and I'll do it.

   [*The tramp of regular marching feet is heard loudly now, accompanied by orders shouted by the leader of the company, as Monica comes down the ladder, and Feelim goes up. The leader's commands are given in stentorian tones, the first word being slightly drawn out, the second delivered in a roar.*

Home Guard Leader [*outside*]. R-i-g-h-t wheel ! [*More quietly*] In the line, in the line. Left, left. [*A roar*] A-b-o-u-t turn ! [*Short, sharp tone*] Left, left, left. [*Quietly*] In the file, in the file.

Feelim [*clicking his tongue in scorn*]. Dtch dtch ! It's pathetic. They think they're marchin' through Georgia.

Leader [*in an extra loud order*]. L-e-f-t wheel !

   [*There is a crash of breaking glass. Feelim slips quickly down the ladder as the spearhead of a pike shoots through the window he is covering.*

Feelim [*soberly, but in anger*]. See that ? They won't leave a single thing whole in the place before they're done. It's only by God's mercy that I wasn't impaled !

Voice of 2nd Constable [*outside — shouting*]. Put out that light !

Feelim [*running over to the switch to do so — in anguish*]. Ooh ! There's the eye that never sleeps again. [*To Monica*] Shove the blackout into its place, and we'll do something to the broken pane tomorrow. God only knows what damage would be done were these fellas armed with slings and smooth pebbles from a runnin' brook. Danger from within an' danger from without. [*He switches on the light again.*] Now we can see through the silly, sombre fantasies of the darkness.

Monica [*seriously*]. I hear Drishogue and Edgar coming — I shouldn't say anything about the dancers. No use of letting sad thoughts invade the quiet liveliness of their outlook.

Feelim. Is it me mention it ? Even if I did, Drishogue wouldn't believe a word of it, no more'n meself. And I've something else to think of beyond shadows — where's me schedule ? [*He searches on the table.*] Here it is. [*He runs a finger through the leaves of an exercise-book and reads from it.*] " Stirrup-pump class ; Fire-drill exercise ; Gas-mask practice ; Discussion on Hens most suitable for people and disthrict ; Red Cross meeting ; Dig for Victory Committee " ; no end to them. [*To Monica*] Monica, darling, for all we know, sinisther persons may be playin' thricks about the house, an' it might be well to put a Home Guard man on duty at nights.

Monica [*warningly*]. Sshush !

or displayed on their chests like Bulat, who was in front of the horde, chanting that word—*vedma*.

"It was her! She did it!" shouted Bulat. "Baba Yaga flew up to my sister's bedchamber in a cloud of smoke just as night descended and abducted her in her mortar!"

I was truly mystified. Flying? In my tiny mortar?

"Why would she abduct your sister?" Yersh, the village elder, stepped forward. Before Zora's arrival, I had treated his gout.

"Why do you think?" demanded Bulat. "The witch is in love with me and was desperate! Give up my sister, vedma, or face my wrath!"

I scoffed just as his eyes fixed behind me. "Sister, thank God you are alive!" He beckoned to her. "Come, the vedma can no longer turn you into a statue!"

I could not help smiling. I searched for the answering smile in Zora, who had come to stand beside me. But her head was lowered, her hands drawn over her breasts, the shift billowing about her legs like the skirts from the night before. Uncharacteristically meek, she started to walk— toward her brother.

"Zora?" I whispered, my insides curdling with dread, with heat, with hurt.

She stopped at Bulat's side. Her eyes, strange and purple, met mine for a second before flicking away. Bulat threw a protective arm around his sister's shoulders, and I understood all. Bulat had orchestrated for Zora to flee from him, knowing she would seek me out, and I would not deny her. He had long blamed me for corrupting her. Now, he could act the savior *and* demonize me, an evil vedma, Baba Yaga, a lonely woman living by herself. And Zora had merely been able to recognize when she had lost.

Afterward, I discovered the lies Bulat had spread about me—that at night, I wore a toadskin cap and a snakeskin coat, that fangs and nostril hair grew in my sleep, that I had horns on my head and huge ears.

But that night, all I could do was stare at Zora. This had been my friend, a woman whom I had helped, and she had gone along with her she be the last. "Bulat," I tried again, "we have known each other a long time. Do not force your sister into—"

"Hand her over, vedma."

I blinked, not knowing the word. Suddenly, there was a glimmer—from a cross, all in gold, hanging near his heart. I had seen such crosses before, on buildings that had sprung up with domes shaped like onion heads and bright colors putting the rainbow to shame. A new religion with a new god had been spreading across Rus' for some time, since before the start of the millennium when Vladimir the Great had brought Christianity to Russia and destroyed the shrines to my gods that he himself had erected. Even the idols on the hills of Kiev dedicated to Mother and the other major gods. But I didn't know much about it; most people continued to worship the old gods.

My eyes did not stray from his cross. "If you cannot be reasoned with, Bulat, then you should leave."

He stomped his foot, his red face reddening even more.

But he was inherently a coward, all his battles fought by his soldiers, and he left soon after. I did not know he would be back, and not alone. That night, I jolted awake suddenly. I glanced about, still in a haze. Zora and I had fallen asleep on the pech, huddled together for warmth. She raised her head sleepily as I stood.

"Stay hidden, Zora," I told her, approaching the window.

In the chink between the shutters, orange light flickered. I tightened my hold on my shawl and, with extreme trepidation, unfastened the shutters.

Outside, torches blazed, illuminating the crowd gathered in front of my izba.

There was no time for fear. Not caring that I was in my shift, begging my heart to stay steady and my head clear, I threw open the door. The crowd gave a great big roar, then surged toward me until I felt their heat, sensed their hands on me, heard their shouts in my ears, loud and jarring. They thrust their pitchforks and blades into the air with a treacherous glint. Their wooden crosses, too, which they hoisted up on their shoulders

[*Drishogue and Edgar come in slowly, looking rather bored. When Drishogue sees Monica his face brightens into a wide smile. He is a tall lad of twenty or so; a thoughtful, tense face, which is somewhat mocked at by a turned-up, freckled nose. Edgar, nearly as tall, is of the same age; his face is plump where Drishogue's is lean; careless good nature, and, perhaps, less imagination, tends to make it, maybe, a trifle too placid. The two young men wear the uniform of Air Force Cadets.*

Drishogue [*sighing with boredom*]. Well, we'll know soon; as for me, I know I've passed the tests. Oh, how I long to take the sky by storm! [*Going over to Monica — eagerly*] Monica, dear, are you going to work all night? I thought you'd be ready to come out an hour ago.

Monica. I won't be long now; I'll run off and change.

Edgar. If you see Jennie, tell her I'm waiting here.

Monica. I'll tell her; she's resting; we'll probably come down together.   [*She goes out.*

Edgar [*to Drishogue*]. A bonny lass, boy; and a brave one, too.

Feelim. Sensible and sound enough, if her mind wasn't adorned with a lot of nonsense.

Drishogue. Nonsense? What nonsense?

Feelim [*carelessly*]. Oh, a restless readiness to believe that the deeply dead, who once lived here, can come again to counterfeit in shadow the life they lived before; and men as shrewd as we can hear the silent stir of their ghostly dancing.

[*There are a few moments of silence as Drishogue and Edgar look at each other.*

Drishogue [*to Edgar*]. There, I told you! I'd swear I heard last night the timid music of a frightened minuet.

Edgar [*with good-natured mockery*]. Newcomers always hear strange things in an old house, Drishogue. They expect them, and they come ; a Londoner here, recently, swore he saw shadows in his room peggin' away in the Lambeth Walk. If Feelim sees them, he's sure to see them doing an Irish jig. Let's be sensible : the past is gone for ever, and can never have any influence upon us. A new life, broken from everything gone before, will shortly be before us.

Drishogue. No, Edgar, you're wrong : the past has woven us into what we are. [*With a yawn*] How I wish the fight to come closer ! This coloured idleness is killing me.

Edgar. Take care ; you may get your wish. This idleness is giving us a longer life. Eight weeks — the average life of an airman : not long enough for me. I don't want to come toppling down in the drink. I can endure many more evenings with Jennie.

Drishogue. Don't you ever get tired of walking or lying with Jennie ?

Edgar. Often ; but with her the tiredness is always restful. She's grand for the time being.

Drishogue. But you don't value her enough to want to spend a lifetime with her ?

Edgar. Well, hardly ; in the cool of the evening, in the deep dusk of the night, she is lovely ; but I shouldn't care to have to welcome her the first thing in the morning.

Feelim. A woman's a blessing when th' sun's setting, but a burden when she's rising. But don't talk too loud, boys — I've got to divide the district into sections for delivery of gas-masks.

        [He busies himself at the table with the job.

Edgar [ignoring Feelim's warning]. Our sun is setting, Drishogue. What have we young men got to do with the hope and pleasure of a lifetime ? Where our fathers went, we must go, and whatever sons we may have, will follow us.

Drishogue. Take care, for we may have to wear out ; so be fair to yourself in being fair to Jennie.

Edgar [laughing, with a tinge of bitterness in it]. How can a man be fair where fair is foul and foul is fair ; when life is a long hover in the fog and the filthy air ? No ; let those who know they die tomorrow be merry today.

    [Mrs. Watchit comes trotting in carrying a tray on which are a small teapot, covered with a cosy, a cup and saucer, tiny jug of milk, and some sugar in a bowl. She lays it on a table in front of Feelim. She is a woman of fifty, with soft eyes in a lined face ; her hair, almost white, is elaborately permed. She is dressed in bodice and skirt of purple, over which is a small apron trimmed with green. She moves with a slow, stiff trot.

Mrs. Watchit [beamingly]. Us knew as you'd like a tot o' tea. 'Usband says as 'ow 'ee thinks as it would buck you up like.

Feelim [with delight]. Your 'usband's a wise one, me dear lady. Set it down, set it down ; someone must ha' been prayin' for me.

Mrs. Watchit [*as she lays it down*]. Shall us pour a cup for 'ee ?

Feelim. No, no ; not yet. Let it draw an' thicken a little, an' brew. [*He goes on to work, and Mrs. Watchit goes out again. With satisfaction — to all in the room*] Thoughtful woman, that. Efficient, too, Always doing something, and always doin' it well. [*Musing on the problem*] Division H.I.1, Sub-Division H.I.J.2 ; District O.1.D, Sub-District O.1.D.E ; Section K.L.1, Sub-Section K.L.M.2. Now who th' hell ought to be put there ? I can't see with all these letthers an' integers dazzlin' me.

Drishogue. No, Edgar, though we have more to face than cannon-fire and flak — the frantic wind tearing at our tender house, the hardy, heartless frost flinging his icy coat over us to weigh us down, the lightning's flame stabbing at our entrails, the sea tossing up her highest waves to drench us when we go wounded, limping home ; yet, in spite of all, more than many will never have had their names written down in the little black book ; and, years hence, they will be seen, with shrunken shanks, rheumy eyes, the grey beard and the wasting hair, trying to get their treble voices down to the pitch of youth. [*Speaking a little more slowly*] And even though we should die, then, damn it all, we shall die for a fair cause !

Edgar [*impatiently*]. Oh, all causes are fair to those who believe in them ; I believe in none. I have no cause to die for, such as you love ; no principle ; only an old, doting mother who's jutting close to death herself : my old and dying mother and myself, but I cannot die for him.

Drishogue. For England, then.

Edgar [*more impatiently*]. Which England ? There are so many of them : Conservative England, Liberal England, Labour England, and your own Communist England — for which of them shall I go forth to fight, and, perchance, to die ?

Drishogue. For all of them in the greatness of England's mighty human soul set forth in what Shakespeare, Shelley, Keats, and Milton sang ; in the mighty compass of Darwin's mind, sweeping back to the beginning and stretching forward to the end ; for what your Faraday did in taming the lightning to stream quietly about in the service of man ; and, if these be indifferent things to you, then fight and die, if need be, in the halo of healing from the tiny light carried in the lovely, delicate hands of Florence Nightingale. Go forth to fight, perchance to die, for the great human soul of England. Go forth to fight and to destroy, not the enemies of this or that belief, but the enemies of mankind. In this fight, Edgar, righteousness and war have kissed each other : Christ, Mahomet, Confucius, and Buddha are one.

Edgar [*with a sigh*]. I daresay you are right. I will, I think, fight heartily ; but the young love life, and I am young.

Drishogue. And death is but a part of life, my friend. Dying, we shall not feel lonely, for the great cloud of witnesses who die will all be young. If death be the end, then there is nothing ; if it be but a passage from one place to another, then we shall mingle with a great, gay crowd !
    [*The dark cloth panel in the wireless cabinet suddenly lights up, showing the German sign of the swastika in*

its centre in flaming red; the notes of the first line of
" Deutschland über Alles" are played, and a voice, in
ordinary confident tones, calls: " Germany calling,
Germany calling, Germany calling". Then the swastika
disappears, and the cloth panel of the cabinet is dark
again.

[*The two young men sit with thoughtful faces, their thoughts*
on themselves; Feelim sits upright, a puzzled, listening
look on his face. Then he rises, his face a puzzled pucker
of lines.

Feelim. Wha' was that? [*Without turning — his back is*
towards the two young men] Did yous hear anything?
[*They do not answer.*] Me brain is turning dark an'
dazzled with all these problems of figures, calculations,
an' expository confusion of form an' pamphlet. [*He*
sees the tea.] Ah! a cup of tea to save a life! It must
be well brewed be now. A woman efficient as she is
considerate, is Mrs. Watchit. [*He lifts the cosy off and*
pours a stream of hot water into the cup, and a look of
half-demented disappointment emblazons his face when he
realises Mrs. Watchit has forgotten to put in the tea. With
an agonised yelp] Good God! The old fool forgot to
put the tea in! Nothing that woman lays a hand on
that she doesn't mar. A very pest in the place. She
thought of everything but to put in the tea. Escaped
her notice. How do they think they're ever goin' to
win th' war this way! *" A nice cup o' tea'll tune you*
up", she says; she's tuned me up, right enough, but
not with tea. [*He lets an agonised roar out of him.*]
Mrs. Watchit! [*He savagely pushes an electric bell near*
the fireplace. He waits a moment for an answer that doesn't
come, then goes over to the doorway, the teapot held out in
his hand. Venomously — striding to the doorway] Gallivantin' after soldiers, I suppose. They're all at that

game. Women of ninety gettin' their hair permed. [*He roars at doorway*] Mrs. Watchit! Mrs. Watchit! [*To the two airmen*] A lovely rest camp this place ud make, wouldn't it?

Drishogue [*annoyed*]. For goodness' sake go down and get the tea, if you want it so bad.

Feelim [*vehemently*]. I haven't time to stir, man — I've too much to do! [*He gives a long-sustained roar.*] Mrs. Watchit!

> [*Mark, the Home Guardsman, in shirt, trousers, and high rubber boots with a pike having a shaft fourteen feet long and a blade two feet long, comes hurrying in, excited and wary.*]

Mark [*excitedly*]. What's th' rumble goin' on round here? What's wrong, eh? Quick, show us!

Feelim [*as he sees the pike poking about*]. Mind that pike! Mind that pike, there!

Mark. What's amiss? Us heard fierce shoutin' fr'm garden.

Feelim [*thrusting teapot towards Mark*]. Nothin's amiss; only bring this back to that woman, Watchit, an' tell her Mr. O'Morrigun would be obliged if she'd thry to make tea in the only way known to mortals. [*As Mark, taking hold of teapot, releases hold of pike which crashes over the table*] Mind that pike, I'm tellin' you!

Mark. 'Tain't no use bringin' teapot down — Mrs. Watchit's gone to market to try ferret out a few eggs.

Feelim [*resignedly*]. Then, like a good man, you brew a pot of tea for a man dyin' of drouth.

Mark. That 'tain't no use either.   Afore she went, Mrs.
Watchit cut off gas from main and put key in pocket
to 'usband fuel.

Feelim [*madly*]. Oh, is it any wonder revolutions are
threatenin' all over the world !   Ah, a wise woman,
that Watchit one !   Well, look here, tell Farmer
Frome that it'll be hours yet, days, maybe weeks even,
before I can give him a hand with the Egg Inspector's
report, or the Butter Inspector's report, or the Noxious
Weeds Inspector's report, or the Warble Fly Inspector's report.

Mark [*hesitating*]. Us doesn't like goin' near 'ee.   'Ee's up
t' knees in forms, an' is wild-eyed an' roarin'.

Feelim. Go on — we've all to take risks these days.   [*As
Mark is going*] Hold on a second !   [*He goes to table, and
comes back with a slip of paper in his hand.*]   Tell him that
a new Ordher, X.123 plus 789, concernin' growers of
rhubarb, says, " A grower of rhubarb in relation to,
or conception of, the meaning of the order appertaining
to the cultivation of live plants or herbs for appropriate
culinary purposes, and concerning the growth of the
particular herb already specified, or otherwise mentioned, to wit the plant commonly known under the
name of rhubarb, is a person set down in the affirmative
sense in Form 05321.YX, and includes any person in
whom the property in rhubarb is, or has been, invested
before its severance thereof from any land in which the
said herb, or plant, may be in process of cultivation.
For additional information, see Form Y.321, 789.A."
Tell that to Farmer Frome from me.   It's all about
rhubarb.

Mark. Us'll do me best.

[*He goes out, balancing his pike, and Feelim returns to the table to resume his calculations, carefully replacing, with a sigh, the teapot on the tray.*

Drishogue [*who for the last few moments has been watching the thoughtful drooping head of Edgar*]. Come, buddy, come, wake up ! The sheep's in the meadow, the cow's in the corn ! Death never comes so swift as life imagines. And if she comes too swift, why then, The flower that blooms and dies all in a day is fair as one that lingers to decay.

Feelim [*irritated, and perhaps a little frightened*]. Why persevere with this gloomy talk ? God's truth, I prefer th' saucy talk of Jennie herself.

Drishogue. However it may be, when we have passed tne end, no-one shall know that he is dead ; for still the curlews call, the plovers cry, and linnets sing as sweetly and as loud.

[*A moment after, Jennie comes tripping in, gay and expectant. She is dressed in her Land Girl walking-out costume — broad-brimmed brown hat, vivid green jersey, brown breeches, long green-grey stockings, and brown shoes.*

Jennie [*gaily*]. Hello, my merry men all ! [*Coming over to Edgar, and lightly ruffling his hair.*] Come along ; the curfew's tolled the knell of parting day, and Diana's lamp is lit to show a silver path to where we go. [*Seeing how serious they look.*] What th' hell has you all so glum-looking ?

Feelim [*with dignity*]. We were talkin' serious, Jennie.

Jennie. So am I. What's more serious than the life of this fair world that's in the sidelong glance of a maid at a man ? What were you talkin' about ?

Drishogue. We were talking of death : the fear of it, and how to face it firmly, Jennie.

Jennie [*sympathetically — to Edgar*]. My poor boy ! Were they trying to measure your troubled thoughts with sky-blown rules again ? The best prayers for giving courage and hope are ripe kisses on a young girl's red mouth ! Though life's uncertain, we ought to edge its darkness with a song !

Feelim. He has a right to be serious when he wants to.

Jennie. Come on, strong boy. You can be as serious as you like with me. You'll find in me the loaf of bread, the jug of wine, the book of verse, and the maid singing in the wilderness. [*Seizing him by the arm to raise him from his seat*] Up !

Edgar [*hesitantly*]. Just a minute, dear ; there's a time for everything.

Jennie. There's no out-marked hour for love : it is the very breath of time and space.

Feelim [*monitorily*]. It's good to think occasionally of God.

Jennie [*mockingly*]. Which of them ? There were hundreds. One was in every thunderclap, one flew in every breeze, one lay under every tree ; and now we seek safety in crosses of tin, in a touch of St. Jude's toe, or an eyelash of a St. Camberwell ; forgetting that the stately or nimble song in verse, stone, or picture, and the urge of a young man and woman into each other's arms, are the gay instruments of God's best melodies. [*As Monica enters, dressed for a walk in short skirt, jacket, and blouse, covered by a dark-blue mackintosh*] Ah, dear, we're just in time to deliver our boys from bondage. Get hold of yours, and come along. [*Getting Edgar to his feet, and putting an arm round him*] I'm all cased up in a costume ; but a hand can slip under the jersey, and the girdle's easy undone.

Drishogue [*slipping an arm round Monica as he goes out with her*]. We'll pull aside shy-buttoned bodice, to glimpse fair perfection beneath.

Jennie [*singing saucily*] :
    She stood where th' primroses blow,
    Looking modest an' shy as a daisy ;
    Come an' kiss me, sweet maid, said a beau,
    Or are you too shy an' too lazy ?

Jennie [*as she goes out with Edgar*] :
    I can canter like any gee-gee,
    Said th' maid to th' man, with a bow, sir ;
    An' if you'll be rider to me,
    I'll willingly show you how, now, sir !

                          [*The couples go out.*

[*Outside again can be heard the tramping feet of the Home Guard drilling ; the non-com., or officer in charge, intoning, " Left. . . . Left. Into file. . . . Right turn. . . . Left. . . . Left "; the sound of the marching feet, distant at first, coming nearer, till the sound passes by the window, and moving off, fades away again into the distance.*

Feelim [*clicking his tongue in irritated disdain*]. Dtch dtch ! Boys of the Old Brigade.

    [*Dame Hatherleigh comes in by the piano on left. She often has a brisk manner, but almost always a look of anxiety clouds her face. She is a woman of forty-five or so, well figured, though tending, ever so slightly, towards plumpness. She still holds on to a good part of an earlier loveliness shown in a heavy mass of brown hair, tinged now with grey specks ; fine, oval face, and eyes, deep, dark, alert, and intelligent, perhaps a little brighter than they should be. She is simply, almost austerely dressed in a tailor-made suit of dark green, relieved by a scarf of deep orange, flecked with crimson, round her neck, and a belt of the same colours round her waist.*

[*She is carrying a V-for-Victory sign of white, some two feet in height, which she places upright on the table in its centre. Feelim rises, and becomes the obedient and attentive butler at once.*

Dame Hatherleigh. Sit down, Feelim ; sit down. You're more important now than I am. [*As she places the V sign on the table*] There's something now to remind all who may be in the room that victory is sure.

Feelim. It'll be sudden, too, ma'am, never fear.

Dame Hatherleigh. I hope so : for my husband's sake and my son's ; for all our sakes. [*With a long and sad sigh.*] It's a bad thing, Feelim, for one's love and hopes to be depending on one child only. [*Her body grows tense, and her face becomes drawn with anxiety and fear, while her eyes stare out in front of her.*] I sometimes dread the things I seem to see and hear, threatening woe to husband and to son. When there is silence in my mind, I see and hear them. [*In a sharper tone*] I see and hear them now : — the cold clang of a horde of tramping jackboots, bound with steel ; the sharp windy scream of a thousand German warplanes, with a pillar of fire moving before them, showing itself in the shape of a whirling swastika ! In the centre of the red fire my son is a perishing white flame ; and the steel-shod jackboots pound down heavy on my husband's body !

[*Before she fancies these things the cloth panel of the wireless cabinet has lit up, showing the bold, brazen sign of the swastika, more clearly than before, and a trumpet sounds confidently, but not loudly, the first line of " Deutschland über Alles", an aggressive voice proclaims, " Germany calling, Germany calling, Germany calling !" While she speaks, the tramp of many marching feet can be heard, sounding some distance away ; heavier and more rhythmic than the march of the Home Guards, and accompanied with a cold, keen clash, as if every jackboot was shod with steel. The sound does not come near, and fades away when Feelim begins to speak.*]

Feelim [*encouragingly*]. Both'll be all right, me lady, never fear. It'll all be over before your son can get his wings.

Dame Hatherleigh. He's got them, and so has your Drishogue. I know, though it isn't official yet : he's got his wings, but the war isn't over yet.

Feelim. Both of them'll be all right, ma'am. I know it ; I feel sure of it.

Dame Hatherleigh. It's all in God's hands. All we're sure of is that England must win : British Israel can never fail.

Feelim [*glad to change the subject*]. Never, no ; how could it ?

Dame Hatherleigh [*becoming more eager*]. Isn't it thrilling to feel that we are soul of the soul of the lost Ten Tribes of Israel, and are being held firm in the hands of Deity for a special purpose !

Feelim [*echoing her elation*]. Thrillin' ? Don't be talkin', me lady !

Dame Hatherleigh [*enthusiastically*]. Heremon's children have a great destiny. [*Suddenly — to Feelim*] You've heard of Heremon ?

Feelim. Is it me ? 'Course I have ! Our own ancesthor !

Dame Hatherleigh. Yes, our ancestor, the son of a Milesian father and a Tuatha de Danaan mother, the first of the line of Zarah, the mother of the line of Dan.

Feelim [*echoing*]. Line o' Dan — that's right.

Dame Hatherleigh. These are the two tribes who came over with Simeon of Wales, you know — the ancient Kymri or Simonii, who were the remnants of the Ten Tribes, dispersed after the fall of the Assyrian Empire. [*Ecstatically*] Isn't it wonderful !

Feelim [*just as ecstatically*]. There was always somethin' wonderful, somethin' sthrange, somethin', somethin' thremendous about th' Irish people !

Dame Hatherleigh [*correcting him*]. British people, Feelim. [*Solemnly and impressively*] We've got to dig, Feelim !
  [*Mrs. Watchit trots in, looks at them, halts a second, and then resumes her trip to the table, where she sits down.*

Feelim [*relieved that he knows at last what he is talking about*]. You're right there, ma'am. Dig we must while them U-boats are prowlin' about. Dig f'r victory !

Dame Hatherleigh [*a little impatiently*]. Not that digging ! We must dig for the Ark !

Feelim [*astounded*]. Th' Ark ?

Dame Hatherleigh. Oh, Feelim, don't you know that under the Hill of Tara lies the Ark of the Covenant ?

Feelim [*more astounded than ever*]. No !

Dame Hatherleigh. Fact. And we must dig it up. The Tara that Heremon gave to his wife as a dowry and burial-place — Teea-Mur — the town of Teea, or Tara as we call it now.

Feelim [feelingly]. Home o' th' High Kings ! D'ye know, me lady, I wouldn't be a bit surprised if when you took a top off an Irish mountain, you'd find Noah's Ark restin' in a boggy bed o' moss, with the dove, herself, nestin' near th' tiller !

Dame Hatherleigh. We must get the other one first, Feelim. You remember the glorious destiny in store for us, revealed in the Book of Daniel, don't you ?

Mrs. Watchit [nodding her head]. Ay, us knows Daniel.

Feelim. Daniel ? Yes, of course — the fella who fooled about with the lions an' — an' things.

Dame Hatherleigh [a little impatiently]. Not the lions, Feelim ; the image of brass and gold with the feet of clay that the rock from the mountain cut to pieces in poor Nebuchadnezzar's dream.

Feelim [emphatically]. Nebuchadnezzar ! That's th' fella I've been thryin' to think of — a boyo, if ever there was one.

Dame Hatherleigh. It's only when the Stone of Destiny is returned to the Davidic line that Great Britain and America will become one happy and united family, having one baptism, and holding one faith. Mind you, it's no myth, Feelim.

Mrs. Watchit [nodding head]. No, no myth ; all on us knows Nebuchadnezzar.

Feelim. Myth is it ? I'd like to meet th' one would say

it was ! Didn't I see it all with me own eyes, an' I in the Royal Irish Academy one day, written down in th' Tawny Deeds of th' Triads of Tirawly, set down in the sixth century before Anno Domini. It's only too thrue. Th' only throuble is, me lady, in this unbelievin' age, you'll get few to stand for Nebuchadnezzar's Dream, or th' image, or th' Ten Thribes, or even th' noble lady, Teeaa, who gave her name to Tara.

Dame Hatherleigh. You're forgetting the Ark of the Covenant, Feelim : confront them with that, and they'd be speechless.

Feelim [*earnestly*]. You're right, they would — speechless, be God, they'd be, sure enough !

Dame Hatherleigh [*with ecstatic fanaticism*]. The moment the war ends, we'll set about it ; dig briskly, but ever reverently. You know Tara, Feelim ?

Feelim [*as enthusiastically*]. Every green sod of it, me lady !

Dame Hatherleigh. Well, when you've time, sketch out a detailed plan of the hill, so that we may know where it is best to excavate first — when you've time. And now to war work — I to the Red Cross Committee, and, after that, the provision of billets for the aerodrome workers ; and you ?

Feelim [*indicating Mrs. Watchit*]. We're just about to measure our light an' fuel expenditure so's to keep future records.

Dame Hatherleigh. Patriotic work, my dears. [*She bends to whisper*] When Mr. Edgar returns, say I want to see him. Goodbye for the present.

    [*She goes out. Feelim rises, goes over, opens the door for her, and bows as gracefully as any eighteenth-century courtier.*

Feelim [*as soon as the door is shut — raising his eyes to the ceiling*]. Didja hear that rigmarole ! Dig out Tara, she says, to find th' Ark of the Covenant. Think of your sthrong connection, says she, with the lost Ten Thribes. Abraham, Isaac, an' Jacob, I know, were three of them, but th' names of th' others has escaped me memory.

Mrs. Watchit. Us'll ask 'usband — 'ee's sure t'know.

Feelim. Ah, for God's sake, let th' mania stay with one, and don't spread it on to others ! Is it outa me mind she thinks I am, or what ? What d'ye take me for, woman, says I ? Won't we be tired enough when we're done diggin' for victory, without breakin' our backs diggin' up Tara's Hill ? Wouldn't I look a nice gazebo shovin' th' Ark of th' Covenant through the streets of Dublin or of Cork ? I can hear th' people laughin' from here ! If I was caught diggin' there, they'd ask, What are you diggin' for, Feelim ? Th' Ark of the Covenant, I'd say, what else ? Th' what ? they'd say ; an', when I woke, yours truly would find himself in a padded cell.

Mrs. Watchit. Dame Hatherleigh's a good woman, an' kind, all upset by Mr. Edgar lowerin' himself goin' with that Jennie Frome ; an' her poor mind whirlin' by actin' secretary to seven committees.

Feelim [*savagely*]. You keep your mind from whirlin' when you're makin' tea ; an' when you make it, make it with tea, and don't thry to make it with a miracle !

Mrs. Watchit [*realising*]. Us knew us had forgotten something ! Us'll run down an' slip on kettle for another,

while you lay out plans. Lady was 'ere again, lookin'
for Drishogue.

> [*She whips up tray of things, and runs out. Clearing his
> throat with some short coughs, a lot of hems and haws,
> Feelim clears a space on the table, and arranges on it a
> thick exercise-book, a sheaf of writing paper, a bunch of
> pencils, and a pen and ink. He sits down, and begins
> to pore over the dial plans of the gas and electric meters.
> Mrs. Watchit returns, trotting over to his side, and
> bending down to see what Feelim has arranged. They
> straighten their backs, and carefully put on their spec-
> tacles, with some more short coughs and hems and haws.*

Feelim [*confidently*]. Now, we're all set, an' do thry to
keep your mind from whirlin'. Now here's th' plan
of the electric dial. Yes ; yes. Now, there's three
dials, no, four ; no, five dials altogether.

Mrs. Watchit. Us thought us counted six.

Feelim. One's a test dial, an' no concern of ours. One
ten thousand, one thousand, one hundred, one ten,
and one one — five altogether. See ?

Mrs. Watchit. See what ?

Feelim. I mean, understand ?

Mrs. Watchit. But unnerstand what ?

Feelim [*sharply*]. Five dials, ma'am, showin' th' amounts
of electricity we're consumin'.

Mrs. Watchit. I says t' my 'usband, us says to 'ee, I says
five dials I says — fancy !

Feelim. Let's get to the units — tens o' thousands,
thousands, hundreds, an' ones. Now let's see what it
says, keeping th' units in our heads.

Mrs. Watchit. 'Usband says to me, five dials 'ee says ; an' another red one, says us to 'ee ; fancy, now, says 'ee, why, 'ee says, suppose they does it to puzzle folks.

Feelim. Wait a minute.   What we have to do is to subtract th' amount of currency shown today——

Mrs. Watchit. Add it, isn't it ?   'Usband says t' us amount used since before we see'd last figure, 'ee says, must be added t' quantity, 'ee says, consumed, previous t' calculation made at first.

Feelim [*beginning to be annoyed — imitating her*]. Listen, ma'am — 'ee says 'ere — [*he taps the plan sharply with a finger*] — 'ee says, " Read your meter ; take down th' total on the dials ", 'ee says.

>   [*Mark peeps into the room from the doorway.*

Mark. Any chance of spot of tea for us an' mates ?

Feelim [*annoyed — gesturing for him to go away*]. We're busy, now, we're busy !

Mrs. Watchit [*waving him away*]. Checkin' our 'lectricity ; mustn't think of tea now.   Us's on war work.

Mark [*coming over to the table on tiptoe, and cautiously bending over to watch the work*]. Them dials is enough to fair dazzle a man proper.

Mrs. Watchit [*nodding her head in assent*]. Dials work contrairy, too — a hand goin' left, a hand goin' right, an' t' other movin' left.

Mark. What's Government athinkin' of ?   Drill, I says, yes, night an' day, manœuvrin', trench diggin', an' camoflage crawlin', all fair an' square, I says, is what us wants, to be ready to stick parachute Jerries droppin' about, I says, outa clouds, afore he lands, with day's work an' snatch o' sleep, enough t' go round clock, without shovin' of things forward us doesn't know how t' do.

Feelim [*indignantly*]. Who says he doesn't know ? Jot down figures the dials show, and a computation between the figures, here and there, and you get your answer ; but what can a man do with a thunder of talk in his ear ?

Michael [*popping his head in by the doorway*]. Any chance o' thet spot o' tea, Mark ?

Feelim [*clicking his tongue in annoyance*]. Dtch dtch !

Mrs. Watchit [*waving him away*]. We're too busy now. Us's on war work !

Mark [*warningly — to Michael*]. Hshush ! Us's questionin' th' dials.
    [*Michael tiptoes over to the table to join the group bending over the plans. He is short, stout, bull-necked ; and he gasps a little after every sentence.*

Mrs. Watchit. Us's all tryin' t' help, no more. 'Usband says only way t' live, 'elp one another, 'ee says, spite of discomforts, denials, an' suchlike hazards, till day breaks an' shadows flee away.

Michael. All sound, Christian doctrine, sensible, too, us'll all agree.

Feelim [*with icy anger*]. We're not concerned now with sound Christian doctrine, good people, but with secular instruments ticking out problems it takes concentration to solve.

Mark. Best way conserve fuel, I says, is keep aturnin' down gas-tap, don't light fires, keep poker locked up,

mark time with hot water, riddle-me-ree th' ashes, an'
don't light no light that 'tisn't necessary.

Feelim [*mockingly*]. And never get outa bed ! What we've
got to do is to find the kilowatt-hours an' th' job's done.

Michael. Aay, find 'em, but that's hard as what they calls
asplittin' of that there addem.

Mrs. Watchit [*nodding her head in profound assent*]. 'Tis that ;
though it's all a knack, asplittin' of the addem, or
ferretin' out them vitamins, 'usband said tonight, a
week ago, comin' from Three Pigeons — once get th'
knack, 'ee says, an' everythin's no more'n openin' door
an' shuttin' she behind you.

Feelim [*emphatically*]. Keep silent, th' lot of you, or go
away, till I set me mind on these figures.
         [*A jet of dirty steam streams suddenly in through the
         doorway.*

Mark and Michael [*together — alarmed*]. Th' house afire, or
somethin' !

Mrs. Watchit [*aghast — springing to her feet*]. The kettle for
th' tea ! God ! Us forgot th' 'lectric kettle on stove !
         [*She trots madly out, followed by Mark and Michael.*

Feelim [*in agony*]. Th' current, the current ! Waste,
waste ! A year won't save what we've lost today in
half an hour ! [*The big door flies open, and Monica,
pursued by Drishogue, runs in. He catches her half-way
across the room, presses her in his arms, and kisses her hotly
several times. Leaning back in his chair, exhausted*] I
dunno, I dunno ; instead of gettin' them down, th'
war seems to be gettin' them all hit up !

Monica [*breathless — striving to free herself*]. Please, Drishogue, I must take the class ; they're waiting. It is very important ; it may separate life from death at grips in some wounded body to meet one quick to fix a pad, a bandage, or a tourniquet — let me go !

Drishogue [*releasing her*]. Tonight, then, for it's a dark joy to have to leave you now.

Monica. Yes ; tonight !
[*She runs out, and Drishogue flings himself into chair, Feelim watching him reprovingly.*

Feelim. For goodness' sake go a little more orderly — we're not in Russia now.

Drishogue. Wish to God we were.

Feelim [*sarcastically*]. Perfection there, eh ?

Drishogue. Far from it ; only a hard, bitter, glorious struggle towards it.
[*Mrs. Watchit comes in by the big door ; she is wearing an air of importance, and she is followed by Joy and another Land Girl, both of whom are in walking-out uniform ; a member of the A.T.S., one of the W.A.A.F., a Girl Warden, and Mark.*

Mrs. Watchit [*to Feelim — beamingly*]. Us was just in time to save house fr'm fire ! [*To Drishogue*] A very talented young lady, an Em Ay an' all . . . wants t' have a word with 'ee.

Feelim [*sitting straight in his chair — to Drishogue*]. An Em Ay an' all. Came several times. [*To Deeda*] Here he is, ma'am.
[*Mrs. Deeda Tutting comes strutting towards Drishogue through the lane formed by the others. She is a tall, gaunt, plain-faced woman of forty or so. Her hair,*

turning grey slowly, is rather untidy, with wisps hanging down her neck and over her ears. Deep clefts connect a very querulous mouth with the butt of a thick and aggressive nose. Her forehead stretches too far back, giving her face a longer look than it really has. She is wearing big, round, horn-rimmed glasses, and carries a big, loose-bodied, black handbag, bulging with papers. She is dressed in a vivid green skirt, blue blouse, and thick-soled brogues. A black kerchief, striped with white, encircles her neck. Her voice is loud, rather shrill, and her manner positive and dogmatic.

Mrs. Watchit [*with all possible refinement — introducing her*]. Us has great pleasure in introducin' Mrs. Deeda Tutting.

Deeda [*thrusting out a big hand which Drishogue shakes gloomily and warily — with dogmatic familiarity*]. Hello there ! So you're the young man who adores the Soviet Union ? I don't blame you : Lenin began well, and we all had hopes for Russia's future ; but that's a lost dream now !

Feelim. Hear that, now, Drishogue ?

Mrs. Watchit. Us always had suspicions.

Deeda. I and my husband worked there on Committees, Comintern and Light Industries, so I know. If you were there, you'd see a look of fear in every sunken eye, misery chiselled on every pallid face, rags trying to cling to every shrunken body, and all steeped in the drab life they have to live.

Drishogue. Others with eyes as clear as yours, lady, have seen brighter and manlier things there. The fear you say you saw may have been the deep, dark fire of courage ; the chiselled lines in pallid faces, the insignia of resolution ; the ragged garments, the hurried shelter worn by sturdy hope striding down the street. If you want, woman, to see fear in th' eye, the pinched and pallid face, the shrunken figure, the tattered garment, ribbed to welcome every gusty wintry .wind, look here at home — you'll find them plentiful in every town and city !

Deeda [*more shrill and positive*]. Can't you listen ? I know !

Feelim. Listen to the lady, son, who has had experience. Things happen when th' world turns from God.

Deeda. My husband worked beside me. He, too, found his dream was false. [*With a shrill and positive whine.*] He suddenly disappeared like thousands of others — perhaps millions — into a concentration camp. [*In a modified scream.*] If it weren't for you and other Liberals here, Stalin daren't have done it !

Drishogue [*mockingly*]. You'll be telling me in a minute that Stalin himself is the one man left outside a concentration camp !

Feelim. Odd things happen, Drishogue, when th' people turn from God.

> [*Michael rushes in, excited and angry, and pushes his way to Feelim, waving a big official form in his hand.*

Michael. Ere, looka, read this one !

Mrs. Watchit [*warningly*]. Shush, man, we're talkin' serious.

Michael [*ignoring her — loudly*]. Government, she says, will acquire total egg output of keepers of thirteen hens or more, at thruppence an egg, 'n us's spent a tenner or more on hencoop an' fowl-run !

Joy [*angrily — to Michael*]. Can't you see us's in middle of important discussion ?

Michael [*persistent*]. An' th' balance of meal allowed for fowl is same f'r twelve as f'r twenty, so's plain owner of twenty uses no more'n 'im of twelve, so's owner of twenty is consumin' no more'n owner of twelve's, so's his balance o' meal's no more'n owner of twelve's, so why penalise one more'n other by she makin' compulsory purchase of egg output ? [*Indignantly*] Us'll not stick it !

Feelim [*to Deeda*]. Go on, lady ; never mind him.

Deeda [*tearfully continuing her story*]. Arrested without a word, without a sign, my poor husband's dead by now for certain. Listen. [*She bangs the table with her fist.*] They lay hands on whom they like to send them to forced labour. What can your subtle Irish mind say to that, eh ?

Drishogue [*calmly*]. Well, if the behaviour you're showing now is usual with you, I don't wonder your husband disappeared — it was the wisest thing he could do.

Feelim [*reproachfully while Deeda stands silent, viciously looking at Drishogue*]. Aw now, Drishogue, aw now ! Th' Gestapo took him, Drishogue ; th' Gestapo took him.

Joy. Who else, I ask ?

Deeda [*to Feelim*]. The Ogpu, sir, not the Gestapo. [*To Drishogue — violently*] I tell you, young man, the National Socialism of Germany, in many respects, is far superior to Soviet Rule ; and if it only gives up its racial animosity, and its spirit of conquest, it's Germany will become more cultured than even

Britain's or France's pompous and hypocritical imperialism !

Drishogue. You're asking a lot of Fascism, lady — you're asking it to cease to be itself.

Deeda [*furiously*]. Germany has as much right to *Lebensraum* as we have, and peace with her is the one chance of saving ourselves ; for if America and England war with Germany, it may well bring about a fusion of Hitlerism and Stalinism into one mighty movement of destruction !

Michael [*violently breaking out again*]. What about a little *Lebensraum* for decent people's hens ! What's use of blamin' governments away off when our own at home's worse ?

Feelim [*angrily*]. You don't know what you're sayin', man!

Michael. Well, us knows what us's sayin', but no-one wants t' listen t' uns. Us'll soon 'ave Inspectors be'ind every bush watchin' hens layin'. What's become of that 'ere Magna Charta, us asks ?

Feelim [*indignantly*]. Good God, man, can't you realise there's a lady speakin' ? Can't you realise that your hens and everyone's hens an' cocks are insignificant things compared with the tremendous thruths this lady is enunciatin' ?

Joy [*solemnly*]. Nothin' can prevail against truth.

Drishogue [*to Deeda*]. There must be something great in what the rank and gaudy privilege of the world's power, secular and clerical, is afraid of : but this great people know only a rational fear, for at the top of their resolution is the spearhead of their Red Army.

Deeda [*wheeling round to face the crowd*]. Are you listening to this miserable, besotted, and belated nonsense! [*She wheels round to face Drishogue again.*] Don't be a fool, man! I've seen them, and I know — a deformed, ill-nourished, tatter-clad crowd! Their rifles are soft-tube toys; the wings of their warplanes fall off in a sturdy wind; their big guns melt away after a few shots; and their tanks crumple into scrap when they strike a stone in the roadway!

Drishogue [*sarcastically*]. They do, do they? What a pity!

Mrs. Watchit [*nodding her head in assent*]. Us guessed it all along.

Deeda [*carried away — almost screaming*]. Behind your boasting façade of Soviet achievement lies a chaos of incompetence, a mass of sullen terror, a swamp of ignorance; at war, your Red Army will be so stupidly led and so wretchedly supplied that it will scatter from the field in utter rout before a month of war has passed. [*She bends down till her face is close to that of Drishogue.*] And I will be glad, delighted, over-joyed at its overthrow! If there is any honesty or truth left in us, we'll be at war with them soon to sweep away the horrid falsity of them and their master!

Drishogue [*springing to his feet — fiercely and loudly*]. Woe unto any nation making war on the Soviet Union! She will slash open the snout, and tear out the guts of any power crossing her borders!

Deeda [*coldly*]. Nice language, I must say!

3rd Home Guard [*shouting in from doorway*]. Sarge, Captin's callin' for 'ee all over place.

Michael [*answering back as loudly*]. Let 'im — us 'as to see 'bout 'ens !

Drishogue [*fiercely still*]. The people cannot stop for you to catch them up ; if you can't go fast enough to keep in step, then pray for death, for you've lost a use for life !

Feelim [*as fiercely as Drishogue*]. Remember the lady's a lady, man, an' an Em Ay, too ! It's that Red Dean an' his book that has turned your mind asthray. He didn't tell you that four-sixths of his sixth of a Socialist world was naught but snow an' ice an' frozen soil, where no animal plays, no bird flies, no creatures crawl, no man can live ; naught but stunted birch, a biting, bitter wind, an' endless night where shivering Death himself stands idle and alone !

Drishogue [*to Deeda — fiercely*]. You waste God's time and mine, woman. Over in the east, the people took their first fine step forward, and they look over the rim of the world now. Many can see them clearly, and many more can hear them cheering. We know full well the hardships all before us. Our spring will still have many a frosty morning and a frosty night ; our summers hot hold many a burden for us ; our autumn glory will still be tinged with many a starless night, the sound of sorrow loud beneath their shrouded silence ; but winter's night of hopeless woe is gone forever, and the people's energetic joy shall sound like well-cast bells through every passing season !

Deeda [*furiously*]. You seem to be unspeakably intolerant ! I must say I cannot understand the mystery of the Irish mind.

Drishogue. There you show your weakness. [*Pointing to*

Feelim] His mind's as Irish as mine, yet you understand it well.

Deeda [*beyond herself*]. I tell you the workers in the Soviet Union are worse than ever they were ; and you must be a starry-eyed sucker not to see it !

Feelim [*angrily*]. An' add to that her poor husband bein' whipped away to a lingerin' death be th' Gestapo !

Deeda [*to Feelim — angrily*]. How often have I to tell you ? Not the Gestapo, you old fool — the Ogpu !
> [*Deeda's venomous remark half stuns Feelim, and while he is staring at her, the globe over the clock shines into a vivid purple light.*
> [*Dame Hatherleigh enters briskly, but stops, and stands still to watch, and listen to, the disputants, a look of indignation on her face. She is in fire-fighting dress. The cloth panel of the wireless cabinet is illumined with the swastika, the trumpets play " Deutschland über Alles " ; but the animated crowd take notice of nothing but themselves.*

Feelim [*recovering from the shock — while the trumpets are sounding*]. I think you're after makin' a mistake, madam ; while you may be no lady, I'm no fool !

Deeda [*with irritation*]. Oh ! be silent, please ! I'm not concerned with you — [*pointing to Drishogue*] I'm addressing this young man here.

Feelim [*angrily*]. Well, I'm addressing you ! You're no messenger from Mars in th' guise of a lady born an' bred, causin' commotion with tawdry stories of starvin' shadows slinkin' through crooked streets, disappearin' husbands, armies formed o' scarecrows, till our brains are dizzy — well, here's one, anyway, who doesn't believe you ever seen a sthreak o' sunlight shinin', or a snowflake fall, on Soviet soil !

Dame Hatherleigh [*with quiet indignation*]. Oh, you pack of glittering daws ! There you crowd bickering while death, in a moment, is certain for some, grievous injury for many, and terror for us all ! Look at the purple light ! Set out the splints, bandages, and pads ; see to the incendiary fire tools ; and man the stirrup-pumps.

Feelim [*alert in an instant — putting on equipment*]. To our posts — all of us !
   [*All but the Dame, Drishogue, and Feelim go out in different ways.*

Drishogue. Where can I go, Dad ? What can I do ?

Dame Hatherleigh [*putting a hand on his shoulder*]. Find the safest shelter you can — we shall need you for finer and more terrible work before long.

Drishogue. Where's Monica ?

Dame Hatherleigh. At her post.
   [*Feelim, having put on his steel hat and other equipment, goes out with Dame Hatherleigh as the warning siren is wailing, while Drishogue stares out of the window.*

END OF ACT I

Act II

The scene is the same as before, but it is early morning with a nip of frost in the air ; the birds are beginning their preliminary chittering and the crows their cawing, before the day's work, and a cock crows afar off. The lights are on, for the blackout has to remain up for some time yet. Joy, in full working dress of the Land Girl, is waiting by the door for Jennie who is coquettishly arranging her bright-coloured kerchief around her handsome head.

Jennie [shivering a little]. God, it's cold ! You'd never think so many birds would be so near a town.

Joy. Six hours alert lasted. Thank goodness none came near'n five miles away. Duxton got it hot. Was you nervous ?

Jennie. Hardly, dear. It was a godsend to me. With all out on duty, and too tired to move when they came back, it meant a glorious night of fulfilling a feminine duty with Edgar.

Joy [giggling]. Same 'ere with Sergeant Mark.

Jennie. That's the fitter on the aerodrome works ? Clever fellow, me lass ; keep tight hold on 'im.

Joy [giggling, but trying to be solemn]. Us 'as more'n us can do t' keep 'im fr'm keepin' tight 'old of me ! Us never knew till las' night how unruly 'ee could be.

Jennie. Nice, but naughty. Ruffled you a lot, eh ?

Joy. God forgive uns all ! [*With prim piety*] 'Taint right, somehow. What if us caused a curse on all us's doin' ?

Fine thing if harvest failed, an' all them U-boats sinkin'
ships on sea !

Jennie [*impatiently*]. Oh, come off it, Joy ! Don't be
trying to afflict us with the old wife's tale of the knife,
the victim tied to an altar, waiting for fire from heaven
to set alight the logs below it. The stormy night of
your harum-scarum god is over. Don't be afraid when
your hair gets tangled in the stem and leaf of the
myrtle.

Joy. Hurry up, dear ; I can hear th' other girls waitin'
below for us.

Jennie [*opening bureau, and rummaging about in it*]. Christ !
if anyone told me a year ago I'd be up at dawn to
plant, to mow, to reap, and to sow, and to be a
farmer's boy, I'd have brained him with his lady's
fan ! Ah ! here it is — behind the bible. [*She takes
out a bottle of gin and two glasses, pouring some gin into each.*]
Now the dawn won't appear so dangerous. [*She hands
a glass to the giggling Joy.*] To the old Dame and all her
Ten Tribes !   [*She and Joy drink the gin.*

Joy. All th' same us is anxious. D'ye think th' Jerries'll
invade 'ere ? We're not far f'm th' coast.

Jennie [*carelessly*]. We'll stick it if they do.

Joy. What would you do if they come ?

Jennie. Live on if I can ; die in my lover's arms, or die
fighting them, if I can't.

Girls' Voices [*outside*]. Eh, you two — hurry up !

Jennie [*shouting back*]. Eager for work, what ! [*To Joy*]
Another before we entice ourselves out into the cold.
[*She fills glasses again, giving one to Joy, and holding on to*

*the second herself.   She raises the glass on high, and sings ;
drinking the gin when she finishes the verse :]*

Oh, here's to the trousers and green jersey, too,
That are out in the sun, and the rain, and the dew,
Under the sky when it's black or it's blue,
Digging hard, digging deep, in the morning !

[*Girls, chorusing outside, while Jennie shoves back bottle and
glasses into the bureau.*

Girls :

Maiden that's bashful, and maiden who's bold,
Forget all th' tales about love ever told ;
And think of your toiling on farm and in wold,
Digging hard, digging deep, in the morning !

Jennie [*singing*] :

Make way for the Land Girls true, and as brave
As soldier in battle, or seaman on wave ;
Giving back in her work some of what England gave,
Digging deep, digging hard, in the morning !

[*Jennie and Joy, having switched off the light, go out, and,
with the other girls, can be heard singing the chorus of
the song, till it dies away in the distance.*

[*After a few moments, a beam of light comes in from the
doorway, followed by Monica who is holding a torch in
her hand.   She is dressed in a white nightgown, slashed
with blue on the shoulders, a black dressing-gown, with
blue trimmings almost covering it.   Dark-blue slippers
cover her bare feet.*

Monica [*turning towards the doorway, after switching on a
light*]. There they go, singing to their work. After
last night's worry, the rest won't rise for a little longer.

[*Drishogue comes in now, dressed in his Air Force uniform,
the new white wings sparkling on his breast.   He is*

*buttoning his coat, and his shoes remain unlaced. He is
a little shy and awkward-looking.*

Monica [*rallying him*]. Don't look so glum, dear. We
haven't done anything so terrible as you may do
before long : isn't it nobler to bring one life into the
world than to hunt a hundred out of it ?

Drishogue. Depends on the kind you kill. Besides, I
don't want a scene — your father going for you because
you're gone on me, and mine for me because I'm gone
on you.

Monica. What they say or do down in a hollow matters
little to what we say or do up on a hill. Oh, Drishogue,
darling, I am very anxious ! I'm always thinking of
you passing in your plane, the countless flaming
fingers of death clutching at you, as you fly by, to pull
you down ! Don't you fear it, too ?

Drishogue [*thoughtfully*]. No, not fear ; a little nervous at
the forging of a will into a new adventure.

Monica [*shuddering*]. I wish I could keep away from the
thoughts of death : were you to go, I should be a
desolate little ship lost on a lonely sea.

Drishogue. It is inevitable we should think of what is
everywhere around us.

Monica [*clinging to him*]. Oh, Drishogue, surely death
cannot mean the loss of life !

Drishogue. Perhaps not ; I only know it means the loss
of many lovely things : the moving patterns of flying
birds ; the stroll through crowded streets, crudely
strewn about, that the moon regenerates into silvered
haunts of meditative men ; the musical wile of waves

racing towards us, or slowly bidding us farewell ; the wild flowers tossing themselves on to the field and into the hedgerow ; the sober ecstasy, or jewelled laugh, of children playing ; the river's rowdy rush or graceful gliding into sea or lake ; the sun asthride the hills, or rainfall teeming down aslant behind them ; a charming girl, shy, but ready with her finest favours — oh, these are dear and lovely things to lose !

Monica. They may be shadows of finer things to come.

Drishogue. Give me but these, and God can keep whatever is behind them. But let us get away before the others come. We ought to go before the house awakens.

Monica [*a little impatiently*]. Oh, let them come ! To be afraid of what we've done is to be like a young oak shivering in a summer breeze. Sometimes a quiet life becomes too precious to us all. Why should you fear the taunt in the rosy hours spent with the girl you like ?

Drishogue. And love, too, darling.

Monica. For the time being, anyway.

Drishogue. Till time has grown so old that things remembered lose their colour, and are growing grey.

Monica. Dark woe to think how things have changed so sudden ! [*In the distance, they hear faintly the drilling of the Home Guard in the rhythmic murmur of " Left right, left right, left right ".*] Drill on, drill on, Home Guard, first thing at morning, last thing at night, for England sorely needs you now ; for France is gone, and England's good right arm hangs helpless by her side !

Drishogue. And you must be as the Irish lass of twice a hundred years ago, who sold her rock and sold her reel and sold her only spinning-wheel, to buy her love a sword of steel to fix him fitly in the fight for the rights of man.

Monica. I'll have to do it soon enough ; but first come, love, to my room again, to dream away from us a moment more of restless turnings to the sound of war ; and give darkness another chance to hush a lover and his lass into the sweet secrecy of themselves.

[*He goes to the window, pulls down a blackout, and looks out.*

Drishogue. I ought to go before the house awakens. Look ! the moon is pale and worn after dancing through the sky as the beauty of the night, and is bidding goodbye at the door of dawn.

Monica. False dawn, with hate in all its lovely face ! [*Suddenly the window is shaken, and the house trembles.*] God, what's that !

Drishogue. Blast, I suppose, from a distant bomb exploding.

Monica [*shivering*]. They sometimes say that this old house is haunted.

Drishogue [*merrily*]. You're as superstitious as my father, who, if he had his way, would have my neck ajingle with his holy medals. [*He opens the window.*] That was no ghostly tremor. Let the light o' day come in to banish the shadows of the mind's imagining. There now's the enlivening air of the morning, bringing with it, too, the innocent, elegant scent of lavender.

Monica [*a little hysterical*]. Not lavender ! Anything but lavender !

Drishogue [*dreamily*]. It is mixed with the air stealing in through the window from the mauvy blossoms of the plant outside.

Monica. There's none outside ; none, I tell you ! It's your imagination. It's musk, or myrtle, or mignonette that scents the air to touch our senses with a silent sadness.

Drishogue [*quietly insistent*]. It's lavender. When we sheltered in your room, it was there ; and it has followed us here.

Monica [*clinging to him*]. Drishogue, my love, do not seek the centre of danger, but keep warily to the fringe of fighting ! Though I should never have seen you, had you not come to us, I sometimes wish you hadn't ventured into danger for the love of England !

Drishogue [*starting away from her — with startled indignation*]. Love of England ! Good God, woman, I have no love for England !

Monica [*startled too*]. But aren't you fighting for her ?

Drishogue [*passionately*]. No, I'm not ! I'm fighting for the people. I'm fighting against the stormy pillagers who blackened the time-old walls of Guernica, and tore them down ; who loaded their cannon in th' name of Christ to kill the best men Spain could boast of ; who stripped the olive groves and tore up orange trees to make deep graves for men, heaping the women on the men, and the children on the women. I was too young then to go out armed for battle, but time has lengthened an arm long enough to pull the Heinkels and the Dorniers out of the sky, and send them tumbling down to hell !

Monica [*soothingly*]. There, there ! I meant no harm, and, anyway, I'm not an English girl, but a thoroughbred Cornish lass.

Drishogue [*delightedly*]. A Kelt! How well I knew some jewel of nature hid in how you looked and what you did and all you said! A Keltic kiss for my Cornish girl.   [*He kisses her.*

Monica. But Jennie Frome's English, Drishogue, and you like her well.

Drishogue. I like her well, but are you sure she's English?

Monica. She's English right enough.

Drishogue [*doubtfully*]. I don't know. You search back far enough, and you'll find some Kymric, Scottish, or Irish ancestor who has saved her soul alive. [*Whipping her up in his arms with a wild movement*] Now for another wild welcome to my own dear Cornish lass! [*As he bears her out, the house shivers again, and the windows shake. He stops, and lets her slide from his arms. Awed.*] There it is again — the house is quivering over us! And there goes the scent of lavender again — no longer coy — but the scent of lavender a long time dead!

Monica [*frightened*]. Oh, come away, for God's sake!
    [*Abraham Penrhyn — Monica's father — appears at the window. He is a moist-eyed, high-foreheaded man of fifty or more. His bushy grizzled hair, longer at the back than it ought to be for a farmer, is strictly brushed back from his forehead. A long grizzled beard flows from his chin down over his breast; he would look venerable but for the thin-lipped mouth, and the stern and unhappy wrinkled lines at each corner of it. When he climbs into the room, he is seen to be dressed in brown corduroy trousers, tight brown leggings, heavy black boots,*

thick brown tweed coat, with a cap of same colour and material on his grizzled head. For a moment or two he stares at the couple, and a look of silent and bitter anger spreads over his face.

Abraham. You be there, ah, yes ; the two of ye ; full o' th' malice of sin ; thought, word, an' deed conspirin' to flare out in opposition t' God's commandments ! Worse 'n all, too, encompassed by th' arms of a man o' war. Things is bad f'r a once innocent girl sunk down on th' breast of a man o' blood. All th' wonders o' creation, all mercies o' grace, all glory of un eternal future set as naught against a dream of lasciviousness. Is it a wonder house trembles ? No more be a flood of water, God's promise holds ; but a flood o' flame may burn th' world, for the evil's great, an' th' time favourable. [*He climbs over sill, and comes into the room.*] Are ye daughter o' mine, or be ye some shamed shadow, stuffed wi' venom against th' good ye cannot own yourself ?

Monica [*storming into dialect*]. Shamed body I am to have to call such a shape as you a feyther !

Abraham. What of your mother in her grave ? [*Almost screaming.*] What of your dear mother, I says ! Wrigglin' in agony in her abode of bliss she are to see you slinkin' off an' slidin' down away off afar from she an' God t' where th' means of sin float thick as semmer swerms of gaily-banded bees, their colours hidin' stings !

Monica [*fiercely*]. Don't 'ee jerk name o' mother from th' very rest that cries shame at 'ee, f'r 'ee never raised she higher 'n her knees ! She hurried there t' hide fr'm 'ee. A coloured kerchief on head, a wee brooch on breast to 'ee were signs fr'm Satan aseekin' out her soul !

Abraham [*vehemently*]. So they was, an' so they does remain ! But f'r us'n timely warnin's, she'd ha' been as you is now. Be ye me daughter, or be ye not, 'tisn't f'r us t' say, for ye have no look about ye of a decent bringin'-up !

Drishogue [*catching Monica's arm*]. Monica, come away, come away !

Monica [*fiercely — shaking his hand away*]. Not since mother left 'ee for ever, when I was ten, ha' I been near you as daughter or friend, and am no more ; no, never. Dame Hatherleigh has had to do me f'r mother an' f'r feyther since. [*More fiercely*] Get away from me ; get far away from me lover 'n me !

Abraham [*with bitter reproach*]. Us fattened bullocks for she an' 'ee, didn' I ? An' reared sheep, an' ploughed land, an' sowed corn, an' watched sun, rain, an' worked, waitin', watchin' crops agrowin' f'r 'ee an' she ; t' furnish roof over heads, meat f'r table, an' clothes f'r backs, didn' I ? An' now to know taste of what 'ee do an' what 'ee thinks, us 'as to steal along at nights, an' in the dawn ; steal an' creep afther 'ee t' end up in seein' of 'ee near t' nakedness in arms of man of war ! [*Violently*] No daughter of mine ; no, never, even, f'r 'ee to go on bended knee, an' ask forgiveness !

Monica [*violently*]. Get away fr'm me ; away, far away fr'm lover an' me ! [*Flinging open her dressing-gown to show her nightdress*] Near nakedness, an' us isn't ashamed ! No, never while love has word to whisper or arm strong enough t' fondle. [*To Drishogue*] Take

me in your arms to my room again, an' show him I
am lost for ever !

> [*Feelim appears at the opposite side of the room. He is
> half-dressed — trousers, shirt, and boots unlaced, with
> his tin hat on his head. He carries a torch which sends a
> stream of light over the couple. He is angry, and looks
> a little scared.*

Feelim. Put out that light !   Turn off that switch !
Don't you know it's not near off blackout time yet ?
D'ye want th' special police-pathrols to come prancin'
in on us, or wha' ?   An' th' house thremblin' over us
an' undher us, an' all !   What are th' two o' yous
doin' ?   What has yous ramblin' round th' house at
this hour for, eh ?   Nice conduct goin' on, an' th'
Germans only nine waves away from th' shore !   I
suppose you know there's no Tuatha de Danaan magic
round here to raise a mist, either, to hide th' shore
from th' enemy ?   Or raise a terrible storm, either,
so's to send their ships an' barges scattherin' to th' icy
seas in th' north, or the icier oceans to th' far south ?
Can't yous see for yourselves th' way we're tearin'
down the road-signs, whippin' off the destination
names from bus, thram, an' perambulator ?   Surely,
it's a warnin' for sensible behaviour to see the military
goin' mad at shovin' up concrete pillars at every
turnin', and — and hewin' deep declivities outa every
road to check th' tanks that'll soon be thundherin' down
on top of us !   [*To Abraham Penrhyn*] An', Farmer
Penrhyn, why are you found in the middle of mahogany
an' cushions, instead of bein' in the centre of a field,
or an orchard, tendin' growin' corn or ripenin' apples ?

Abraham. Why don't 'ee keep your son fr'm molestin'
me daughter ?

Feelim. Why don't 'ee keep your daughter from molestin' me son ?

Abraham [*taking a pint bottle of whisky from inner pocket of coat*]. See that ? An enemy of man. Us'll make friend of she, an' spite ye all ! [*He takes out cork, and drinks deep.*] That's only th' beginnin'. Us'll drink till us goes out of th' way with it, and is ready to perish ; us'll drink till ragin' comes, an' come in an' go out howlin', an' fair disgrace ye all !

Feelim. A lot of it, maybe, 'ill make you a little reasonable.

Abraham. Ye is all bent in fear, an' adread of th' poppin' of bombs. T' hell with ye all ! Hear that ? It's only th' beginnin'. Maybe, now, you'll keep your son away fr'm me daughter.

Feelim. I'll do that same when you keep your daughter away from me son.
[*Abraham goes to the window, climbs over the sill, and looks at them again.*

Drishogue. Why don't the pair of you raise your voice, and cry out halt to life ?

Abraham [*warningly*]. Mind ye, I'll be worse, ay, far worse, when ye see me again !
[*He goes down ladder, and disappears.*
[*Outside, in the distance, is heard the faint tramp of the Home Guard, and the orders of their leader, more clear than the tramp of the feet, " R-i-g-h-t wheel ! Left right, left right ; left . . . left."*

Feelim. There — listen to that, yous ! Isn't it a wondher yous wouldn't take pattern by those gallant men, trainin', trainin', trainin' themselves to fight against the things to come ! [*He suddenly wheels right round.*] What's that ! I thought I heard a shadowy step, an' the swish of a satin flounce against me instep ! Oh, isn't it enough to have to contend with corporal enemies, without havin' to deal with spiritual ones too ! [*To the couple*] Are you sure yous didn't hear anything ?

Drishogue. We've heard a lot from you.

Feelim [*angry again*]. You're goin' to hear more. You might have some regard for me predicamented attention to the crowd of betther people surgin' round Dame Hatherleigh tryin', through her, to touch American bankers, ambassadors, an' consuls, in an effort to get their children an' relatives quick to the States ; with military critics urgin' them on with maps showin' we'll soon see the coal-scuttle helmets comin' over the hills, an' hear the jackboots poundin' th' roads to the town's centre, to hang their hats in our own hall a moment afther. [*An electric bell gives a loud peal outside.*] There's another, now, hot-foot after a berth in a ship for America !
[*Special Constable Dillery appears in the doorway, flashing a huge torch over the couple and then over Feelim. He is long and lanky, pale-faced and melancholy-looking, with a drooping grey moustache. He is dressed in ordinary civilian attire, covered with a fawn mackintosh, but wears a prodigiously big, hard, round-topped, thrust-out peaked cap, with a gigantic silver badge coruscating in front of it.*

Dillery [*flashing his torch on Feelim*]. What d'ye mean in havin' that unobscured light there flashing about, an' th' blackout down ? Have you no thought of th' dreadful danger you may bring on people ?

[*Constable Sillery's head is thrust through the open window, preceded by a big hand holding a lighted torch many times larger than that held by Feelim. He is dressed like Dillery, and the same huge hat, with the protruding peak, almost hides a fat, red, excitable face.*

Sillery [*angrily — flashing his torch on Feelim*]. 'Oo's 'ee's showin' an exposed light before blackout's over ?

Feelim [*impatiently — putting his torch out*]. Aw, don't go rousin' th' neighbourhood about a pin-point of light !
    [*Voice of Home Guard leader away in the distance :* " *Left right, left right, left right* ".

Dillery [*indignantly*]. Pin-point was it ? It was visible half a mile down the road.

Sillery. An' mile or more acomin' downhill.

Dillery. Th' gleam of it dazzled me eyes moment I stepped outside of house. Farmer Dodge said she was a searchlight gone wrong.

Sillery [*portentously*]. She'll 'ave t' be taken seriously, if she happens again.
    [*Dame Hatherleigh sweeps in energetically around the piano on the left, carrying a large torch that flings a purplish-silver beam of light over the room. Her night attire is almost completely covered with a warm, dark-green dressing-gown, and her feet are in slippers of the same hue.*

Dame Hatherleigh. What is all this ? Sillery, Dillery, what are you doin' here, instead of being on patrol ? [*Before they can answer.*] Monica, dear, what are you doing ? You should be asleep after being up so late last night. The whole place is flooded with light, the curtain is down, and the blackout time not yet

ended.   Constables, you surprise me who should be a
good example to others.   Did any of you feel the house
shake ?   Did you hear me asking you a question,
Dillery — what are you doing here ?

Dillery. Us seen an exposed light astream fr'm window,
an' came t' investigate.

Sillery. Us seen a bright light awaverin' over country, an',
in duty bound so to do, investigated, an' traced it 'ere.

Dame Hatherleigh. Nonsense !   I hope you two men
haven't stayed too long in the Three Pigeons.   Will
you extinguish those torches at once !   You should be
a good example to everyone else, and here you both are
flooding the place with light that can be seen miles
away.

Dillery [*putting out torch*]. As proper authorities, we seen
naked light away off, and, after conference, traced
she 'ere.

Dame Hatherleigh. That won't do, Dillery.   When I came
in, you both had your torches flaming big as beacons.
But we'll say no more this time.   But this is no time
for careless conduct.   No quondam goings-on from
this on ;   we must be men, and put childish things
from us.   Don't you two agree ?

Constables [*together*]. 'Ess indeed, ma'am.

Dame Hatherleigh. Of course you do, as sensible men.   It
was senseless to floodlight the place, but inexperience
explains it all.   We'll let you two constables off this
time.   It'll never do to bring quiet houses into chaos
by banging on doors and ringing of bells.   Mark every
circumstance well, and ponder it, before you decide to
act.   Don't you agree ?

Constables [*together*]. 'Ess indeed, ma'am.

Dame Hatherleigh. Of course you do. Don't go painting terrors all over the place to frighten people out of their commonplace composure. If you are frightened at anything yourselves, hide it, as brave men wearing the King's uniform, for it may in the end be nothing. No brave soldier lets his gun off at a shadow. Follow what I say, constables ?

Constables [*together*]. Us follows you, ma'am, quick an' right.

Dame Hatherleigh. Well, off you go home, now. [*She makes the V sign by raising the first two fingers of her right hand. The two constables, followed by Feelim, do the same.*] Victory ! [*She goes over to the window — to Sillery.*] Now, Sillery, mind how you go down that ladder with your game leg ! I don't want your wife to come complaining that I shoved you into needless danger. Step at a time, now.

Sillery [*disappearing*]. Never fear, ma'am. [*Popping head over sill again.*] No use bein' afraid — us may, like as not, be all dead soon.   [*He goes.*

Dame Hatherleigh [*to Dillery*]. A merry thought to leave with us ! Eveleen doing well in the A.T.S. ?

Dillery [*with pride*]. Lass's corporal now.

Dame Hatherleigh. Fancy that, now ! Tell her I'm delighted to hear it. Off you go ; and give a hand when you can at the digging of the trench.

Dillery [*as he goes out, making the V sign again*]. I will that ! Thank you, ma'am, f'r your kindness. Mornin' all. Goodbye. Cheerio all.   [*He goes.*

Dame Hatherleigh [*half to herself*]. Dear me, how far away some seem to be from the discipline and dignity of the lost Ten Tribes ! [*To Monica*] Monica, dear, go up and dress, for now we have all so much to do that some of us will surely end our little day before the half of it be done.   Give Drishogue a swift kiss, and be off.

Drishogue [*kissing Monica*]. Seven days of leave left yet, Monica, so we'll be often together, and closer than ever before.

Monica. And may time be weary of speed at last, creep ahead like a snail, and halt for a long rest at every passing hour !
  [*She goes, and Dame Hatherleigh comes over to place a hand affectionately on Drishogue's shoulder.*

Dame Hatherleigh. Now, my lad, who is my boy's friend, don't stay lively too long at a time, even for your love's sake.   You need all the rest you can snatch away from what is still to do.   Our lives no longer now are free enough to call our own.   Each life is owned by all.

Drishogue [*jauntily*]. Never fear : Edgar and I'll do all things needful.   We'll whizz through the sky, and turn every pouncing enemy plane into a vanishing wisp o' smoke.

Dame Hatherleigh. I know you will do your bit, and God be wi' you both. [*She goes to turn away, hesitates, and turns to face him again.*] But listen, Drishogue, dear, and don't laugh at me or him : I cabled forty dollars over to Saskatoon's bishop for a symbol guaranteeing instant admission to heaven to the bearer, should he fall in the fight ; and a subsidiary guarantee bringing

the bearer safely home. Please don't smile, if he
mentions it to you, for my son is very dear to me.

Drishogue. No, no, Dame Hatherleigh, I shan't make fun
of it, though I advise you not to press it in his thoughts
too much ; remember his life depends on his swift
and steady nerve, how quick his muscles answer to
their tensioned call ; how taut he is to the tip of his
finger when danger flies into the sky ; and let his
guns speak straight and steady to the very heart of what
he aims at. Let him do all this, and his little symbol
will never shame him.

Dame Hatherleigh. Ah ! those words, dear Drishogue, are
little more than a well-mannered mockery. [*In
anguish*] Oh, Drishogue ! we are all now in the midst
of exploding death and a consuming fire, and don't
know where to turn.

Feelim [*vehemently*]. Don't mind that fellow, ma'am —
he's alive only when he's conthradictin' ! You done
right. You couldn't have done a wiser or a better
thing, believe you me. What does he know to allow
him to go cock-a-hoop against the faith an' belief of
th' whole fightin' world ?

Dame Hatherleigh [*vehemently — almost fiercely*]. Feelim's
right ! What do you know, what can you know of
things beyond the ken of man !

Drishogue [*calmly*]. Nothing, my lady. Beyond the
common news of the day, I know nothing, save that
on sunny days the sky is blue ; that grass is green ;
and that one day leaves the house of man to let another
enter.   [*With a bow to Dame Hatherleigh, he goes out.*
   [*Through the doorway, Mark and Michael come into the
   room. Mark carries a big cylinder tin of window*

security paint by its wire handle, and Michael carries rolls of strip, adhesive paper used to criss-cross glass to prevent splintering. They come close to Dame Hatherleigh, and stand one on either side of her.

Mark [*hurriedly*]. Listen, now, Dame Hatherleigh ; listen t' me.

Michael [*hurriedly*]. You just listen t' me, me lady ; wiser 'n better it would be.

Mark. That's 'ee's opinion — 'tain't mine.

Dame Hatherleigh. Now, one at a time ; you, Mark.

Mark [*speaking rapidly*]. Us says as how it's plain as plain as how window painted over with — with — just a second — [*he raises cylinder to read the label*] — as how window painted whole with guaranteed unsplinterable gum is as it must be more endoorable than window criss-crossed with fancy thingamajigs which is all calculated t' — t' explode like, an' pierce an' penetrate bodies that happens to be plump in the way of glassy spikes aflyin' about reckless like.

Michael. 'Tain't no use, Dame, us is convinced. Spread over window endoorableness is disorganised like, us says ; an' when bomb falls — [*he puffs out his cheeks, and blows out his breath explosively*] — concussion comes on window full force, an' glass goes *Bang !*

Feelim [*in disgust*]. Dtch dtch — we'll never get anything done this way.

Mark [*roughly — to Michael*]. 'Tain't no use, yours, us knows. [*To Dame Hatherleigh*] 'Ee ain't right, me lady. See th' flaw in she ?

Feelim. There's a flaw in the hees, too !

Mark [*holding up the rolls*]. Not in them no. Guaranteed. Look ! Printed on 'em t' show there's no deception. See ! 'Gainst any concussion, explosion, or blast, however severe ; no flaw 'ere. Stan' behind window criss-crossed with these 'ere paper strips, an' blast fr'm thousand-ton bomb couldn't rustle hair on un's head !

Dame Hatherleigh [*doubtfully*]. I don't know — I think I prefer the sandbags.

Michael [*fervently — to Dame Hatherleigh*]. Look, lady, us'll be fair. Drop thousand-ton bomb front of window painted with she, an' I'll abide results if someone like Mr. O'Morrigun, there, can be got to stan' th' test.

Feelim [*most indignant*]. You're damn kind, you are ! Don't you be bringin' Mr. O'Morrigun's name into it, man ! There's no reason whatever for mentionin' Mr. O'Morrigun's name in th' matter at all. When are you fellows goin' to realise that what's left of our Army's been snatched out of Dunkirk, weary an' worn an' sad, leavin' us th' way we're without a tank, a rifle, a hand-grenade, or a hope, with the Germans in millions pilin' into barges all long the coasts less than twenty miles away from us ? If you're goin' to put th' stuff on, put it on without any further argument !

Mark. Us thinks it's about time for an Irishman livin' here to take an odd risk f'r th' sake of all.

Feelim. That risk would be a little too odd for this Irishman to take. Look, man, when bombs are droppin', if he's quick enough, and can, this Irishman dives behind a ten-foot-thick stone wall !

[*Mrs. Watchit comes trotting in, followed by Mr. Peter Constant, who comes close to the group, while Mrs. Watchit stands a little aside, nodding her head vigorously*

in agreement whenever Mr. Constant speaks. He is a
very tall fellow, thin as a rake, with a brown moustache
pointing east and west, and a V-shaped beard, whose
pointed end faces due south. He is dressed in blue shirt,
green tie, grey coat, and yellow trousers, but most of
these are hidden by a long, heavy overcoat reaching almost
to his heels. He carries a bunch of green moss in his hand.

Mrs. Watchit [*to Home Guards*]. Mind th' way, there. [*To Dame Hatherleigh*] Mr. Constant, ma'am ; poor man wants to get his wife away to America, an' can't ; he's all awry with the knowledge of them Germans comin' to tear 'im limb fr'm limb.

Constant [*to Dame Hatherleigh*]. I want you to help me to get my wife out of England. You must act quick. I've done all except get a guarantee that an American friend will take charge of her. I know none there. Please cable for this guarantee. Our income would allow both of us to live there quite well ; but this stupid Government won't let us take more than a miserable amount out of the country. I can lodge enough with you to assure your friend that he or she will suffer no financial loss.

Mrs. Watchit [*pitiful*]. Poor man — 'ee is in a way !

Dame Hatherleigh [*coldly*]. I'm afraid I can't help you, Mr. Constant. She and you will just do what we all have to do — stay put, and do all we can to save our country.

Mrs. Watchit [*nervous*]. We're all aquivery with what's happened, for us knows now what t' expect when a raid comes again.

Constant [*to Dame Hatherleigh*]. My case is quite, quite

different. As soon as the raids began, my wife became certain that she was going to have a baby.

Dame Hatherleigh. We'll all just have to stick it. There's no escape.

Constant [*hysterically*]. There must be ! I should be going too. I am a Liberal, and I wrote several letters to *The Times*. They'll know this, and if I'm still here, it means torture and the concentration camp for me !

Dame Hatherleigh. That is why we must resist. If we don't, it will mean these things for us all.

Constant [*hysterically*]. But my wife's having a baby — don't you realise that ?

Feelim [*impatiently*]. Man alive, that's a common occurrence round here ! That's a side issue, man. We have to use our time to prepare for the possibility of anythin' happenin'. Worse things than the raids that have already passed us.

Mrs. Watchit. God defend we ! Mrs. Splender of the Black Diamond told 'usband that in last raid blast come in on door, ran upstairs, caught she in bath, whipped 'er un' bath outa window, un' set she down in middle of street. Ashamed of 'er life, she was, 'usband says, un' refused to budge till Fire Brigade brought blanket. 'Usband says she says she'll never forgive them Germans.

[*A car accelerating is heard outside.*

Mrs. Watchit. What's that, what's that ? Is it a plane ?

Constant [*squealing at her*]. Can't you hear, damn you ! You'll have us all as jumpy as yourself. [*Shouting*] It's a car, woman !

Mark [*to Constant*]. Easy, easy, there, mate.   No need to go panicky.

Constant [*savagely*]. What th' hell does she want to go all whimpering and shaking for when she hears a car !

Michael. Her heart's not shakin'.   If all does as she done, ashiverin', bombs fallin' near 'n far, amakin' tea for us as needed it, us'll do well enough.

[*Constable Sillery comes in, spick and span in his uniform, with the George Medal sparkling on his breast.   It can be seen now that he walks with a slight limp.*

Sillery [*importantly*]. There's a goodish crowd outside clamourin' about th' shelters promised.   Us tried to persuade them to disperse, an' couldn't, so us selected a man of them to come along f'r proper interrogation. [*He calls*] Come on in, Jack !

[*A short, stout, sturdy man comes in, roughly dressed, with a tweed cap in his hand.   He is embarrassed, but carries it off with a defiant manner.   He is followed by a trickle from the crowd, who group themselves by the door.*

Man. We wants to know when shelters is acomin'.   We works hard ; an' durin' nights we want to feel our wives an' children is somewhat safe.   We can get no proper information nowhere ; so we come t' see Head Warden, Mr. O'Morrigun.   [*He coughs, and waits for comment.   After a silence, he resumes.*] People's gettin' restless, y'know.   [*In a burst of anger*] D'ye think we're made o' steel ?   Damn your eyes, give us shelters !

Crowd [*round door — chanting*] :
Oh, give us shelters deep and lonely,
Where we can hide our screaming children,
To save them from the peril of living,
And from the bomb's exploding terror.

Our little homes are flaming sadly,
Death's staring in through every window ;
Each thoroughfare is cover'd thickly
With twisted things that once were lov'd ones.

Man. Coventry has got it ; London has got it, and
is gettin' it still.   Th' East End's smokin' rubble.
Thousands of houses are down, an' nothin' but th'
poor back doors stay standin'.   Th' buildin's left with
their backs to th' sky are shakin'.   Th' people are
fightin' to live on in a forest o' fire.   We've had a
taste of it ; but a fuller shower's bound to come our
way yet.   Blast your eyes, give us shelters !

Crowd [*chanting*] :
Oh, give us shelters deep and lonely,
Where we can sit in darkness quietly,
With warm arms round cold, frightened children,
Till evil things are banish'd utterly !

Feelim [*rising to his feet*].   We'll do all we can.   We've done
what we could, as the medal on Sillery's breast shows.

Mrs. Watchit [*enthusiastically*].   Ay, an' th' George Cross
won be Farmer Penrhyn f'r pickin' lives fr'm blazin'
buildin's !

Mark [*slightly jealous*].   'Ee was in drink when 'ee done she.

Feelim.   Just as well he was : few men in their sober
senses could have done what he did.   [*Argumentatively*]
People, listen.   Two things we have to do — fight the
raids and fight invasion.   Fight it on the beaches,
among the meadows, in the streets.

Michael [*angrily*].   How fight ?   Where be th' rifles ?
Where be anything ?   With Bren-guns hosin' bullets
on us, bombs separatin' us, tanks cannonadin' us, us'll

have no chance ! Die in th' last ditch ? Us'll die in th' first one jumped into !

Chorus [*outside the door*]. Give us th' shelters, give us th' shelters !

Dame Hatherleigh. Friends, we can't fight if we live all the time in shelters.

[*Dillery, pushing crowd aside, rushes in excitedly, his fingers of right hand raised in the V victory sign.*

Dillery [*wild with excitement*]. They've come ; at last they've come, fr'm America — arms, arms, arms !

Rest [*together*]. Arms, arms, arms !

Dillery. Tanks, planes, an' big guns f'r th' Army, an' Bren-guns, grenades, machine-guns, an' rifles f'r th' Home Guard !

Feelim. Listen, boys ; don't get excited ; listen ! [*Excitedly he jumps on to a chair.*] Get them windows done so's you can do some serious work — learnin' th' stirrup-pump ; how to handle incendiaries ; dig threnches ; camouflagin' yourselves ; an' how to crawl, jump, run to cover of stone, three, or bush ; how to cut telephone wires, an' how to signal with flag, light, hand, and foot. We've all got to stay put, an' more than stayin' put, everyone sthrong enough to bend a blade of grass's got to get goin', do his bit. We've got to keep th' Jerries out ; an' if they manage to get in, we've got to keep them fully occupied. Forward ! [*His eloquence breaks into song :*]

> To arms, to arms, to arms !
> To arms, your ranks advance !
> March on, march on, serfdom is past,
> Set free th' world at last !

[*He jumps down.*]   Come on, me lads an' lasses !
[*He rushes through the crowd, and leads them out, cheering.*
[*Dame Hatherleigh stands listening to the cheering for a few
    moments, then Mrs. Watchit comes in, carrying a
    telegram which she gives to the Dame.*

Mrs. Watchit. Telegram for you, me lady.   Boy waitin'.
[*As Dame Hatherleigh tears open the envelope and reads the
    telegram, the crowd break from the cheering into the singing
    again.*

Crowd [*outside — singing*] :
            To arms, your ranks advance !
            Give death a passing glance !
            March on, march on, serfdom is past,
            Set free th' world at last !

Dame Hatherleigh. Tell the boy there is no answer,
    Watchit ; and tell Mr. O'Morrigun I want him at
    once.
[*Dame Hatherleigh sits slowly down in a chair.   Mrs.
    Watchit goes out, and after a few moments Feelim comes
    into the room.*

Feelim. Anything wrong, me lady ?   Aren't you feeling
    well ?

Dame Hatherleigh. Get me a drink, Feelim, please.
    [*Feelim hurries to the bureau, fills some whisky into a glass,
    adds a little water from a carafe, gives it to the Dame, and
    she drinks it slowly.*]   Thanks.   A woman I know well,
    Feelim, has just heard that her dear husband lies dead
    at the front.

Feelim. A God's pity that, ma'am ; but I wouldn't
    worry, me lady.   We've too many things to think of
    ourselves now without bothering about the trouble an'

sorrow of others. [*After a short silence.*] Hundreds are in th' same plight, and soon that black band of mournin' will circle the arms of thousands.

Dame Hatherleigh. It's hard for her who has had to suffer it.

Feelim. 'Course 'tis ; but we have to try to remember that life's comin' into th' world as fast as it's goin' out of it.

> [*Drishogue comes in with an arm around Monica. He is in uniform, and has his equipment strapped on him. He appears to be elated, while Monica looks very unhappy.*

Dame Hatherleigh [*surprised*]. Drishogue ! Where are you going with your harness on your back ?

Drishogue [*taken somewhat aback*]. Didn't Edgar tell you that we got sudden orders to return to squadron, and are about to say goodbye ?

Dame Hatherleigh [*hurt*]. No. [*Quickly*] Couldn't find me, probably. Where is Edgar ?

Drishogue [*jauntily*]. Bidding farewell to his lady-love, as I am.

Dame Hatherleigh. I see. [*Impulsively clasping Drishogue's hand in both of hers.*] Goodbye, my dear boy, and God be with you both !

Feelim [*piously*]. Amen ! [*To Drishogue — trying to say it coldly*] Well, goodbye for th' present, Drishogue.

Drishogue. Goodbye, Dad.

Dame Hatherleigh [*to Feelim*]. Let's give them the last moment to themselves.

> [*Dame Hatherleigh and Feelim go out.*

Monica. Oh ! Drishogue, God and myself only know how much I'll miss you !

Drishogue. Cheer up, darling ! It won't be long till the golden net of reunion again entangles us in each other's arms.

Monica. However far from Monica Drishogue may be, her love will stretch to where he is, and added length of thought will weave caresses and a prayer around him.

Drishogue. However far from Drishogue Monica may be, her slim body shall feel the pressure of his arms, and her lips the warmth of his kindling kisses.

Monica. And when he comes again, the bells shall ring his name alone ; the birds shall sing his bravery ; and Monica shall lead him to where all that she has shall be his.

Drishogue. And a kiss shall be the song the world is singing.

Monica. A kiss like this !   [*She kisses him.*

Drishogue. Oh ! my love, a lover's kiss is an eternal thought !

Monica. Here they're coming.

Drishogue. Goodbye !

Monica. Goodbye ! A beggarly word braving it out to parting lovers like sorrow in a coloured coat.
    [*Edgar, garbed like Drishogue, comes in with Jennie,
    followed by Dame Hatherleigh, Feelim, Mrs. Watchit,
    and the others. The Purple Light appears again. The
    cloth panel in the wireless cabinet shows the swastika.*

Edgar [*cheerily*]. Come, it's kind of all of you to gather to say goodbye to England's newest flyers.

Jennie. When I see you again, let the breast of your Air Force blue glitter with stars like the sky of a winter's night !
  [*The trumpets sound the first line of " Deutschland über Alles " louder than ever, and a clear, threatening voice proclaims, " Germany calling, Germany calling ", immediately followed by the wail of the air-raid warning.*

Crowd [*to the airmen*]. Goodbye, goodbye !
  [*The two young flyers go out. The rush of the German warplanes is heard in the rushing swing of the music of " The Ride of the Valkyries " coming close, and then fading into the distance, as several tongues of flame shoot up into the sky seen through the windows. The crowd, led by Mark, chant encouragement to the flyers and to themselves.*

Mark [*chanting*] :

Young, lusty lads in Air Force blue,
Go forth wearing red rose and rue ;
Our life, our dreams, depend on you,
Sons of England !

Crowd [*chanting*] :

The mothers, wives, and children here,
Are nursing thoughts that death is near ;
Show them the way to cast out fear,
Shield of England !

Mark [*chanting*] :

When German proud planes zoom on high,
Teach them in th' tormented sky,
Who come to kill, remain to die,
Sword of England !

Crowd [*chanting*] :
>   Time shall be dead, and England, too,
>   Ere we forget red rose and rue,
>   So bravely, blithely worn by you,
>   Sons of England !

[" *The Ride of the Valkyries* " *swings into its loudest
sound as Feelim, in steel hat and equipment, accompanied
by the Home Guard, Monica, Jennie, Joy, and the rest
stream out to do all they can to modify the destruction
and uproar in the bombed town and district, leaving
Dame Hatherleigh alone gazing steadily towards the
window at the rising tongues of crimson and yellow
flames.*

END OF ACT II

ACT III

The scene is the same, but the aspect of the big room has changed with the changing world outside it. Its broad and pleasing panelling has become like the ties, the belts, and bars connecting various parts of machinery together, and making of them an active, unified whole. The capacious fireplace, resembling it before, has now assumed the almost similar — though something stylised — shape of a great drop-hammer. The columns flanking the doorway have become machinery shafts. The bureau has become a lathe, though still preserving the vague outlines of what it once was. The two lesser windows have turned into wheels carrying belts to the chandeliers, now turned up on their sides, and ready to revolve, too, in unison with the rest of the machinery. Though the great room still has the shape of its old existence, everything in it is touched strongly with the form of its first existence. The wireless cabinet at the back, between the windows, is still the same. In a corner is a rack on which half a dozen rifles, the same number of steel hats, and various pieces of equipment hang. Beside them, a stirrup-pump and several long-handled shovels for dealing with incendiary bombs. Near the cabinet, someone is lying covered by a blanket; and on the other side a form is lying, hidden in a rug. Outside tongues of flame are intermittently leaping up and down, and they can be seen through the window at the back. The black silhouette of a crane's jib passes through the red flame as if destruction and construction were battling each other. Before the central window, some dozen or so sandbags are piled in an effort to strengthen the wall under it. Dame Hatherleigh is standing rigid before them, staring out of the window, as if she had never moved from it. Occasionally a deep spasmodic shudder passes through her body, then, with a quiver, her body becomes rigid once more. Through a good part of the scene, men in overalls and dungarees, blue and brown, cross the room, left to right, and right to left. At a table, near the jutting piano, to the left, Feelim is sitting, writing out some report or other, and, now and again, giving anxious glances at Dame Hatherleigh. Mark comes in, grimy-faced, and with his uniform dusty, and the tin hat on the back of his head. He carries a long-handled shovel which he puts among the others. He looks at the Dame, nods meaningly to Feelim, who shakes his head, and looks again at the Dame. As he is depositing his shovel with the others, Ernest Pobjoy slinks rather than walks in, carrying a basket of newly-dug potatoes on his arm. He is thirty years of age, well-made, slim, and intelligent in a curious aloof way. He can do a lot of things with his hands, is clever at vegetable culture, and has read a little. He is dark-haired, and brushes it back straight from his forehead. He can be alert when he likes, but usually goes about with his head down, and moves as if he were offering an apology for being alive. He is dressed in khaki shorts, blue shirt, grey coat, and sandals. He hesitates when he comes in, glancing at Feelim, at the Dame, and at Mark. Then he slinks over to where Feelim is sitting.

Pobjoy [*to Feelim*]. What am I to do with these spuds, please ?

Feelim [*curtly*]. Don't know.

Pobjoy [*slinking over to the Dame*]. What am I to do with these spuds, ma'am, please ?   [*She takes no notice.*

Pobjoy [*slinking over to Mark*]. Can you tell me where I'm expected to leave these spuds ?

Mark [*roughly and fiercely*]. Go to hell !
          [*After some slight hesitation, Pobjoy goes slinking out by*

the door.   The cloth panel on the wireless cabinet is lighted to show a V sign, while some mean musical notes corresponding to the letters of B.B.C. are repeated three times.   Then a voice calls out : " When the siren goes, take shelter.   Keep away from windows.   When bombs fall, lie down."   Then the panel becomes dark once more.

Feelim [*scornfully towards the wireless set*]. An' when you can't keep awake, go asleep !   'J'ever hear such nonsense !   [*To Mark*] Any more news ?

Mark. Didn' come on any more yet.   New shift adiggin'.

Feelim. Hear how many were brought down ?

Mark. Story goes there were near to twenty o' th' bastards perished.

Feelim [*delighted*]. It's mountin', it's mountin' !   How many of ours missin' ?

Mark [*with an apprehensive glance at the Dame*]. Dunno right ; some say three ; some say more'n that.   God !   Us is tired !

Feelim. Get some sleep, boy.   Watchit'll give you a sandwich ;   can't get tea — no water, no gas, no nothin', be God !   Heard anythin' of Jennie ?

Mark [*almost falling with sleep*]. No, never a word.

Feelim. Get some sleep, boy.   [*Mark goes sleepily out. After a pause — to Dame Hatherleigh*] If I were you, I wouldn't get into th' habit of standin' in front of windows, ma'am.   [*She takes no notice.   Feelim speaks louder.*]   I shouldn't get into th' habit of standin' in front of windows !

Dame Hatherleigh [*turning slowly and rigidly round*]. I must watch the sky. Were I away, he might call, and I shouldn't hear.

    [*She turns slowly and rigidly to face the window again.*

Feelim. Y'know, you got no sleep last night, or th' night before. It won't do. He'll be all right. Somethin's tellin' me that. Besides, Drishogue'll keep an eye on him.

Dame Hatherleigh [*musingly — in a toneless even voice*]. When twilight falls, the dancers come. Everywhere I go, there they dance before me.

Feelim [*a little frightened at the mention of the shadows*]. You'd no right to come out th' other night — the bomb that fell near you gave you the shock into imagining things.

Dame Hatherleigh. When Edgar goes, what's left but a poor, tired, daft soul, who, losing her way to the door of death, is seeking a decent way back to it. [*Suddenly*] Who are those, there, below, running round like ants ?

Feelim [*coming to the window*]. Them, me lady ? Oh, them are the workmen repairing the new factory attached to the house here.

Dame Hatherleigh [*puzzled*]. House here ? Not here : this house can never change ; never change. *Per ardua ad astra.* A hard high climb to the stars ! [*A swift momentary flash of flame flickers by the window. She screams.*] The flame ! I saw my son's face, agonising, carried by in the midst of it !

Feelim [*catching her arm firmly*]. Nonsense, Dame Hatherleigh ! Thry to be calm. Thry to centre your mind on Teeaa an' th' lost Ten Thribes.

Dame Hatherleigh [*flinging his hand off with a sudden vigour*].
Get away from me ! You damned Irish ! Why didn't
your selfish people come over to help us !
  [*The form under the rug stirs, flings the covering half aside,
  sits up, and shows the crinkled face of an old woman of
  seventy.*

Old Woman [*angrily*]. Good God ! What kind of a rest
centre's this ! Amn't I to be let get even a minute's
sleep ? What's she squealin' about ? Christ God ! is
she the one an' only one whose remembered things are
the things to forget ? Why don't you shut the old
bitch up somewhere so's poor people can get a little
peace ?
  [*She sinks down again under the rug, and Feelim goes over
  to the other figure lying beneath the blanket, and gently
  shakes it.*

Feelim [*gently*]. Monica, dear ; Monica, darlin', wake up,
will you ? I dunno what to do with the Dame.
  [*Monica, who is fully dressed, slowly sits up from under the
  blanket, and opens her eyes sleepily.*

Monica. What is it ? More dressings and more wounds ?
Oh, why did you wake me, man !

Feelim. I dunno what to do with the old Dame. She's
restless an' obstinate ; I thought you might get her
to keep quiet. I've a hundred reports to make out,
an' a thousand forms to fill, an' I got only a few
hours' sleep meself.
  [*Monica reluctantly rises, and goes over sleepily to the
  Dame. A sturdy young foreman comes in, dressed in
  brown overalls, with an open rule in his hand. He
  stands to watch Monica and the Dame. He speaks with
  an Irish accent.*

Monica [*sleepily, but with decision*]. Now, Dame Hatherleigh, this won't do. You must think of others by keeping quiet. Come.

Dame Hatherleigh. I don't feel able to stir. I saw something odd a minute ago, but I can't remember what it was. Oh! my poor head's gone cold as if a frosty blast had entered it by the ears.

Monica. We'll get you a warm drink somehow, and then you must lie down. Come.

> [*Monica leads the Dame slowly out.*

Foreman [*to Feelim*]. What's wrong with the old Dame?

Feelim. Blast shock. Doctor says time and quietness'll bring her to herself again.

Foreman. Two things hard to come by, me friend.

Feelim. Did you happen to hear who were the two flyers that fell to death on th' aerodrome?

Foreman. They were unrecognisable. They're searching for identity discs among the pile of German burnt-out planes around them. All they found so far is a little image of an angel with outspread wings on th' body of one of them — musta been a Catholic.

Feelim. Good God! [*Looking round to make sure Dame Hatherleigh has gone.*] Hatherleigh wore on his breast a blessed image of an angel with outspread wings!

Foreman. The third one, they say, was some fool of a Land Girl who plunged into th' flames to thry to tear one of them free.

Feelim [*lifting his eyes towards the ceiling — fervently*]. From the hurt of th' burnin', from the lost alliance of loved

ones here on earth, from th' blackened dust of a vanished life, give the vision of perpetual light in th' peace of eternal rest, O God of th' many kindnesses, and th' darin' deeds of mercy !

> [*As Feelim is speaking the cloth panel on the wireless set lights up, and muted trumpets sound the first lines of " Deutschland über Alles ", darkening again when Feelim has finished his appeal.*

Foreman [*uneasy*]. I wouldn't be dwellin' on them things ! I was as near death meself th' other night as I ever want to be. Let's forget it. [*Indicating the blanket and woman under the rug.*] You'll have to get these away, y'know ! Can't have th' place turned into a slap-dash dormitory ; so go to it, boy !

Feelim [*indignantly*]. Who're you talkin' to ? Go to it yourself, boy ; or see the Welfare Officer about it. It's not my job.

Foreman [*sharply*]. Everything's everybody's job these days ; so see the place cleared, and don't argue about it.

Feelim [*a little incoherent with indignation*]. Who th' hell are you to give orders ? We're no way inclined to reverence fellows fresh from th' bog ; so keep your devalerian authoritarianism quiet till you know your way betther about !

Foreman [*indignant now*]. You shut up about De Valera. There's damn few like him anywhere.

Feelim. Don't I know that well — leadin' th' country to ruin an' revolution ! Turnin' th' poor people into shock brigades of confraternities an' holy sight-seein' sodalities, so that they're numb with kneelin', an' hoarse with th' dint of recitin' litany an' prayer !

Foreman [*ready to go*]. He done one good thing, anyway.
He kept us all outa th' war !

> [*He goes. Feelim goes back to the table, and sits down.
> After a moment or two, Joy, with other Land Girls,
> Wrens, A.T.S., farm workers, and Mark come in, half
> pulling Pobjoy in with them, followed by Mrs. Watchit
> who stations herself at the side of Feelim. The Land
> Girls come up to the table ; Pobjoy stands, hesitant,
> nearer the doorway. His features are now faintly
> defined as of a face appearing in vacancy. Any old lines
> of determination he may have had have lost their vigour ;
> and the face has congealed into a dogged and dead con-
> viction ; faint lines are there still, but fading into
> insignificance, like tarnished spangles lying in a dustbin.*

Joy [*to Feelim*]. Eh, you, what d'ye think us girls are ?

Feelim [*gallantly*]. If I told yous what I think yous are,
it's not diggin' th' land yous would be, but sportin'
about in the whitest o' linen an' gayest of silks, with
young an' handsome gallants festooned with ordhers,
an' swords danglin' from their hips, cravin' a dance
in a lighted hall, or a long kiss outside, under a tree,
an' the twilight fallin' !

Joy [*in no way displeased at Feelim's praise*]. None of your
blarney, now ! We've come to tell you to take Pobjoy
out of the fields, or we down tools ; for we won't
work with a damned Conchie.

Felicity. If he comes near where us girls work, we'll pull
a limb outa him !

Feelim. An' where is he to go ?

Joy [*violently*]. To hell, where all his likes are stuffed !

Feelim. Now, now ; no bad language, girls ! We'll have

to thry to look at this in a sensible way.   If you refuse
to work with him, he'll be a nuisance ;   if you suffer
him to work, he'll be, at least, a help.

Felicity. A hindrance, you mean.   It's against my conscience, he says, to do anything that would lead, even
indirectly, to the killing of another.   [*Violently — over
to Pobjoy*] If y'ever come within reach of my arm, you
vacant worm, born be sleight o' hand instead of
woman, I'll give your napper the weight of whatever
tool I'm handlin' !

Feelim. Now, now, Felicity, darlin', be more moderate.
[*Over to Pobjoy*] Come over nearer, man, an' let's have
a dacent look at you.   [*Pobjoy comes nearer.*]   See all the
trouble you're causin' ?   What are we to do with you ?

Pobjoy. I've been ordered to work on the land.

Feelim. Well, you see they refuse to work with you ?

Pobjoy. That's your problem.   I won't waste time
thinking of it.

Feelim. That's grand !   I shouldn't, if I were you.   But
seriously, thry to be reasonable.   [*With a wink.*]   Your
heart's weak, isn't it, an' you were rejected for military
service ?   That makes it easier for everyone.

Pobjoy. Heart's all right.   I don't want to make it easier
for myself or for anyone ;   besides, I don't tell lies.

Feelim. No ?   [*Exasperated.*]   Why don't you say your
head is weak, then, an' clear your conscience ?

Pobjoy. I gave my reasons to the court.

Feelim. An' what did the court say ?

Pobjoy. Said I was a skunk. I don't mind : I'm used to it.

Feelim [*wonderingly*]. I daresay a man can get used to anything in time. Had it been said to me, I'd have cleared the court !

Pobjoy. I don't believe in violence.

Feelim. Neither do I ; but life is full of violence, and we're in the middle of life. Birth is noisy, and death isn't quite a quiet thing. [*Getting eloquent.*] There's violence in fire, wind, and water ; in th' blast that brings a well to being ; in the plough that cleaves th' ground ; there is violence even in th' push that sends the leaves fluttering to the ground in the autumn ; man alive, there's violence in th' struggle that gets me early up in th' morning !

Pobjoy. Things you mention are natural, subsentient things — I have a conscience.

Mrs. Watchit [*impatiently*]. Waste o' time talkin' teh 'ee. Smack in th' jaw is grace o' God teh folks like 'im, 'usband says.

Feelim [*to Mrs. Watchit*]. Wait a minute. [*To Mark, who bends down to whisper something*] Wait a minute, wait a minute, can't you ! [*To Pobjoy*] Haven't you got anything in your country you admire, love, and would defend ? Surely, if they were bein' attacked, you'd defend your old churches ; the graves in which your great men and women lie ; the places where they lived ; your folk-song and your music ?

Pobjoy [*scornfully*]. No, thanks. I've no wish to dash round with the smoothing iron.

Feelim. Come now, you do honour Stratford-on-Avon, an' the fella who wrote *Paradise Lost* ?

Mrs. Watchit [*ecstatically*]. Us 'eard tell of 'im — wunnerful !

Feelim [*to Pobjoy*]. Where's this he was born ?

Mrs. Watchit. Ah ! where indeed ?

Pobjoy. I don't know — you tell us, knowall.

Feelim. Ay, will I ; he was born in Bread Street, London, if you want to know. Well, where was he buried ?

Pobjoy. The Abbey, I suppose ; I don't know.

Mrs. Watchit. 'Ee don't know, an' 'ee don't care. 'Ee only guessed about th' Abbey. Knowin' 'is own land's people's no importance.

Feelim [*importantly*]. Milton wasn't buried in th' Abbey ; he lies in th' churchyard of St. Giles, Cripplegate — where th' bombs are fallin' now.

Pobjoy [*sarcastically*]. That's hot news !

1st Farm Worker [*muttering angrily*]. We don't want no foreigners to come 'ere tellin' us things.

Feelim [*ignoring the interruption*]. And Nelson — come now, the greatest sailor, maybe, that ever lived : what about him, eh ? He's an inspiration to Englishmen, isn't he ? [*He stands up to sing :*]
Too well the gallant hero fought for England, home, an' beauty.
He cried, as 'midst th' fire he ran,
Nelson confides that every man this day will do his duty !

Come, you take pride in Nelson ; and remember his courage an' glory to give you resolution an' — an' fortitude in th' day o' testin', don't you ?

Pobjoy. Let them who take the sword perish by it — that is their funeral.

Feelim. Thousands of children who never took the sword perished by it ; perished by it because we took it into our hands a little late.

Pobjoy [*sourly*]. If you want to joke, go back to your Ireland where they like it.

Feelim [*stormily*]. Is there no fight in you at all ! D'ye never feel like killin' someone ?

Pobjoy. No ; do you ?

Feelim. I feel like it now, man ! You take your rations damn quick, don't you ? Yet you let brave men risk their lives to bring them here to you and your like.

Pobjoy [*coldly*]. They're riskin' their lives, too, for you and your crowd in Ireland, though you and they stay snug at home, safe and cheerful. Those brave men are blown to bits while your Irish eyes are smiling. Get your own rats to go into the fight, and then you'll have a surer right to lecture us.

Old Woman [*suddenly flinging her rug half-way off her, and sitting bolt upright*]. Ay, an' if he doesn't like us, it's easy to go to where he came from ! Oh ! I heard him, with his Stratford-on-Avon, Stoke-on-Trent, an' Bognor Regis. But he's too comfortable here, makin' a nice livin' outa th' soft-hearted English.

Feelim [*to the old woman*]. I was asked here, me girl : I was solicited to come here, an' give a hand with things.

Felicity [*fiercely*]. An' you come quick ! Yous are beginnin' to miss English rule, an' are flockin' here to oust us of our rights !

Old Woman. As for me, no-one's prouder than me of the North-eastern Irish, who are men, an' not rattle-snakes or scum, for they belong to a different race altogether.

Feelim [*sarcastically*]. Didja not know that before, me girl ? We Irish are only human. The North-eastern boyos are specially adapted for divine purposes.

Old Woman [*furiously*]. North-east Ireland will remain where it is, in spite of your venom, ignorance, an' audacious intolerance. That's why your tribe never gets anywhere. After all, th' whole world knows we English are th' supreme examples of unity an' orderliness ! I hope to see all foreigners sent back to where you came from ; an', regardin' yourself, I wish you a bomb-strewn passage over your Irish Sea !

[*While the argument has been going on, Pobjoy has been edging back through the crowd towards the door ; and, later on, he slips away, unnoticed by the disputants.*

Joy. Us's gettin' tired of th' yarn about th' Irish as a fightin' race — if they are, where are they in this war — tell me that ?

Feelim [*afire with racial pride*]. Where are they, is it ? If you were only near enough to th' centre of the flame an' th' fighting, you'd know where they were ! Thousands of us left our bones to bleach in th' Vale of Tamar, th' time Harold tried to prevent th' Norman pennon from becomin' England's banner. Th' leopards on your banner would have jumped from th' flag had not the Irish held firm on the flank of the King's army at Crécy. Ay, an' when your gay an' godly King Harry th' Fifth got ringed round with horsemen an' spears at Agincourt, an' surrendered himself into God's care, he didn't forget to put th' Irish in th' front of the field.

Old Woman [*mocking*]. Oh ! that time's too far off to be brought in front of us now.

Mark [*bending down close to Feelim to say in a loud, hoarse whisper*]. What are they to do with them hens us was tellin' you about ?

Feelim [*stormily*]. What hens, what hens ?

Mark. Y'know, them hens th' Food Officer wants th' children of school teh bring 'ome on holidays, because she can't allocate rations f'r 'em while owners iss absent ?

Feelim. Can't you see, man, I'm engaged on an important discussion ? Let th' damned hens wait a minute ! Tell th' Food Officer th' girls'll bring th' hens home in their handbags ! [*To the crowd*] We'll bring things a bit nearer. We were at Waterloo ; we were frozen to th' ground in th' bastions of Sebastopol ; we were fightin' for yous in Egypt while our mothers an' fathers were gettin' evicted outa their poor hovels be th' landlords, as th' song of " Th' Irish Dragoons " shows. [*He stands up to sing :*]
    An' th' tears rolled down his sun-burned cheeks,
    An' dhropped on th' letther in his hand ;
    Is it thrue ? Too thrue ;
    More throuble in me native land !

Mark [*in an insistent, loud, and hoarse whisper*]. What iss us teh tell officer about hens ?

Feelim [*ignoring him*]. An' not only yous, but others revelled in our courage an' skill. Did any of you ever hear of the Pennsylvanian Line? [*After a short silence — shouting*] D'ye hear me? Did yous ever hear tell of th' Pennsylvanian Line? [*A short silence.*] None of yous, no! Well, they were th' best regiments in Washington's Army, an' almost all of them were Irish!

Old Woman. Ay, so you say.

Joy [*scornfully*]. Ah! for God's sake!

Feelim [*rising, and advancing towards them so that they back a little away from him*]. Ah, for God's sake, yourself! An' we climbed th' heights of Gettysburg, with sprigs of green in our caps: an' thousands of us terraced the slopes with our bodies that lie there quiet to this very day.
   [*Abe Penrhyn rushes in, somewhat wild and dishevelled. He pushes through the crowd till he is directly facing Feelim.*

Abe [*violently*]. There yeh are, asittin' in state, an' full of audacity in doin' a neebor harm! But God's ever thinkin' of how best to punish ill deeds, all an' sundry. Nawthin's 'id fr'm 'Ee. Where were your pumpers when farm was afire, eh?

Feelim. What pumpers?

Abe. Stirrup-pumpers, fool! An' y'ur fire guards an' shovellers?

Feelim. They were thryin' to be in ten places at once; and five of them are dead.

Abe. So'm I; near. What's left now of what stood proud, an' full of good things, with a throng o' work, makin' day pass quick, but a sulky heap o' ashes, an' coils of vicious smoke, stingin' honest men's eyes out o' them ! O God, un's all too hard to bear proper an' fit into what's meet teh say about Thy werks an' ways teh man !

Old Woman. Aw, poor man. A good, honest, reasonable Christian soul ! An example to all of Christian cherity en defiance.

Abe [*slumping down on a chair*]. All is ashes an' all is dust. Us's a broken man.

Old Woman. Aw, th' poor man. Jeopardy 'as done for 'im !

Feelim [*to Abe*]. Get a gun in your hand an' you'll feel betther.

Old Woman. Good an' proper advice. A gun's no hindrance to a neighbourly feelin'.

Mrs. Watchit. Ay, a sturdy un' steady gun's good thing teh have about house.

Abe [*vehemently*]. No, never ! Never took life — not even rabbit's. Us always got th' men about farm teh kill th' rabbits. [*Violently*] Ah, God, You're too hard on them as loves You more, an' serves You better'n far 'an others !

Feelim [*indignantly*]. I'll not let you insult God ! Say what you like about Feelim O'Morrigun ; but you must show ordinary respect to God Almighty !

Abe [*rising to his feet*]. I'll show ye ! Us'll spite ye all ! I've somethin' hid away ; but us'll bring she into light o' day !

Feelim [*earnestly*]. Take my advice an' leave th' dhrink alone.

Old Woman [*interested — going over to Abe*]. Ay, do ; bring it out, son. When a person feels low, a drop of stimulant has a tremendous way o' workin' good to soul an' body. Come on, son, an' we'll get it together.
          [*She half leads out Abe around the piano.*
     [*As they go out, the telephone on the table rings a call.*
     Feelim puts the receiver to his ear.

Feelim. Eh ? What is it, what is it ? Your husband must be given another billet ? Why ? Can't get any sleep at night because of th' fleas ? Well, what d'ye want me to do — organise a hunting exhibition ? Well, I can't help it if he does get a breakdown because of th' fleas. Complain to th' Billeting Officer. Oh ! you have ? Said there were worse things in th' world than little fleas ? I can't help it if they're eatin' him alive ! [*Impatiently*] Look here, I'm right in th' middle of an important conference, an' can't talk, now ; ring me up later on. [*He rings off, and gives his attention again to the crowd.*] Listen, yous. Yous didn't know all I'm after tellin' yous. And, if yous even did, aself, yous wouldn't believe it, for you have your doubts that there are stars in the sky. Who discovered quarternions ? Who was th' Father of Chemisthry ? [*He is nearly roaring by this time.*] There's nothin' that we didn't do, for in our time we were ministers, governors, an' chancererlors. Everywhere, without skippin' a single counthry of any known size, with a Christian thrace, or without one ! But yous have forgotten your own greatness. What about your saints, with your Ha ! St. George, instead of Ha ! St. Edward ? Where, today, is your St. Peter of York, St. Wilfrid of Ripon,

St. John o' Beverley ?   Forgotten as well as gone !
  [*Tired and breathless, he staggers to the chair, and sits
  down, panting.*

Mrs. Watchit. I wouldn't excite meself, if us was you,
Mr. O'Morrigun ; for it's a strain, 'usband says, as
over-estimates th' system.

Feelim [*leaping to his feet again in a final outburst*]. An' we're
here still, pierced be every bullet, scorched be every
bomb, shook be every shell ; an' here I am with death
as close as life to me, an' a son waitin' to gamble his
life in the skies for England's sake !
                    [*He sinks into the chair again.*
  [*The old woman comes rushing back alone, a look of wild
  fright on her face. She plunges through the astonished
  crowd.*

Old Woman [*as she rushes in*]. Make a passage there ! He's
on me tail ! Holy God, keep th' thing quiet for a
little longer ! Clear a way there !
                  [*She rushes out by big doorway.*

Feelim [*in wonderment*]. What th' hell's happened now ?
  [*Abe comes in, staggering a little. He carries a winged
  bomb in his arms. When the crowd see what he has,
  they press back to the walls. Some put chairs in front
  of them ; others crouch behind the table.*

Abe [*jubilantly*]. Us found she nestin' on window-sill.
[*Jeering*] Why do ye all look so anxious ? Fair surprise
for ye, varmints all !

Mark. What th' hell did 'ee meddle with bombs for ?
Us knows Government warned all not to touch
unfamiliar objects.

Feelim [*appealing to Mark*]. Don't excite him, Mark.

Abe. Bombs ain't no unfamiliar objects now.   Couldn't leave she sizzlin' on window-sill, could I ?

Feelim [soothingly]. There's a good man, now ; Abe, oul' son, take it away.   Give it to a policeman, or hand it over to the Home Guard.

Mark [angrily]. Us isn't trained to handle them things !

Feelim. He must give it to someone ; it can't be left on the mantelpiece.
 [*The Dame comes in slowly.   She is covered with a long black robe ; the one bright thing about her is a silver cap. Her face is mask-like in its lines of resignation.   No colour, and little life is in her voice.*

Dame Hatherleigh. What is this I hear you have, Abe ? You must carry it to where it can do no harm.   The house must change ; but it must not die.   ·[*She lays a hand on Abe's arm.*] Each of us is very near the other now.   Your home is gone ; mine is going.

Abe [fiercely]. Us's a wicked daughter, ma'am, and she's brought a double woe on us.

Dame Hatherleigh. Your daughter's a fine girl, Abe.   She must look before her ; we can only look behind.   [*To Feelim*] Feelim, guard well and cherish dearly all that may be coming to you.   [*To Abe*] Come, my friend — we shall go together.
 [*They go out together.   There is a silent pause of a few moments.*

Feelim [in a whisper]. Look outa th' window, Mark, an' see if you see them.

Mark [going to the window, and looking out]. There they go, dimly ; goin' down the concrete way that was once th' garden path.   All th' flowers are gone, though there

be some do say their scents is still about th' place,
'n stronger than before. [*As the house trembles and the
windows shake*] My God, what's that !

Crowd [*together*]. The house is trembling and the windows
shake !

Feelim [*leaning his head in his hands*]. Woe is bein' born
somewhere. Jesus ! Whoever thought God would
ever bother His head about th' English !

Mark [*at window*]. An' here's Penrhyn's daughter, Monica,
acomin' up what was once the garden path, an' now's
th' concrete way ; acomin' slow, but acomin' sure.

   [*The cloth panel of the wireless cabinet lights up, and shows
   the Union Jack and the Soviet Flag crossed, and fluttering,
   together, while a voice speaks from the cabinet.*

Voice. We wage a desperate war till death seizes the evil
thing born from Germany's belly, and trained to
destroy the world ! British people, the Red Army's
with us now ! To work ! Tanks for us and for them ;
planes for them and for us ; guns for us and for them !
To arms ! To work ! [*Voices heard singing :*]

   Heart of oak are our ships,
   Heart of oak are our men :
      We always are ready ;
      Steady, boys, steady !
   We'll fight and we'll conquer again and again !

   [*The panel darkens again. The young foreman comes in,
   and goes across the room. Outside, a distinct, but not
   loud, hum of moving machinery can be heard, with an
   occasional sharp clank of steel meeting steel.*

Foreman [*briskly*]. Now, ladies and gentlemen, murmur
your last farewell, and take your last look at the house

of your fathers ; for in a few minutes' time we link
this with the other factory turning out tanks for the
Red Army, and tanks for our own.

> [*Away in the distance, trumpets and drums play soft, very
> slowly, and low the melody covering one or two verses
> of the lament, " Oh, Bend Low the Head ". No-one
> apparently hears, though Feelim gives a slight indication
> of hearing the music.*

Monica [*calling outside*]. Feelim ! oh, Feelim ! [*Monica,
looking distraught, and a little dishevelled, comes in towards
Feelim. He rises, on seeing her so distressed, and she enters
softly into his arms.*] Oh ! Feelim, Feelim, pity me,
and hold me close ; for he was the other flyer who
fell aflame from the sky !

Feelim [*bravely, but a little brokenly*]. I guessed it all along ;
I knew it, Monica. My Drishogue, my son ! One was
Edgar ; the other was Drishogue. Who was the girl ?

Monica. Jennie. She tried to reach her lover, to hold him
in her burning arms, and calmly died beside him !

Feelim. We must be brave. My Drishogue ! His
father's lost him, but his mother has him by the hand.
[*After a pause*] Does th' poor Dame know ?

Monica. She knows, though she seems to be dying on her
feet. She insisted that as they died together, so they
should be buried together, and one covering shelters
the dust of lover and son and friend. They are here,
and are to be buried now.

Feelim [*as if in a stupor*]. God knows I'll miss you,
Drishogue !

Monica. Are you listening, Feelim ? They're about to be

carried out for burial now. Dame Hatherleigh is to stand by the window to see the last of them as long as she can.

Crowd [*who stand round with bent heads*]. They died for us all. God be good to them !

Mark [*softly — to Feelim*]. Us'll see teh th' hens — don't ee worry no more.

Monica [*gently shaking Feelim's arm*]. Listen, Feelim ! The casket's covered with our English flag ; and to keep his spirit calm beside his comrades, I draped a silken strip of green above our English colours.

Feelim. That was real kind of you, now, Monica. Th' old colour. Ay, a brave oul' flag. Is there e'er a war known to man where it wasn't seen ? I'd be obliged to any man who'd mention one. [*He pauses.*] Age has twisted a little stiffness into me ; but th' oul' eye is still clear, and th' oul' legs are still sturdy. [*To the crowd*] Yous are askin' me silently what'll I do now, an' will I go back to where I come from ? [*With a shout*] Give me me steel hat, one o' yous ! [*Mark hands it to him, and he fixes it firmly on his head.*] Let the grey hair be hid behind it, for steel's a sensible embroidery for an ageing head today. [*Savagely*] Th' damned villains, bloodied all over with th' rent-out lives of child an' woman ! They owe Feelim O'Morrigun a son ; an', be Christ ! old as he is, he'll help to make them pay to th' uttermost farthing in th' blood of their youngest an' their best ! Let their bombs explode, an' wreck an' tear, an' tumble everything ! It'll take more than they can make an' carry to punch us out of where we stand to fight them ! [*He raises his hands in an eloquent gesture*] Hearts of steel, well tempered

with hate, is what we are today — hearts of steel !
Hearts of oak don't last ; so hearts of steel we are !

Crowd [*enthusiastically*]. Ay, all of us — hearts of steel !

Feelim [*more vehemently than ever*]. Ay, from now on to
fight, harry, an' rend th' Germans till they're glad to
go goose-steppin' into th' grave ! Here on this spot,
at this moment, Feelim O'Morrigun takes up th'
fight where Drishogue laid it down ! [*Brokenly —
laying a hand on Monica's shoulder*] A cap-badge an' a few
buttons are all that's left of my boy !

Monica [*nestling closer to him, and speaking as if it were a
secret*]. There's more to come ; a living spark from
himself that will soon be a buoyant symbol of our
Drishogue who is gone !

Feelim [*his puritan nature asserting itself*]. Oh ! that was
wrong of him ! I knew somethin' dangerous would
come of the two of you bein' so often together !

Monica [*fiercely*]. It was right and proper of him, for I
wanted a pledge of all he meant to me ; and I got it ;
and I'm glad. Besides, we were married a month ago
at a registry office ; but his dad and my dad were so
contrairy that we didn't say anything about it.

Feelim [*shocked*]. Woman, woman, that isn't anythin' in
th' nature of a marriage at all !

Monica. It satisfies me. My dad won't, so you must
stand by me now.

Feelim. Ay, ay ; yes, yes ; but the gettin' o' children
should be done accordin' to rule !

Mark. Us'll all stand by you ; an' th' babe shall become
th' child of th' community.

Crowd. The babe shall become the child of the community.

Feelim. Oh ! Which is worse — th' burden of th' dead who are with us now ; or that of the living still to come !

> [*The trumpets and drums outside, just below the window, play the melody going with the first verse of the lament " Oh, Bend Low the Head ".*

> [*Dame Hatherleigh moves in very slowly, and stands, facing forward, right in front of the window. The Dame is dressed in a long sable cloak, similar to that worn by The Son of Time, which covers her completely, showing no sign of green ; and her head is covered by a silver cap, similar too to the one worn by Time's son. Her face is white, and set impassively like a mask. The coffin — half covered with a Union Jack, and half by a vivid strip of green silk — is borne in by Home Guards and farm workers, and crosses the room slowly to go out by the doorway on the right. Dame Hatherleigh turns round slowly to gaze rigidly out of the window. As the trumpets play the melody a second time, those in the room and outside sing the words of the lament :*

Oh ! bend low the head to this casket of clay,
Where young life lies darken'd while yet it is day.

Their laughter so young and so careless is o'er,
And their feet, prone to dance, shall be dancing no more.

No longer th' white apple-blossom is nigh,
And silent for ever the lassie's fond sigh ;

Th' lark's song is gone ; and they'll ne'er stir to see
A sky bravely blue o'er an autumn-bronz'd tree !

> [*Preceded by Feelim and Monica, the crowd follows the coffin out ; the two Home Guards bringing up the rear.*

[*When the music becomes faint in the distance, the young
foreman, taking no notice of Dame Hatherleigh still
standing rigid by the window, blows a whistle sharply,
and the room becomes alive with movement — the belts
travel, the wheels turn, and the drop-hammer rises and
falls.   The central wheel is yellow as the ripening corn ;
the smaller ones red as the setting sun ; and the travelling-
belts green as dewy grass on a fine spring morning.
Through the window, the silhouette of the great crane's
jib is seen, holding in its beak the silhouette of a tank
that is swung by the window, down to the ground.   The
modified clank of steel touching steel is heard, accompanied
by the sounds indicating the busy and orderly hustle of a
factory.   In a few moments the room rapidly darkens,
and at once lightens again into a vague twilight, showing
the shadowy dancers grouped in the room, triangularly
facing   towards   the   window.   Dame `Hatherleigh,
wrapped in her sable cloak, and wearing the silver cap,
stands rigid where Time's young son had previously stood
beside the clock.   Very faintly in the distance the melody
— now near as vague as the twilight — of the lament
can still be heard.*

1st Lady Dancer [*to her companion*]. Do you hear anything,
Maurice ?   Listen !   The sound of some very faint
music sounding like a sad, a very sad, valse ?   Listen !
The sound of silent steps around us !   The dead —
they make me shiver !

1st Gentleman Dancer. Some new souls seeking out com-
panionship from shadows.   But you and I can only
yield a thought to them.

1st Lady Dancer. Ah ! how quick the place is changing.
Smooth-faced memory is turning rough, and thrusts us
out from places well beloved.

Dame Hatherleigh [*in a sad voice, beginning to grow toneless*].
We must all go soon. Our end makes but a beginning
for others.

1st Lady Dancer. Where can we go, Maurice, oh ! where
can we go ? This place only has the wistful look of
eternal life.

1st Gentleman Dancer. Fear not, sweet lady : our hands
still mingle, though they do not touch. Fear not,
sweet lass, for shadows are immortal.

Dame Hatherleigh. Only the rottenness and ruin must die.
Great things we did and said ; things graceful, and
things that had a charm, live on to dance before the
eyes of men admiring.

2nd Lady Dancer. See St. Paul's standing sturdy out
against the sky ; and see, the people's heads are holding
high, and swing is in their carriage.
    [*The sound of marching feet is heard : not of a squad of
    Home Guards, but of a mighty host.*

2nd Gentleman Dancer [*sadly*]. The people need our swords
no longer.

1st and 3rd Gentlemen Dancers [*sadly — echoing him*]. The
people need our swords no longer.

Lady Dancers [*together*]. Well-a-day ! that ye had no
swords to offer !

3rd Gentleman Dancer. Look at the endless columns of
marching men in brown ! Gracious God ! has colour
gone from life !

3rd Lady Dancer. Don't look, don't look ! You frighten
me with a vision of a dulled-out world !

Dame Hatherleigh. Is the crimson cherry brown ? The

apple-blossom black? The sky for ever grey? No, no! The cherry is as red as ever; the apple-blossom rosy; and the sky is often blue; sweet lavender rears tops of gentle purple; many a sturdy oak shall strut from a dying acorn; and a maiden's lips still quiver for a kiss.

3rd Gentleman Dancer. The lavender will bloom again, and oak leaves laugh at the wind in the storm.

Dame Hatherleigh. And every factory and every home will carve a niche for a graceful coloured candle. [*A little more wakeful.*] The scent of lavender's in every breath I draw, and the dancers are very close. Wait a moment for me, friends, for I am one of you, and will join you when I find my son.
[*She slowly sinks down to lean her body against the clock.*

1st Gentleman Dancer. The lavender shall bloom again!

The Others [*together*]. The lavender shall bloom again!
[*They begin to dance their stiff, slow, but graceful minuet; the music, as before, accompanying them is slow, and somewhat staccato, as if the player found it hard to press down the notes. While they are dancing, the voice of the Lavender Seller is heard again chanting her wares.*

Lavender Seller [*singing outside in the street*]:
Ladies, buy my bonnie lavender,
Incense for your snowy sheetings,
Giving charm to all the ruling joys
Measur'd out in lovers' meetings!
    Lavender, lavender,
Ladies, buy my bonnie laven-lavender!

CURTAIN

LAVENDER

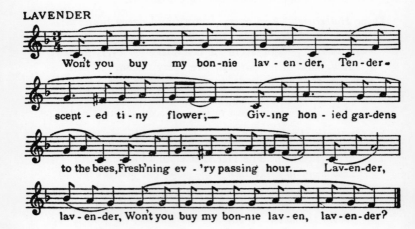

Won't you buy my bon-nie lav - en - der, Ten-der-
scent - ed ti - ny flower;— Giv-ing hon - ied gar-dens
to the bees, Fresh'ning ev - 'ry passing hour.— Lav-en-der,
lav - en-der, Won't you buy my bon-nie lav - en, lav-en-der?

RED-HEADED JOHNNY AND ME

When we stretch'd our-selves down in a hur-ry,— Be-
-neath the soft shade of a tree,— Th' moon threw her man-tle of
sil-ver— O'er red-head-ed John-ny and me.— Stars
twink-led a wel-come an' won-der'd— How we
far'd un-der Cyn-thi-a's shawl; No girl ev-er suf-fer'd such
pleas-ure,— Since Ad-am gave Eve her first fall!—
Ho, then, for young man an' maiden— Fair jewels of love fiercely a-
-glow— Who save life e-ter-nal from fad-in',— An'
keep a tir'd world on th' go!—

SHY LASS

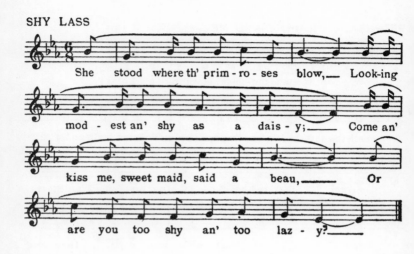

She stood where th' prim-ro-ses blow,— Look-ing mod-est an' shy as a dais-y;— Come an' kiss me, sweet maid, said a beau,— Or are you too shy an' too laz-y?—

DIGGING FOR VICTORY

Oh, here's to the trous-ers and green jer-sey, too, That are out in the sun, and the rain and the dew, Un-der the sky when it's black or it's blue, Dig-ging hard, dig-ging deep, in the morn - ing!

GIVE US SHELTERS

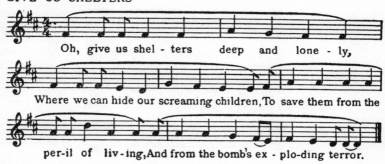

Oh, give us shel - ters deep and lone - ly, Where we can hide our screaming children, To save them from the per-il of liv-ing, And from the bomb's ex - plo-ding terror.

LADS IN AIR FORCE BLUE

Young lust - y lads in Air Force blue, Go forth wear - ing red rose and rue; Our life, our dreams, de--pend___ on you,___ Sons of Eng - land!

IRISH DRAGOON'S SONG

An' th' tears rolled down his sun-burned cheeks, An'
dropped on th' let-ter in his hand.   Is   it
thrue? Too true—More troub-le in me nat-ive   land!

BEND LOW THE HEAD (Lament)

Slow and sad

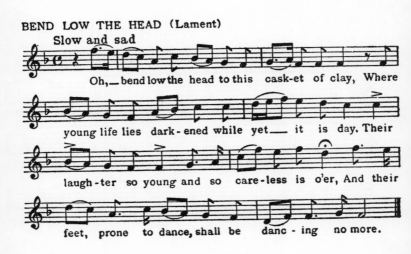

Oh,— bend low the head to this cask-et of clay, Where
young life lies dark-ened while yet__ it is day. Their
laugh-ter so young and so care-less is o'er, And their
feet, prone to dance, shall be   danc-ing no more.

COCK-A-DOODLE DANDY

TO

JAMES STEPHENS

THE JESTING POET

WITH A RADIANT STAR

IN'S COXCOMB

CHARACTERS IN THE PLAY

THE COCK

MICHAEL MARTHRAUN, *a small farmer, now the owner of a lucrative bog*

SAILOR MAHAN, *once a sailor, now the owner of a fleet of lorries carrying turf from bog to town*

LORNA, *second young wife of Marthraun*

LORELEEN, *Marthraun's daughter by his first young wife*

MARION, *helper in Lorna's house*

SHANAAR, *a " very wise old crawthumper ", really a dangerous old cod*

1ST ROUGH FELLOW ⎫ *peasants working on the bog*
2ND ROUGH FELLOW ⎭

FATHER DOMINEER, *the parish priest of Nyadnanave*

THE SERGEANT, *of the Civic Guard*

JACK, *Mahan's foreman lorry driver*

JULIA, *Lorna's sister, a paralytic on a visit to Lourdes*

HER FATHER

ONE-EYED LARRY, *a peasant lad and potential sacristan*

A MAYOR

A MACE-BEARER

THE MESSENGER, *in love with Marion*

THE BELLMAN, *a kind of town crier*

A PORTER, *of a general store in the near-by town*

SCENES

SCENE I.—The front garden outside Michael Marthraun's
house, in Nyadnanave.
Morning.

SCENE II.—The same.
Midday.

SCENE III.—The same.
Dusk.

Part of the garden outside the house of Michael Marthraun. It is rough and uncared-for, with tough grass everywhere, sprinkled with buttercups and daisies. It is surrounded by a stone wall, three to four feet high, which is pierced by a wooden gate to the right of any visitor entering the garden. To the left, a little way from the gate, a clump of sunflowers, in full bloom, stand stiff and stately, their blossoms big as shields, the petals raying out widely and sharply, like rays from an angry sun. Glancing farther to the left, a visitor would see the gable-end of the house, with a porch jutting from it, and a window above the porch. The porch is supported by twisted pillars of wood, looking like snakes, which are connected with lattice-work shaped like noughts and crosses. These are painted a dazzling white. The framework of the window above is a little on the skew, and the sash-work holding the glass is twisted into irregular lines. A little way from the porch, towards the wall, is a dignified-looking bronze urn holding a stand-offish, cynical-looking evergreen. Farther up, near the wall, the Irish Tricolour flutters from a flag-pole. The house itself is black in colour, the sash and frame of the window in it is a brilliant red.

It is a brilliantly fine day in summer, and as there is nothing in the garden to provide a shade, the place is a deep pool of heat, which, seemingly, has lasted for some time, for the grass has turned to a deep yellow hue, save where the house and porch throw a rich black shadow. Stretching away in the . distance, beyond the wall, is a bog of a rich purple colour, dabbed here and there with black patches. The sky above it is a silvery grey, glittering like an oriental canopy.

Some little distance away, an accordion is heard playing a

*dance tune, and, a few moments after, the Cock comes dancing in
around the gable of the house, circles the dignified urn, and disappears round the farther end of the gable-end as the music ceases.*

*He is of a deep black plumage, fitted to his agile and slender
body like a glove on a lady's hand ; yellow feet and ankles,
bright-green flaps like wings, and a stiff cloak falling like a tail
behind him. A big crimson crest flowers over his head, and
crimson flaps hang from his jaws. His face has the look of a
cynical jester.*

*Michael Marthraun, followed by Sailor Mahan, comes into
the garden by the porch. Each carries a kitchen chair, which
they set down some way from the house. Michael is a man who
is well over sixty years of age, clean-shaven, lean, and grim-
looking. His lips twitch nervously whenever he forgets to keep
his mouth tightly closed. He is dressed in a blackish tweed suit,
and his legs are encased in black leggings. A heavy gold chain
stretches across his waistcoat, and he wears a wide-leafed collar,
under which a prim black bow is tied.*

*Sailor Mahan is a little over fifty, stouter than his com-
panion, and of a more serene countenance. He has a short,
pointed beard, just beginning to show signs of greyness. His
face is of a ruddier hue, and shows that the wind and the stress of
many storms have made it rugged, but in no way unpleasant.
There is, maybe, a touch of the sea-breeze in his way of talking
and his way of walking. He is wearing light-grey flannel
trousers, a double-breasted royal blue coat, and has a white scarf
round his neck, over a light-blue shirt. They come to the two
chairs, and stand there facing each other.*

Michael. Come out here, come on out here, where a body
can talk free. There's whispers an' whispers in that
house, upsettin' a man's mind.

Mahan [puzzled]. Whispers ? What kinda whispers ?

Michael. Sthrange kinds ; whispers good for neither soul nor body.

Mahan. But there's no-one in the house but your wife, Lorna, Marion the maid, and your own girl Loreleen ?

Michael. Ay, so you think ; but I know different.

Mahan [*breezily*]. Nonsense, Mick ; you're haulin' on a rope that isn't there !

Michael [*raising his voice*]. You don't live in th' house, do you ? [*Mahan is silent.*] You don't live in th' house, do you ?

Mahan [*raising his voice too*]. I know I don't live in it, an' if it's like what you say, I don't want to live in it !

Michael. Well, then, keep quiet when a man speaks of what he knows.

Mahan. I know as much about a whisper as you do.

Michael. You know about th' whispers of wind an' wave, harmless an' innocent things ; but I'm talkin' about whispers ebbin' an' flowin' about th' house, with an edge of evil on them, since that painted one, that godless an' laughin' little bitch left London to come here for a long an' leering holiday.

Mahan. Loreleen ? Why, man, she's your own daughter by your first young wife !

Michael. So it was said at th' time, an' so it's believed still ; but I had me doubts then, and I've more doubts now. I dhread meetin' her, dhread it, dhread it. [*With a frightened laugh*] Michael Marthraun's daughter ! [*Gripping Mahan's arm*] Is she anyone's daughter, man ?

Mahan [*impatiently*]. She must be somebody's daughter, man !

Michael [*impatiently*]. Why must she be, man ? Remember what th' Missioner said last night : Sthrange things are foisted by the powers of evil into th' life o' man. Since that one come back from England, where evil things abound, there's sinisther signs appearin' everywhere, evil evocations floatin' through every room.

Mahan [*puzzled*]. What kinda evocation an' significality is there ?

Michael [*looking suspiciously at the porch, then at the window above it, and drawing Mahan farther away from the house*]. Looka, Sailor Mahan [*he speaks furtively*], there's always a stern commotion among th' holy objects of th' house, when that one, Loreleen, goes sailin' by ; an invisible wind blows th' pictures out, an' turns their frenzied faces to th' wall ; once I seen the statue of St. Crankarius standin' on his head to circumvent th' lurin' quality of her presence ; an' another time, I seen th' image of our own St. Pathrick makin' a skelp at her with his crozier ; fallin' flat on his face, stunned, when he missed !

Mahan [*doubtful, but a little impressed*]. Good God, them's serious things, Michael Marthraun ! [*A pause.*] Are you sure, now, Mick, you're not deludin' yourself ?

Michael. Have sense, man ! An' me own wife, Lorna Marthraun, is mixin' herself with th' disordher, fondlin' herself with all sorts o' dismayin' decorations. Th' other day, I caught her gapin' into a lookin'-glass, an' when I looked meself, I seen gay-coloured horns branchin' from her head !

Mahan. No ! Oh, Mick, you're fancyin' things. Lorna's a fine, upstandin' woman, an' should be respected.

Michael. Are you gone on her, too ? I tell you, I seen the way th' eyes of young men stare at her face, an' follow th' movements of her lurin' legs — there's evil in that woman !

Mahan. But there's nothin' evil in a pretty face, or in a pair of lurin' legs.

Michael. Oh, man, your religion should tell you th' biggest fight th' holy saints ever had was with temptations from good-lookin' women.

Mahan [*getting nervous, and eager to change the subject*]. Looka, let's sit down, an' thry to settle about what you're willin' to pay for th' cartage of th' turf.

Michael [*ignoring Mahan's attempt to change the tide of talk*]. Up there in that room [*he points to the window above the porch*] she often dances be herself, but dancin' in her mind with hefty lads, plum'd with youth, an' spurred with looser thoughts of love. [*As he speaks, the sounds of a gentle waltz are heard, played by harp, lute, or violin, or by all three, the sounds coming, apparently, from the room whose window is above the porch. Bitterly*] There, d'ye hear that, man ! Mockin' me. She'll hurt her soul, if she isn't careful.

Mahan. She's young enough yet to nourish th' need o' dancin'. An' anyway, why did you insist on marryin' her, an' she so young ; an' she so gay ? She was all again' it herself.

Michael. She consented to it, at last, didn't she ?

Mahan. Ay, when you, her father, an' th' priest had

badgered th' girl's mind into disordered attention over th' catch she was gettin'.

Michael. Oh, well you know, Sailor Mahan, that she had her blue eye on th' fat little farm undher me feet ; th' taut roof over me head ; an' th' kind cushion I had in th' bank, against a hard day.

Mahan. I seen you meself throtting afther her from starboard to port, from poop to quarther-deck, hoistin' before her th' fancy of ribbon an' lace, silver-buckled shoes, an' a silk dhress for Sunday.

Michael. An' what had she but a patched petticoat, a worn look, an' broken brogues to wear to Mass on Sundays ? An' didn't I give her oul' fella fifty solid pounds so that her ailin' sisther could thravel to Lourdes to get undher th' aegis of th' Blessed Virgin ? An' what did I get for them but a scraggy oul' bog of two hundhred acres ?

Mahan. An' you're makin' a good thing out of it since turf came into its own. It's made you a Councillor, a Justice of th' Peace, an' th' fair-haired boy of th' clergy.

Michael. As you mentioned turf, we'd betther settle this question of you demandin', for carting it, an exthra amount I couldn't possibly pay.

Mahan [*stiffness coming into his voice*]. You'll have to, Michael Marthraun, for it can't be done now for a cent less.

Michael. We'll have a drink while we're discussin'. I have a bottle of th' best, ten years maturin', inside. Sit down there till I get it. [*He goes into the porch and, after a few moments, comes quickly out again, his mouth twitching, his voice toned to fear and hate.*] That one, Loreleen's comin' down th' stairs, an' I don't want to come too near her. We'll wait till she goes. Let's talk of our affairs, quietly, while she passes by. Th' thing to do, as Shanaar would tell you, when you hear a sound or see a shape of anything evil, is to take no notice of it. [*Whispering impatiently*] Sit down, man !

Mahan [*sitting down — dubiously*]. Are you sure, Mick, you have a close-hauled comprehension of th' way you're thinkin' ?

Michael. Ay, am I sure ; as sure as I am that a cock crows !
  [*A cock suddenly crows lustily as Loreleen appears in the doorway of the porch. She is a very attractive young woman with an air of her own. A jaunty air it is, indicating that it is the sign of a handsome, gay, and intelligent woman. She is dressed in a darkish green dress, with dark-red flashes on bodice and side of skirt. A saucy hat of a brighter green than the dress sports a scarlet ornament, its shape suggestive of a cock's crimson crest. Her legs — very charming ones — are clad in brown silk stockings ; brown that flashes a golden sheen.*
  [*Michael, who has sat down, jumps startled to his feet at the sudden sound of the cock's crow and, stretching over the table, grips Mahan by the shoulder.*

Michael. What's that, what's that ?

Mahan [*startled by Michael's frightened movement*]. What's what, man ?

Michael [*trying to recover himself*]. Nothin', I heard nothin'. What was it you were sayin' ? [*In a whisper*] Get goin' on th' turf, man.

Mahan [*mystified, but doing his best*]. You'll have to grant
th' two shillin's additional on each load, Mick. I'd
work me lorries at a loss if I took less. [*Placing an
affectionate hand on Michael's shoulder*] An' you know well,
you're such an oul' an' valued friend, I'd do it for
affection's sake, if I only could.

Michael [*forgetting about Loreleen*]. Don't I know that well,
Sailor Mahan ; an' I'd do th' same, an' more, be you ;
but if I surrendhered two shillin's, I might as well
give you th' bog as well. I have to live, Sailor Mahan.

Mahan. Damn it, man, haven't I to live too ? How th'
hell am I goin' to give th' men a shillin' more without
th' exthra two shillin's from you ? Pray to th' saints
to let them fall like rain from heaven, eh ?

Michael [*putting his face closer to Mahan's, hotly*]. Looka here,
Sailor Mahan, you're not goin' to magicfy me into th'
dhream of believin' you're not addin', every hurryin'
week, a fine bundle o' notes to th' jubilant store you've
there already, forcin' overtime on th' poor men o' th'
bank, flickin' th' notes into imperial ordher.

Mahan [*as fiercely — standing up to say it, his face close to the
face of Michael*]. An' you yourself, Michael Marthraun,
aren't worn away with th' punishment of poverty !
Puttin' on a poor mouth, an' if you set out to count
graciously all you have in hidlins, you'd be workin'
many a long, glad day, without supper or sleep, be daylight an' candle-light, till your mind centhred on th'
sum dominated be th' last note fluttherin' from your
fingers !

Loreleen [*who has strolled slowly over to the gate, listening to the
talk the while, turning at the gate to watch as well as listen*].

Lay not up for yourselves treasures upon earth, where moth and rust doth corrupt, and where thieves break through and steal !

Michael [*in a frightened whisper*]. Don't turn your head ; take no notice.   Don't pretend to hear her lyin' hallucinations !

> [*A young, rough-looking Fellow, well-set and strong, comes running along the pathway to the gate.   He is wearing dark-brown corduroy trousers, belted at waist, grey shirt, and scarf of bright green, with yellow dots. He pushes Loreleen aside.*

1st Rough Fellow [*pushing Loreleen out of his way*]. Outa me way, woman !   [*He sees how charming she is as he swings her aside.*]   Be God, but you're th' good-lookin' lass ! What are you doin' in this hole ?

Loreleen. Seeking happiness, an' failing to find it.

1st Rough Fellow. It isn't here you should be, lost among th' rough stones, th' twisty grass, an' th' moody misery of th' brown bog ; but it's lyin' laughin' you should be where th' palms are tall, an' wherever a foot is planted, a scarlet flower is crushed ;   where there's levity living its life, an' not loneliness dyin' as it is here.

Loreleen [*dropping him a deep curtsy*]. Thank you, sir knight, for th' silken compliments to your handmaiden.

> [*She turns to go out, and the Rough Fellow hurries in through the gate, down to the two men.*

1st Rough Fellow [*going through the gate down to where the two men are, and turning to speak up to Loreleen, still standing at the gate*]. If you wait till I'm done with these fellas [*he*

indicates Michael and Mahan] I could go to th' bend o' th'
road with you, for it's meself would surrendher a long
spell of heaven's ease to go a long day's journey with a
lass like you !

> [*Another Rough Fellow hurries in along the pathway out-
> side to the gate, pulling Loreleen aside when he finds her in
> his way. He wears light-brown corduroy trousers, check
> shirt, and has a scarf of light yellow, with green stripes,
> round his neck.*

2nd Rough Fellow [*pulling Loreleen out of his way*]. Eh, there,
woman — outa me way ! [*He sees, as she swings around,
how charming she is.*] Arra, what winsome wind blew
such a flower into this dread, dhried-up desert ? Deirdre
come to life again, not to sorrow, but to dance ! If Eve
was as you are, no wondher Adam fell, for a lass like
you could shutther th' world away with a kiss !

> [*He goes through the gate, and down to the other men,
> pausing to look up at Loreleen again.*

2nd Rough Fellow [*to Loreleen*]. Wait, lass, till I'm done
with these fellas, an' I'll go with you till youth's a
shadow a long way left behind !

Loreleen [*down to the two Rough Fellows*]. I'm not for you,
friends, for I'm not good for decent men. The two old
cronies will tell you a kiss from me must be taken
undher a canopy of dangerous darkness. [*She kisses a
hand to them.*] Goodbye !   [*She goes out.*

Michael ⎱ [*together*]. What d'ye th' two of yous want here ?
Mahan ⎰   Why aren't yous at work ?

1st Rough Fellow [*laying a hand sternly on the shoulder of
Mahan*]. Looka, you ; you give us th' exthra shillin', or

we leave your lorries standin', helpless an' naked on th' roads!

2nd Rough Fellow [*laying a hand sternly on Michael's shoulder*]. Looka, you; looka that! [*He throws a cheque contemptuously on to the table.*] D'ye think a good week's wages is in a cheque for tuppence?

Michael. You didn't work a week, because of th' rain, an' canteen contribution an' insurance brought your wage for the week to tuppence.

2nd Rough Fellow. Tell me how I'm goin' to live a week on tuppence?

1st Rough Fellow. Seein' th' both of them's Knights o' Columbanus, they should be able to say.

Michael. That's a social question to be solved by th' Rerum Novarum.

2nd Rough Fellow. Fifty years old; not worth much when it was born, an' not worth a damn now. You give a guaranteed week, or th' men come off your bog!
[*He goes off towards the gate.*

1st Rough Fellow [*going to the gate — to Mahan*]. Take our demand serious, or your lorries stand still on th' highways!

2nd Rough Fellow [*impatiently*]. Looka, there she is! [*He points a finger in front.*] Let's hurry, an' we'll ketch up on th' fine, fair lady.
[*They hurry along the path, but suddenly stop to stare ahead.*

1st Rough Fellow [*with awe in his voice*]. What's happenin' to her? A cloud closin' in on her, flashes like lightning whirlin' round her head, an' her whole figure ripplin'!

2nd Rough Fellow [*frightened*]. Jasus, she's changin' into th' look of a fancy-bred fowl ! It's turnin' to face us ; it's openin' its bake as big as a bayonet !

> [*The crow of a cock is heard in the distance.*

1st Rough Fellow [*frightened*]. Here, man, th' other way for us ! It's an omen, a warnin', a reminder of what th' Missioner said last night that young men should think of good-lookin' things in skirts only in th' presence of, an' undher th' guidance of, old and pious people.

> [*The two of them hurry away in the opposite direction.*

Michael [*to Mahan*]. Did you hear that ? I'm askin' you, Sailor Mahan, did you hear what them two graspin' rascals said ?

Mahan. I heard, but I can see no significality in it, unless th' two of them had dhrink taken.

Michael [*warningly*]. Looka, Sailor Mahan, if you aren't careful, your wilful disbelief in things'll lead you asthray ! Loreleen isn't me daughter ; she isn't even a woman : she's either undher a spell, or she's a possessed person.

Mahan [*with contempt*]. Aw, for God's sake, Mick, have sense, an' get that bottle o' whiskey out to put a spell on us.

Michael [*almost shouting*]. Have you forgotten already th' case of th' Widow Malone who could turn, twinklin', into a dog or a hare, when she wanted to hide herself ? An' how, one day, th' dogs followed what they thought was a hare that made for th' widow's cottage, an' dived through an open window, one o' th' dogs snappin' a leg off before it could get through. An' when th' door was burst open, there was th' oul' witch-widow screamin' on her oul' bed, one leg gone, with blood spoutin' from th' stump, so that all th' people heard her last screechin' as she went sliddherin' down to hell!

Mahan. I heard tell of it months after, when I come back from Valparaiso.

Michael. Well, if you heard of it, you know it must have happened. An' here you are, thinkin' only of whiskey, and showin' how ready you are to ruin me be askin' more than I'm able to give. You, a good Christian, a Knight of St. Columbanus, a student in th' Circle studyin' th' Rerum Novarum, you should show a sign of charity an' justice, recognisin' th' needs of th' people rather than your own. [*Suddenly*] Here, I'll add thruppence, an' make th' offer ninepence. Hold out th' hand, an' clinch th' bargain.

Mahan. I'll be scuppered if I will! You'll not use me like th' oul' father of th' good woman within, who sold you th' bog when he thought it was derelict, though you're makin' thousands out of it now.

Michael. You forget I gave th' oul' cod enough to bring his other daughter to Lourdes for a cure!

Mahan. You know th' way th' men are actin' now — goin' slow, an' doin' two journeys where they used to do three.

Michael. An' aren't my men threatenin' to come off th' bog altogether? It's this materialism's doin' it — edgin' into revolt against Christian conduct. If they'd only judge o' things in th' proper Christian way, as we do, there'd be no disputes. Now let's be good sons of

Columbanus — you thinkin' of my difficulties, an' me thinkin' of yours.

Mahan. Make your offer one an' sixpence, an' I'll hoist th' pennant of agreement ?

Michael. I couldn't.   Looka, Sailor Mahan, it would ruin me.

Mahan [*viciously*]. You'd rather throw th' money after a tall-hat so that you could controvert yourself into a dapper disturbance th' time the president comes to view th' workin' of th' turf.   Talk about Loreleen castin' a spell !   Th' whole disthrict'll be paralysed in a spell when your top-hat comes out to meet the president's top-hat, th' two poor things tryin' to keep people from noticin' what's undher them !   Two shillin's, now, or nothin'.   [*He sits down in disgust.*
      [*Behind the wall, Shanaar is seen coming along the road ;*
      he opens the gate, and comes slowly down to where the two
      men are.   He is a very, very old man, wrinkled like a
      walnut, bent at the shoulders, with longish white hair,
      and a white beard — a bit dirty — reaching to his belly.
      He is dressed peasant-wise, thin, threadbare frieze coat,
      patched blackish corduroy trousers, thick boots, good and
      strong, a vivid blue muffler round his neck, and a sack-
      cloth waistcoat, on which hangs a brass cross, suspended
      round his neck by twine.   A round, wide-brimmed, black
      hat is on his head.

Shanaar [*lifting his hat as he comes in by the gate*]. God save all here !   God save all that may be in th' house, barrin' th' cat an' th' dog !

Michael [*with great respect*]. An' you, too, Shanaar, old, old man, full of wisdom an' th' knowledge of deeper things.

Shanaar. Old is it ? Ever so old, thousands of years, thousands of years if all were told.

Michael. Me an' Sailor Mahan here were talkin' some time ago, about th' sthrange dodges of unseen powers, an' of what the Missioner said about them last night, but th' easiness of his mind hasn't been hindhered.

Shanaar [*bending lower, and shoving his bearded face between the two men*]. If it doesn't hindher th' easiness of his mind now, it will one day ! Maybe this very day in this very place.

Michael [*to Mahan*]. What d'ye say to that, now ?

Mahan [*trying to be firm, but a little uneasy*]. Nothin', nothin'.

Shanaar [*shoving his face closer to Mahan's*]. Ah, me friend, for years an' years I've thravelled over hollow lands an' hilly lands, an' I know. Big powers of evil, with their little powers, an' them with their littler ones, an' them with their littlest ones, are everywhere. You might meet a bee that wasn't a bee ; a bird that wasn't a bird ; or a beautiful woman who wasn't a woman at all.

Michael [*excitedly*]. I'm tellin' him that, I'm tellin' him that all along !

Mahan [*a little doubtfully — to Shanaar*]. An' how's a poor body to know them ?

Shanaar [*looking round cautiously, then speaking in a tense whisper*]. A sure sign, if only you can get an all-round glimpse of them. [*He looks round him again.*] *Daemones posteriora non habent* — they have no behinds !

Michael [*frightened a lot*]. My God, what an awe-inspiring, expiring experience !

Mahan [*frightened too, but trying to appear brave*]. That may be, but I wouldn't put innocent birds or bees in that category.

Shanaar [*full of pitying scorn for ignorance*]. You wouldn't ! Innocent birds ! Listen all : There was a cuckoo once that led a holy brother to damnation. Th' cuckoo's call enticed th' brother to a silent glade where th' poor man saw a lovely woman, near naked, bathin' her legs in a pool, an' in an instant th' holy man was taken with desire. Lost ! She told him he was handsome, but he must have money if he wanted to get her. Th' brother entered a noble's house, an' demanded a hundhred crowns for his convent ; but the noble was a wise old bird, an' said he'd have to see the prior first. Thereupon, th' brother up with an axe, hidden undher his gown, an' cleft th' noble from skull to chin ; robbed th' noble, dhressed himself in rare velvets, an' searched out all th' rosy rottenness of sin with th' damsel till th' money was gone. Then they caught him. Then they hanged him, an', mind you [*the three heads come closer together*], while this poor brother sobbed on the scaffold, everyone heard th' mocking laughter of a girl and th' calling of a cuckoo !

> [*As Shanaar is speaking the three last things, the mocking laughter of a girl is heard, the call of a cuckoo, and a young man's sobbing, one after the other, at first, then they blend together for a few moments, and cease. Shanaar stands as stiff as his bent back will allow, and the other*]

two rise slowly from their chairs, stiff, too, and
frightened.

Shanaar [*in a tense whisper*]. Say nothing ; take no notice.
Sit down. Thry to continue as if yous hadn't heard !

Mahan [*after a pause*]. Ay, a cuckoo, maybe ; but that's a
foreign bird : no set harbour or home. No genuine
decent Irish bird would do a thing like that on a man.

Michael. Looka here, Sailor Mahan, when th' powers of
evil get goin', I wouldn't put anything past an ordinary
hen !

Shanaar. An' you'd be right, Mr. Marthraun, though, as
a rule, hens is always undher th' eye an' comprehension
of a Christian. Innocent-looking things are often th'
most dangerous. Looka th' lad whose mother had set
her heart on him bein' a priest, an' one day, at home, he
suddenly saw a corncrake flyin' into a house be an
open window. Climbin' in afther it, he spied a glittherin'
brooch on a table, an' couldn't resist th' temptation o'
thievin' it. That lad spent th' next ten years in a
reformatory ; his mother died of a broken heart, and
his father took to dhrink.

[*During the recital of Shanaar's story, the " crek crek, crek
crek " of a corncrake is heard.*

Michael [*in a tense whisper — to Mahan*]. D'ye hear that,
Sailor Mahan ?

Shanaar [*warningly*]. Hush ! Take no vocal notice.
When yous hear anything or see anything suspicious,
give it no notice, unless you know how to deal with it.

Michael [*solemnly*]. A warnin' we'll remember. But
supposin' a hen goes wrong, what are we to do ?

Shanaar [*thoughtfully*]. It isn't aysey to say, an' you have
to go cautious.   The one thing to do, if yous have the
knowledge, is to parley with th' hens in a Latin dis-
sertation.   If among th' fowl there's an illusion of a
hen from Gehenna, it won't endure th' Latin.   She
can't face th' Latin.   Th' Latin downs her.   She
tangles herself in a helluva disordher.   She busts
asundher, an' disappears in a quick column of black
an' blue smoke, a thrue ear ketchin' a screech of agony
from its centre !

Michael [*tremendously impressed*]. Looka that now.   See what
it is to know !   [*A commotion is heard within the house :
a loud cackling, mingled with a short, sharpened crow of a
cock ; the breaking of delf ; the half-angry, half-frightened
cries of women.   A cup, followed by a saucer, flies out
through the open window, over the porch, past the heads of the
three men, who duck violently, and then crouch, amazed, and
a little frightened.*]   What th' hell's happenin' now ?
   [*Marion rushes to the door of the porch, frightened and
   alarmed.   She is a young girl of twenty or so, and very
   good-looking.   Her skirts come just to her knees, for they
   are nice legs, and she likes to show them — and why
   shouldn't she ?   And when she does so, she can add the
   spice of a saucy look to her bright blue eyes.   Instead of the
   usual maid's cap, she wears a scarf-bandeau round her
   head, ornamented with silver strips, joined in the centre
   above her forehead, with an enamelled stone, each strip
   extending along the bandeau as far as either ear.   She
   wears a dark-green uniform, flashed with a brighter green
   on the sleeves and neck, and the buttons of the bodice are of
   the same colour.   Her stockings and shoes are black.   A
   small, neat, white apron, piped with green, protects her
   uniform.*]

Marion [*excitedly — to the men*]. It's flyin' about th' house, an' behavin' outrageous ! I guessed that that Loreleen's cluck, cluck, cluckin' would upset th' bird's respectable way of livin' !

Michael [*frightened*]. What's wrong with you, girl ; what's up ?

Marion. Will one of yous come in, an' ketch it, for God's sake, before it ruins th' house ?

Mahan [*shouting*]. Ketch what, ketch what, woman ?

Marion. A wild goose ! It's sent th' althar light flyin' ; it's clawed the holy pictures ; an' now it's peckin' at th' tall-hat !

Michael. A wild goose ? Are you sure it was a wild one ?

Marion [*in great distress*]. I dunno, I dunno — maybe it's a wild duck. It's some flyin' thing tearin' th' house asundher.

Michael [*trembling — to Shanaar*]. D'ye think it might be what you know ?

Shanaar [*his knees shaking a little*]. It might be, Mr. Marthraun ! it might be, God help us !

Mahan [*nervous himself*]. Keep your heads, keep your heads ! It's nothin'.

Michael [*beside himself with anxiety and dread — shaking Marion roughly by the shoulders*]. Conthrol yourself, girl, an' speak sensibly. Is it a goose or a duck or a hen, or what is it ?

Marion [*wildly*]. It's a goose — no, it's a hen, it must be a hen ! We thried to dhrive it out with flyin' cups and

flyin' saucers, but it didn't notice them. Oh, someone should go in, or it'll peck th' place to pieces !

Shanaar [*prayerfully*]. So long as it's not transmuted, so
long as it's not been transmuted !

Michael [*shaking Marion again*]. Where's Lorna, where's
Lorna ?

Marion [*responding to the shaking listlessly*]. Last I seen of
her, she was barricadin' herself undher th' banisters !

Michael [*pleadingly — to Mahan*]. You've been free with
whales an' dolphins an' octopususas, Sailor Mahan —
you run in, like a good man, an' enthrone yourself on
top of th' thing !

Mahan [*indignant*]. Is it me ? I'm not goin' to squandher
meself conthrollin' live land-fowl !

Michael [*to Shanaar — half-commandingly*]. In case it's what
we're afraid of, you pop in, Shanaar, an' liquidate
whatever it is with your Latin.

Shanaar [*backing towards the wall*]. No good in th' house :
it's effective only in th' open air.

Michael [*in a fury — to Marion — pushing her violently towards
the gate*]. You go, you gapin', frightened fool, an' bring
Father Domineer quick !
   [*All this time, intermittent cackling has been heard, cackling
     with a note of satisfaction, or even victory in it, inter-
     spersed with the whirring sound of wings.*
   [*As Marion rushes out through the gate, she runs into the
     arms of the Messenger, who carries a telegram in his hand.
     He clasps Marion tight in his arms, and kisses her. He
     wears a silvery-grey coat, buttoned over his breast, and*

*trousers.   On the right side of the coat is a flash of a pair
of scarlet wings.   A bright-green beret is set jauntily on
his head and he is wearing green-coloured sandals.*
[*Michael and Mahan have moved farther from the house, and
Shanaar has edged to the gateway, where he stares at the
house, ready to run if anything happens.   His hands are
piously folded in front of him, and his lips move as if he
prayed.*

Messenger [*to Marion*]. Ah, lovely one of grace an' glad-
ness, whose kiss is like a honied flame, where are you
rushin' to in such a hurry ?

Michael [*angrily — up to the Messenger*]. Let her go, you —
she's runnin' for th' priest !

Messenger. Th' priest — why ?
[*The cackling breaks into intensity, the whirring of wings
becomes louder, and a plate flies out through the window,
followed by a squeal from Lorna.*

Messenger [*astonished, but not startled*]. What's goin' on in
th' house ?

Michael. There's a wild goose, or somethin', asthray in
th' house, an' it's sent th' althar bowl flyin' !

Marion. An' it's peckin' th' holy pictures hangin' on th'
walls.

Mahan. Some think it's a wild duck.

Shanaar. It may be a hen, only a hen.

Messenger [*releasing Marion, and handing the telegram to
Michael*]. Here's a telegram for you. [*Michael takes it
mechanically, and stuffs it in a pocket.*]   Is it losin' your

senses yous are to be afraid of a hen ? [*He goes towards the porch.*] I'll soon settle it !

Shanaar [*who is now outside, behind the wall*]. If you value your mortal life, lad, don't go in, for th' hen in there isn't a hen at all !

Messenger If th' hen, that isn't a hen, in there, isn't a hen, then it must be a cock. I'll settle it !

                        [*He rushes into the house.*

Michael [*in agony*]. If it's a cock, we're done !

Shanaar [*fervently*]. Oh, rowelum randee, horrida aidus, sed spero spiro specialii spam !
    [*The head of the Cock, with its huge, handsome crimson comb, is suddenly thrust through the window above the porch, and lets out a violent and triumphant crow. Shanaar disappears behind the wall, and Mahan and Michael fall flat in the garden, as if in a dead faint.*

Michael [*as he is falling*]. Holy saints preserve us — it's th' Cock !

Shanaar [*from behind the wall*]. Oh, dana eirebus, heniba et galli scatterum in multus parvum avic asthorum !
    [*The Cock's head is as suddenly withdrawn, and a louder commotion is heard to be going on in the house ; the Messenger shouting, a Woman's squeal. Then silence for a few moments as puffs of blue-black smoke jet out through the window. When the smoke has gone, the Messenger comes from the house into the garden. His cap is awry on his head, his face is a little flushed, and his mouth is smiling. He carries in his right hand what might have been a broomstick, but is now a silver staff, topped with a rosette of green and red ribbons. He is*

*followed out by the Cock whom he is leading by a green
ribbon, the other end circling the Cock's neck. The Cock
follows the Messenger meekly, stopping when he stops, and
moving when the Messenger moves.*

Shanaar [*peeping over the wall*]. Boys an' girls, take no
notice of it, or you're done ! Talk only of th' first
thing enthcrin' your minds.

Messenger [*looking with astonishment at the two men sitting up
now on the ground, as far as possible from the house, and moving
away when the Cock comes nearer*]. What's th' matther
with yous ? Why are yous dodgin' about on your
bums ? Get up, get up, an' be sensible.
   [*Michael and Mahan scramble to their feet, hurry out
   through the gate, and stand, warily, beside Shanaar.
   Lorna's head appears at the window above the porch, and
   it is at once evident that she is much younger than her
   husband, very good-looking still, but the bright and
   graceful contours of her face are somewhat troubled by a
   vague aspect of worry and inward timidity. Her face
   shows signs of excitement, and she speaks rather loudly
   down to the Messenger.*

Lorna [*to the Messenger*]. Robin Adair, take that bird away
at once. Hand him over to th' Civic Guard, or someone fit to take charge of him.

Messenger [*up to Lorna*]. Looka, lovely lady, there's no
danger, an' there never was. He was lonely, an' was
only goin' about in quest o' company. Instead of
shyin' cups an' saucers at him, if only you'd given him
your lily-white hand, he'd have led you through a wistful
an' wondherful dance. But you frightened th' poor
thing !

Lorna. Frightened him, is it? It was me was frightened
when I seen him tossin' down delf, clawin' holy
pictures, and peckin' to pieces th' brand new tall-hat
that Mr. Marthraun bought to wear, goin' with the
Mayor to greet His Brightness, th' President of Eire,
comin' to inaugerate th' new canteen for th' turf
workers.

Michael [*enraged*]. Is it me new hat he's desthroyed?

Shanaar [*pulling Michael's arm in warning*]. Damnit, man,
take no notice!

Michael [*turning indignantly on Shanaar*]. How'd you like
your sumptuous, silken hat to be mangled into a
monstrosity!

Shanaar [*with concentrated venom*]. Hush, man, hush!

Marion [*who has been looking at the Cock with admiration*].
Sure, he's harmless when you know him.

Messenger [*stroking its back*]. 'Course he is! Just a gay
bird, that's all. A bit unruly at times, but conthroll-
able be th' right persons. [*To the Cock*] Go on, comrade,
lift up th' head an' clap th' wings, black cock, an'
crow!
  [*The Cock lifts up his head, claps his wings, and lets out a
    mighty crow, which is immediately followed by a rumbling
    roll of thunder.*

Michael [*almost in a state of collapse*]. Aw, we're done for!

Shanaar [*violently*]. No notice, no notice!

Lorna [*from the window*]. God bless us, what's that?
[*Down to the Messenger*] Robin, will you take that
damned animal away, before things happen that God
won't know about!

Messenger [*reassuringly — up to Lorna*]. Lovely lady, you can let your little hands lie with idle quietness in your lap, for there's no harm in him beyond gaiety an' fine feelin'. [*To the Cock*] You know th' goose-step done be the Irish Militia in th' city of Cork more'n a hundhred years ago? Well, we'll go home doin' it, to show there's nothing undher th' sun Ireland didn't know, before th' world sensed it. Ready? One, two — quick march!

> [*The Messenger and the Cock march off doing the goose-step. Marion follows them, imitating the step, as far as the end of the garden ; then she stands looking after them, waving them farewell. Michael and Mahan come slowly and stealthily into the garden as the Cock goes out. They go to the chairs, on which they sit, exhausted, wiping their foreheads with their handkerchiefs. Shanaar comes towards them more slowly, keeping an eye in the direction taken by the Cock and the Messenger. When the place is clear, he anchors himself behind the table.*

Lorna [*down to Marion*]. Marion, dear, come on in, an' help me to straighten things up a little.

> [*She goes away from the window.*

Marion [*going slowly towards the house, after having given a last farewell — gleefully*]. Wasn't it a saucy bird! An' th' stately way he done th' goose-step! [*She playfully shakes Michael's shoulder*] Did you see it, sir? [*Michael takes no notice.*] God forgive me, but it gave us all an hilarious time — didn't it, sir?

Michael [*coldly*]. Your misthress called you.

Marion. I heard her, sir. What a clatther it all made! An' yous all quakin', an' even Sailor Mahan there, shakin' in his shoes, sure it was somethin' sinisther!

Mahan [*angrily*]. You go in to your misthress, girl !

Marion [*giggling*]. Th' bould sailor lad ! An' he gettin' rocked in th' cradle of th' deep ! Me faltherin' tongue can't impart th' fun I felt at seein' yous all thinkin' th' anchor was bein' weighed for th' next world !

Michael [*loudly*]. Go to your misthress when you're told.

Marion [*giggling more than ever*]. An' oul' dodderin' Shanaar, there, concoctin' his Latin, an' puttin' th' wall between himself an' th' blast ! Well, while yous sit all alone there in th' gloamin', yous won't be in heart for singin'. [*She chants*] " Only to see his face again, only to hear him crow ! " [*She runs merrily in.*

Shanaar [*warily — in a warning whisper*]. Watch that one !

Michael. Th' ignorant, mockin', saucy face of her afther us bein' in danger of thransportation to where we couldn't know ourselves with agony an' consternation !

Shanaar [*fervently*]. Sweet airs of heaven be round us all ! Watch that one, Mr. Marthraun. Women is more flexible towards th' ungodly than us men, an' well th' old saints knew it. I'd recommend you to compel her, for a start, to lift her bodice higher up, an' pull her skirt lower down ; for th' circumnambulatory nature of a woman's form often has a detonatin' effect on a man's idle thoughts.

Michael [*pensively*]. How thrue, how thrue that is !

Shanaar. What we have to do now, is to keep thought from dwellin' on th' things seen an' heard this day ; for dwellin' on it may bring th' evil back again. So don't let any thought of it, *ab initio extensio*, remain in your minds, though, as a precaution, when I'm passin' th' barracks, I'll acquaint the Civic Guard. Now I must be off, for I've a long way to thravel. [*He goes as far as the gate, and returns.*] Mr. Marthraun, don't forget to have th' room, where th' commotion was manifested, *turbulenta concursio cockolorum*, purified an' surified be an understandin' clergyman. Goodbye. [*Again he goes as far as the gate, and returns.*] Be on your guard against any unfamiliar motion or peculiar conspicuosity or quasimodical addendum, perceivable in any familiar thing or creature common to your general recognisances. A cat barkin' at a dog, or a dog miaouin' be a fire would atthract your attention, give you a shock, but don't, for th' love of God, notice it! It's this scourge of materialism sweepin' th' world, that's incantatin' these evils to our senses and our doorsteps.

Mahan [*pensively*]. That's th' way th' compass is pointin', Shanaar — everyone only thinkin', thinkin' of himself.

Shanaar. An' women's wily exhilarations are abettin' it, so that a man's measure of virtue is now made with money, used to buy ornaments, bestowed on girls to give a gaudy outside to the ugliness of hell.

Michael [*fervently*]. Oh, how thrue, how thrue that is!

Shanaar. An' th' coruscatin' conduct in th' dance-halls is completin' th' ruin.

Mahan [*solemnly*]. Wise words from a wiser man! Afther a night in one of them, there isn't an ounce of energy left in a worker!

Shanaar [*whispering*]. A last warnin'— Don't forget that six thousand six hundhred an' sixty-six evil spirits can find ready lodgin's undher th' skin of a single man!

Michael [*horrified*]. What an appallin' thought !

Shanaar. So be on your guard. Well, goodbye.

Michael [*offering him a note*]. Here's a pound to help you on your way.

Shanaar [*setting the note aside*]. No, thanks. If I took it, I couldn't fuse th' inner with th' outher vision ; I'd lose th' power of spiritual scansion. If you've a shillin' for a meal in th' town till I get to the counthry, where I'm always welcome, I'll take it, an' thank you.

[*Michael gives him a shilling.*

Shanaar. Thank you kindly. [*He goes out through the gate, and along the pathway outside. Just as he is about to disappear, he faces towards the two men, and stretches out a hand in a gesture of blessing. Fervently*] Ab tormentum sed absolvo, non revolvo, cockalorum credulum hibernica !

Michael [*with emotion*]. You too, Shanaar, oul' son ; you too ! [*Shanaar goes off.*

Mahan [*after a pause — viciously*]. That Latin-lustrous oul' cod of a prayer-blower is a positive danger goin' about th' counthry !

Michael [*startled and offended*]. Eh ? I wouldn't go callin' him a cod, Sailor Mahan. A little asthray in a way, now an' again, but no cod. You should be th' last to call th' man a cod, for if it wasn't for his holy Latin aspirations, you mightn't be here now.

Mahan [*with exasperation*]. Aw, th' oul' fool, pipin' a gale into every breeze that blows ! I don't believe there was ever anything engenderogically evil in that

cock as a cock, or denounceable either ! Lardin' a
man's mind with his killakee Latin ! An' looka th'
way he slights th' women. I seen him lookin' at Lorna
an' Marion as if they'd horns on their heads !

Michael [doubtfully]. Maybe he's too down on th' women,
though you have to allow women is temptin'.

Mahan. They wouldn't tempt man if they didn't damn
well know he wanted to be tempted !

Michael. Yes, yes ; but we must suffer th' temptation
accordin' to the cognisances of th' canon law. But
let's have a dhrink, for I'm near dead with th' drouth,
an' we can sensify our discussion about th' increased
price you're demandin' for carryin' th' turf ; though,
honest to God, Sailor Mahan, I can't add a ha'penny
more to what I'm givin'.

Mahan. A dhrink would be welcome, an' we can talk over
th' matter, though, honest to God, Michael Marthraun,
blast th' penny less I'll take than what I'm askin'.

Michael [going to the porch, and shouting into the house].
Marion, bring th' bottle of ten years' maturin', an' two
glasses ! [He returns.] It's th' principle I'm thinkin'
of.

Mahan. That's what's throublin' me, too. [Marion comes in
with the bottle of whiskey and the two glasses. She places them
on the table, getting between the two men to do so. Reading the
label] Flanagan's First ! Nyav na Nyale — th' heaven
of th' clouds ! An' brought be a lass who's a Flanagan's
first too !

Marion [in jovial mood]. G'long with you — you an' your
blarney !

Michael [*enthusiastically*]. Had you lived long ago, Emer would have been jealous of you !

> [*He playfully pinches her bottom.*

Marion [*squealing*]. Ouch ! [*She breaks away, and makes for the porch.*] A pair o' naughty men !

> [*She goes into the house.*

Michael [*calling after her*]. I forgot th' soda, Marion ; bring th' siphon, lass.

Mahan [*complacently*]. I could hold that one in me arms for a long time, Mick.

Michael. Th' man would want to be dead who couldn't.

Mahan [*enthusiastically*]. I'd welcome her, even if I seen her through th' vision of oul' Shanaar — with horns growin' out of her head !

> [*Marion returns with the siphon which she places on the table. The Two Men, looking in front of them, have silly, sly grins on their faces.*
>
> [*The ornament, which Marion wears round her head, has separated into two parts, each of which has risen over her head, forming two branching horns, apparently sprouting from her forehead. The Two Men, shyly gazing in front, or at the table, do not see the change. Marion's face has changed too, and now seems to wear a mocking, cynical look, fitting the aspect of her face to the horns.*

Marion [*joking*]. Two wild men — it's afraid I am to come near yous.

> [*Michael puts his right arm round her waist, and Mahan his left one.*

Mahan [*slyly*]. What about a kiss on your rosy mouth, darlin', to give a honied tang to th' whiskey ?

Michael. An' one for me, too ?

Marion [*with pretended demureness*]. A thrue gentleman'll rise up an' never expect a thrue lady to bend down for a kiss. [*With vigour*] Up an' take it, before yous grow cold !

    [*They rise from their chairs, foolish grins on their faces, settle themselves for a kiss, and then perceive the change that has taken place. They flop back on to the chairs, fright and dismay sweeping over their faces.*

Mahan
Michael } [*together*]. Good God !

    [*They slump in the chairs, overcome, their hands folded in front of their chests, palm to palm, as if in prayer. Marion looks at them in some astonishment.*

Marion. What ails yous ? Was th' excitement too much for yous, or what ?

Michael [*plaintively*]. Saints in heaven help us now !

Marion. What's come over yous ? Th' way yous slumped so sudden down, you'd think I'd horns on me, or somethin' !

Michael [*hoarsely*]. G'way, g'way ! Shanaar, Shanaar, where are you now !

Marion [*going over to Mahan, and putting an arm round his neck*]. What about you, gay one ?

Mahan [*gurgling with fright*]. You're sthranglin' me ! G'way, g'way, girl !

Marion. Looka, a kiss would do yous good. Yous think too much of th' world !

Mahan [*chokingly*]. St. Christopher, mainstay of mariners, be with me now !
   [*Lorna thrusts her head out from the window over the porch.*

Lorna [*down to Marion*]. Let them two oul' life-frighteners fend for themselves, an' come in. From th' back window, I can see th' crowd gathered to give Julia a send-off to Lourdes, so come in to tidy if you want to join them with me.

Marion [*half to herself — as she runs into the house*]. God forgive me — I near forgot ! Here we are followin' laughter, instead of seekin' succour from prayer !
   [*She runs in, and Lorna takes her head back into the room again.*

Michael [*frightened and very angry*]. Now, maybe, you'll quit your jeerin' at oul' Shanaar ! Now, maybe, you'll let your mind concentrate on higher things ! Now, maybe, you won't be runnin' loose afther girls !

Mahan [*indignantly*]. Damnit, man, you were as eager for a cuddle as I was !

Michael [*lifting his eyes skywards*]. Oh, d'ye hear that ! I was only toleratin' your queer declivity, like a fool. An' afther all th' warnin's given be wise oul' Shanaar ! Looka, Sailor Mahan, you'll have to be more on your guard !

Mahan [*trying to defend himself*]. How could any man suspect such a thing ? We'll have to think this thing out.

Michael [*with exasperation*]. Think it out ! Oh, man,

Sailor Mahan, have you nothin' more sensible to say than that we'll have to think it out?

Mahan. Let's have a dhrink, for God's sake, to steady us down!

Michael [*hurriedly putting bottle and glasses under the table*]. What're you thinkin' of, Sailor Mahan? We can't dispense ourselves through a scene of jollification an' poor Julia passin' on her way to Lourdes!

[*Along the path, on a stretcher, carried by the two Rough Fellows, comes Julia, followed by her father. The stretcher is borne to the gate, and there laid down, so that the head of it is flush with the gate-posts, and the rest of it within the garden. The framework of the gate makes a frame for Julia, who is half sitting up, her head supported by a high pillow. Her face is a sad yellowish mask, pierced by wide eyes, surrounded by dark circles. Her father is a sturdy fellow of fifty, a scraggly greyish beard struggling from his chin. He is roughly dressed as a poorer peasant might be, and his clothes are patched in places. He wears a brown muffler, and a faded black trilby-hat is on his head. All the time, he looks straight in front with a passive and stony stare.*

[*Before the stretcher walks the Mayor, rather stout, clean-shaven, wearing a red robe over rough clothing; he has a very wide three-cornered hat, laced with gold, on his head. Behind him walks the Mace-bearer, a big silver and black mace on his shoulder. He is tall, and wears a bright blue robe, trimmed with silver, on his head is a huge cocked hat, laced, too, with silver. These two do not enter the garden, but walk on, and stand waiting near the house, beside the flag-pole, but without the wall.*

[*Lorna, followed by Marion, comes out of the house. Instead of the bright headgear worn before, they have black kerchiefs, worn peasant-wise on their heads — that is, they have been folded triangularly, draped over their heads, with the ends tied beneath their chins.*

[*Lorna runs over to the stretcher, kneels down beside it, and kisses Julia.*

Lorna [*affectionately*]. My sister, my little Julia, oh, how sorry I am that you have to go on this long, sad journey !

Julia [*her voice is low, but there is a hectic note of hope in it*]. A long journey, Lorna darlin', but not a sad one ; oh, no, not a sad one. Hope, Lorna, will have me be the hand all the long way. I go to kneel at the feet of the ever Blessed Virgin.

Lorna. Oh, she will comfort you, me darlin'.

Julia. Yes, she will comfort me, Lorna [*after a pause*] ; an' cure me too. Lorna, say she will cure me too.

Lorna [*stifling a sob*]. An' cure you, too.

Julia [*to Michael*]. Give me your good wishes, Mr. Marthraun.

Michael [*with genuine emotion*]. Julia, me best wishes go with you, an' me best prayers'll follow all th' long way !

Julia [*to Mahan*]. An' you, Sailor Mahan — have you no good wish for the poor voyager ?

Mahan [*fervently*]. Young lass, may you go through healin' wathers, an' come back a clipper, with ne'er a spar, a sail, or a rope asthray !

[*Father Domineer comes quickly in on the path outside. He is a tall, rather heavily built man of forty. He has a*

breezy manner now, heading the forlorn hope. He is
trying to smile now, but crack his mouth as he will, the
tight, surly lines of his face refuse to furnish one. He
is dressed in the usual clerical, outdoor garb, and his hard
head is covered with a soft, rather widely brimmed black
hat.

Father Domineer [*as happily as he can*]. Now, now, no halts
on th' road, little daughter ! The train won't wait,
an' we must have a few minutes to spare to make you
comfortable. Bring her along, Brancardiers ! Forward,
in th' name o' God and of Mary, ever Virgin, ever
blessed, always bending to help poor, banished children
of Eve !

  [*The two Rough Men take up the stretcher and carry it*
   along the pathway outside, the Mayor, followed by his
   Mace-bearer, leading it on. Father Domineer follows
   immediately behind; then come Lorna and Marion,
   followed by Michael and Mahan.

  [*As the stretcher moves along the pathway outside, a band in*
   the distance is heard playing "Star of the Sea", to which
   is added the voice of a crowd singing the words :

      Hail, Queen of Heaven, the ocean Star !
      Guide of the wand'rer here below !
      Thrown on life's surge, we claim thy care —
      Save us from peril and from woe.

      Mother of Christ, Star of the Sea,
      Pray for the wanderer, pray for me.

Father Domineer [*enthusiastically*]. Julia will bring us back
a miracle, a glorious miracle ! To Lourdes !

END OF SCENE I

Scene II

The Scene is the same as before, though the sunshine isn't quite so bright and determined. The Irish Tricolour flies breezily from its flag-pole; the table and chairs stand where they were, and the bottle and glasses are still under it.

No-one is in the garden, all, apparently, having gone to see Julia away on her long, long journey. Away in the distance the band is playing " Star of the Sea ", and the tune can be softly heard from the garden.

After a few moments, Lorna and Marion come along the path outside, enter by the gate, and cross over into the house.

Marion [*anxiously*]. What d'ye think of th' chance of a cure?

Lorna. I'm afraid th' chance is a poor one; but we won't talk about it.

Marion [*piously*]. Well, it was a grand send-off, an' God is good.

Lorna [*coldly*]. An' th' devil's not a bad fella either.
　　[*They both go into the house, and, a few moments later, Michael and Mahan stroll along the path, come into the garden, and go to where the table and chairs are.*

Mahan. Well, th' anchor's weighed.

Michael. It was an edifyin' spectacle, Sailor Mahan, thrustin' us outa this world for th' time bein'. Julia's asked for a sign, Sailor Mahan, an', believe me, she'll get it.

Mahan. She will, she will, though I wouldn't like to bet on it.

Michael. She'll get what she's afther — a complete cure. Me own generous gift of fifty pounds for th' oul' bog'll be rewarded ; an' th' spate o' prayin' goin' on, from th' Mayor to the Bellman, is bound to get th' higher saints goin', persuadin' them to furnish a suitable answer to all we're askin'.

Mahan [*impatiently*]. Arra, man alive, d'ye think th' skipper aloft an' his glitterin' crew is goin' to bother their heads about a call from a tiny town an' disthrict thryin' hard to thrive on turf ?

Michael [*indignantly*]. Looka, if you were only versed in th' endurin' promulgacity of th' gospels, you'd know th' man above's concerned as much about Nyadnanave as he is about a place where a swarm of cardinals saunter secure, decoratin' th' air with all their purple an' gold !

Mahan [*as indignantly*]. Are you goin' to tell me that th' skipper aloft an' his hierarchilogical crew are concerned about th' Mayor, the Messenger, Marion, me, an' you as much as they are about them who've been promoted to th' quarter-deck o' th' world's fame ? Are you goin' to pit our palthry penances an' haltin' hummin' o' hymns against th' piercin' pipin' of th' rosary be Bing Bang Crosby an' other great film stars, who side-stepped from published greatness for a holy minute or two to send a blessed blast over th' wireless, callin' all Catholics to perpetuatin' prayer !

Michael [*sitting down on a chair*]. Sailor Mahan, I ask you to thry to get your thoughts ship-shaped in your mind.

[*While they have been talking, the Messenger has come running along the path outside, and is now leaning on the gate, listening to the two men, unnoticed by them.*

Mahan [*plumping down on the other chair — indignantly*]. D'ye remember who you're talkin' to, man? Ship-shape in me mind! Isn't a man bound to have his mind fitted together in a ship-shape way, who, forced out of his thrue course be a nautical cathastrope, to wit, videliket, an act o' God, ploughed a way through th' Sargasso Sea, reachin' open wathers, long afther hope had troubled him no longer?

Michael [*wearily*]. Aw, Sailor Mahan, what's them things got to do with th' things tantamount to heaven?

Messenger [*over to them*]. Mick's right — them things can't be tantamount to anything bar themselves.

Mahan [*turning fiercely on the Messenger*]. What do you want? What're you doin' here? Your coalition of ignorant knowledge can't comprehend th' things we talk about!

Messenger [*with some excitement*]. Listen, boys — I've a question to ask yous.

Michael [*with a gesture signifying this isn't the time to ask it*]. Ask it some time more convenient. An' don't refer to us as 'boys' — we're gentlemen to you!

Mahan [*to Michael*]. Looka, Mick, if you only listened to Bing Crosby, th' mighty film star, croonin' his Irish lullaby, [*he chants*] "Tooral ooral ooral, tooral ooral ay", you'd have th' visuality to see th' amazin' response he'd have from millions of admirers, if he crooned a hymn!

Messenger. I was never sthruck be Bing Crosby's croonin'.

Michael [*wrathfully — to Messenger*]. You were never sthruck ! An' who th' hell are you to be consulted ? Please don't stand there interferin' with the earnest colloquy of betther men. [*To Mahan*] Looka, Sailor Mahan, any priest'll tell you that in th' eyes of heaven all men are equal an' must be held in respect an' reverence.

Mahan [*mockingly*]. Ay, they'll say that to me an' you, but will they say it to Bing Crosby, or any other famous film star ?

Messenger. Will they hell ! Honour be th' clergy's regulated by how much a man can give !

Michael [*furiously — to the Messenger*]. Get to hell outa here ! With that kinda talk, we won't be able soon to sit steady on our chairs. Oh !

   [*The chair he is sitting on collapses, and he comes down to the ground on his arse.*

Mahan [*astonished*]. Holy saints, what's happened ?

Michael [*in a fierce whisper — to Mahan*]. Take no notice of it, fool. Go on talkin' !

Mahan [*a little confused*]. I'll say you're right, Mick ; th' way things are goin' we won't be able much longer to sit serene on our chairs. Oh !

   [*The chair collapses under Mahan, and he, too, comes down to the ground.*

Michael [*in a fierce whisper*]. Don't notice it ; go on's if nothin' happened !

Messenger [*amused*]. Well, yous have settled down now, anyhow ! Will I get yous chairs sturdy enough to uphold th' wisdom of your talkin' ?

Michael [*angrily — to Messenger*]. There's nothin' wrong
   with th' chairs we have ! You get outa here !
   Nothin's wrong with th' chairs at all. Get outa here —
   I don't trust you either !

Messenger. I've somethin' important to ask yous.

Michael. Well, ask it at some more convenient time.
   [*To Mahan*] It's a blessin' that so many lively-livin' oul'
   holy spots are still in th' land to help us an' keep us
   wary.

Messenger [*scornfully*]. An' where are th' lively holy spots
   still to be found ? Sure, man, they're all gone west
   long ago, an' the whole face o' th' land is pock-marked
   with their ruins !

Michael [*shouting at the Messenger*]. Where are th' lost an'
   ruined holy places ? We've always cared for, an'
   honoured, our holy spots ! Mention one of them,
   either lost or ruined !

Messenger [*shouting back*]. There are thousands of them,
   man ; places founded be Finian, Finbarr, an' th' rest ;
   places that are now only an oul' ruined wall, blighted
   be nettle an' dock, their only glory th' crimson berries
   of th' bright arbutus ! Where's th' Seven Churches of
   Glendalough ? Where's Durrow of Offally, founded
   be Columkille himself ? Known now only be the name
   of the Book of Durrow !

Michael [*ferociously*]. Book o' Durrow ! It's books that
   have us half th' woeful way we are, fillin' broody minds
   with loose scholasticality, infringin' th' holy beliefs
   an' thried impositions that our fathers' fathers' fathers
   gave our fathers' fathers, who gave our fathers what our
   fathers gave to us !

Messenger. Faith, your fathers' faith is fear, an' now fear is your only fun.

Mahan [*impatiently*]. Let him go, Mick, an' let's have that dhrink you mentioned a year ago.
   [*Marion's head appears at the window, looking down at the Messenger. The decorations on her head have now declined to their first place.*

Marion [*down to the Messenger*]. Hallo, Robin Adair! [*He looks up.*] Where are th' two oul' woeful wondhers? [*He points to where they are.*] Oh, they've brought the unsteady chairs out, and now they've broken them up! [*To Michael — angrily*] You knew well th' chairs in the hall were there only to present an appearance.

Messenger [*up to her*]. Oh, Marion, Marion, sweet Marion, come down till I give you a kiss havin' in it all the life an' longin' of th' greater lovers of th' past!

Marion [*leaving the window*]. Now, now, naughty boy!

Michael [*sourly*]. You'd do well to remember, lad, the month in jail you got for kissin' Marion, an' the forty-shillin' fine on Marion, for kissing you in a public place at th' cross-roads.
   [*Marion comes from the house, goes toward the Messenger, who seizes her in his arms and kisses her.*

Messenger. I'd do a year an' a day in a cold cell of pressed-in loneliness, an' come out singin' a song, for a kiss from a lass like Marion!

Marion. Don't think too much of me, Robin Adair, for I've some of th' devil in me, an' th' two fostherers of fear, there, think I wear horns on holy days.

Michael [*impressively*]. See — she's warnin' you, herself, young man !

Marion [*to the Messenger*]. An' what has you here arguin' with them two oul' fools ?

Messenger. I came to ask a question of them, but they were buried in their prayers. Did you see him ? Did he come this way ?

Michael [*suddenly alarmed*]. Come where ?

Mahan [*alarmed*]. See who ?

Messenger. Th' Cock.

Mahan } [*together*]. Th' Cock !
Michael
    [*They carefully creep away from the broken chairs, and stand up when they are some distance from them.*

Messenger. Ay. I thought he'd make for here first.

Michael [*echoing the Messenger*]. Make for here first !
    [*In the distance, the loud, exultant crow of the Cock is heard.*

Messenger [*excitedly*]. There he is ! Away in the direction east of th' bog ! I'll go get him, an' fetch him home.

Marion [*kissing the Messenger*]. Bring him here first, Robin, an' I'll have a wreath of roses ready to hang round his neck.

Messenger [*rushing away*]. I will, I will, fair one !
    [*He goes off. She takes the broken chairs into the house.*

Marion [*carrying in the chairs*]. Next time, you boyos, take out two steady ones.

Michael [*horrified*]. Did you hear what she said, Sailor
Mahan ? Hang a wreath of roses round his neck !
Well, I'll have th' gun ready ! Ay, now !
    [*He goes over to the porch, but Mahan lays a restraining
    hand on his arm.*

Mahan. What good would th' gun be ? Have you forgot
what Shanaar told us ? Your bullet would go clean
through him, an' leave him untouched. Now that
we're in peace here, let's have th' dhrink we were to
have, an' which we both need.

Michael [*halting*]. You're right, Sailor Mahan. If he
comes here, what we have to do is to take no notice.
Look through him, past him, over him, but never at
him. [*He prepares the bottle of whiskey and the glasses.*]
There's sinisther enchantments all around us. God
between us an' all harm ! We'll have to be for ever on
our guard.

Mahan [*impatiently*]. Yis, yis ; fill out th' dhrink for
God's sake !

Michael. May it give us courage. [*He tilts the bottle over
the glass, but none of it spills out.*] Good God, th' bottle's
bewitched too !

Mahan. Bottle bewitched ? How could a bottle be
bewitched ? Steady your nerves, man. Thry givin' it
a shake.

Michael [*who has left the bottle back on the table — retreating
away from it*]. Thry givin' it a shake yourself, since
you're so darin'.
    [*Mahan goes over to the table with a forced swagger, and
    reaches out a cautious hand for the bottle. As he touches
    it, its colour changes to a glowing red.*

Mahan [*fervent and frightened*]. St. Christopher, pathron of all mariners, defend us — th' bottle's changed its colour !

Michael. There's evil things cantherin' an' crawlin' about this place ! You saw th' seal on th' bottle showin' it was untouched since it left th' store. Flanagan's finest, Jamieson's best, ten years maturin' — an' look at it now.

Mahan. How are we goin' to prevent ourselves from bein' the victims of sorcery an' ruin ? You'd think good whiskey would be exempt from injury even be th' lowest of th' low.

Michael. It's th' women who're always intherceptin' our good intentions. Evil things is threatenin' us everywhere. Th' one safe method of turnin' our back to a power like this is to go forward an' meet it half-way. [*He comes close to Mahan, and whispers hoarsely*] Selah !

Mahan [*mystified and frightened at what he thinks may be something sinister*]. Selah ?

Michael [*emphatically*]. Selah !

Mahan [*agonisingly*]. Good God !

Michael. Now, maybe, you'll believe what th' Missioner said last night.

Mahan [*a little dubiously*]. He might have been exaggeratin' a bit, Mick.

Michael. Look at th' bottle, man ! Demons can hide in th' froth of th' beer a man's dhrinkin'. An' all th' time, my turf-workers an' your lorry drivers are screwin' all they can out of us so that they'll haye more to spend on pictures an' in th' dance halls, leavin' us to face th' foe alone.

Mahan [*abjectly*]. What's a poor, good-livin', virtuous man to do then?

Michael. He must always be thinkin' of th' four last things — hell, heaven, death, an' th' judgement.

Mahan [*pitifully*]. But that would sthrain a man's nerves, an' make life hardly worth livin'.

Michael. It's plain, Sailor Mahan, you're still hankerin' afther th' things o' th' world, an' the soft, stimulatin' touch of th' flesh. You're puttin' th' two of us in peril, Sailor Mahan.

Mahan [*protesting*]. You're exaggeratin' now.

Michael. I am not. I seen your eyes followin' that Loreleen when she's about, hurtin' th' tendher muscles of your eye squintin' down at her legs. You'll have to curb your conthradictions, for you're puttin' us both in dire peril, Sailor Mahan. Looka what I've lost already! Me fine silk hat torn to shreds, so that Lorna's had to telephone th' Firm for another, that I may suitably show meself when I meet his Brightness, the President; an' looka th' whiskey there — forced into a mis-undherstandin' of itself be some minor demon devisin' a spell on it! Guess how much good money I sur-rendhered to get that bottle, Sailor Mahan?

Mahan. I've no idea of what whiskey is a gallon now.

Michael [*impatiently*]. What whiskey is a gallon now? Is there some kinda spell on you, too, Sailor Mahan? You can't think of whiskey in gallons now; you have to think of it in terms of sips ; an' sips spaced out from each other like th' holy days of obligation.

Mahan. An' how are we goin' to get rid of it ? We're in some danger while it's standin' there.

Michael. How th' hell do I know how we'll get rid of it ? We'll have to get Shanaar to deal with it, an', mind you, don't go too near it.

[*The Porter appears on the sidewalk outside the wall. He is a middle-aged man with an obstinate face, the chin hidden by a grizzled beard. He is wearing a pair of old brown trousers, an older grey coat, and an old blue shirt. On his head is a big cap, with a long, wide peak jutting out in front of it. The crown of the cap is a high one, and around the crown is a wide band of dazzling scarlet. He is carrying a parcel wrapped in brown paper, either side of which is a little torn. He looks north, south, west, and then, turning east, he sees the two men in the garden.*

Porter [*to the two men*]. Isn't it handy now that I've clapped eyes on two human bein's in this god-forsaken hole ! I've been trudghin' about for hours thryin' to find th' one that'll claim what's in this parcel I'm bearin', an', maybe, th' two of yous, or maybe, one of yous, can tell me where I'll find him. I'm on th' thrack of an oul' fella callin' himself a Councillor an' a Jay Pee.

Michael. What's his name ?

Porter. That's more than I can say, for th' chit of th' girl in th' shop, who took th' ordher, forgot to write down th' name, an' then forgot th' name itself when she started to write it down. All I know is that in this disthrict I'm seekin' a Mr. Councillor So-an'-so ; one havin' Councillor at his head an' Jay Pee at his tail.

Michael [*with importance*]. I'm a Councillor and a Jay Pee.

Porter [*with some scorn*]. D'ye tell me that now? [*He bends over the wall to come closer to Michael.*] Listen, me good man, me journey's been too long an' too dangerous for me to glorify any cod-actin'! It would be a quare place if you were a councillor. You'll have to grow a few more grey hairs before you can take a rise outa me!

Michael [*indignantly*]. Tell us what you've got there, fella, an', if it's not for us, be off about your business!

Porter [*angrily*]. Fella yourself! An' mend your manners, please! It's hardly th' like of you would be standin' in need of a silky, shinin' tall-hat.

Michael. If it's a tall-hat, it's for me! I'm Mr. Councillor Marthraun, Jay Pee — ordhered to be sent express by th' firm of Buckley's.

Porter [*with a quick conciliatory change*]. That's th' firm. I guessed you was th' man at once, at once. That man's a leadher in th' locality, I said, as soon as I clapped me eye on you. A fine, clever, upstandin' individual, I says to meself.

Michael [*shortly*]. Hand over th' hat, and you can go.

Porter. Hould on a minute, sir; wait till I tell you: I'm sorry, but th' hat's been slightly damaged in thransit.   [*He begins to take the hat from the paper.*

Michael. Damaged? How th' hell did you damage it?

Porter. Me, is it? No, not me, sir. [*He stretches over the wall towards them.*] When I was bringin' it here, someone shot a bullet through it, east be west!

Michael. Nonsense, man, who'd be shootin' bullets round here ?

Porter. Who indeed ?   That's th' mystery.   Bullet it was.   People told me the Civic Guards were out thryin' to shoot down an evil spirit flyin' th' air in th' shape of a bird.

Michael [*alarmed*]. Th' Cock !

Porter [*placing the tall-hat on the wall carefully*]. An' seein' how things are, an' th' fright I got, it's welcome a dhrink would be from th' handsome bottle I see paradin' on th' table.

Michael [*in a loud whisper*]. To touch it is to go in danger of your life — th' bottle's bewitched !

Porter. Th' bottle bewitched ?   What sort of a place have me poor, wandherin' feet sthrayed into at all ? Before I ventured to come here at all, I should have stayed at home.   I'm already as uneasy as th' place itself !   [*A shot is heard, and the tall-hat is knocked from the wall on to the road.*]   Saints in glory, there's another one !

Mahan [*excitedly*]. It's your hat, man, th' red band on your hat !

Porter [*to Michael — speaking rapidly, picking the tall-hat from the road and offering it to Michael*]. Here, take your hat, sir, an' keep it safe, an' I'll be goin'.

Michael [*frightened and angry*]. Take it back ; it's damaged ; take it back, fella !

Porter [*loudly and with anger*]. Fella yourself !   Is it takin' th' risk I'd be of a bullet rushin' through me instead of th' oul' hat ?   [*He flings it towards the two men.*]   Here,

take your oul' hat an' th' risk along with it ! Do what
you want with it ; do what you like with it ; do what
you can with it — I'm off !

[*He runs off in the direction he came from, while the two
men gaze doubtfully at the hat lying in the garden.*

Michael [*tremulously*]. The cowards that are in this
counthry — leavin' a poor man alone in his dilemma !
I'd be afraid to wear it now.

Mahan. Aw, give yourself a shake, Mick. You're not
afraid of a poor tall-hat. An' throw away ten good
pounds.

[*He goes toward where the hat is, but Michael holds him by
the arm.*

Michael [*with warning and appeal*]. No, don't touch it till
we see further.

[*The Sergeant appears on the pathway outside. He has a
rifle in his hands ; he leans against the wall looking
towards the two. He is obviously anxious, and in a
state of fear.*

Sergeant. Yous didn't see it ? It didn't come here, did
it ?

Michael [*breathless with the tension of fear*]. No, no ; not
yet. [*With doleful appeal*] Oh, don't be prowlin' round
here — you'll only be attractin' it to th' place !

Sergeant [*ignoring appeal*]. Three times I shot at it ; three
times th' bullets went right through it ; and twice th'
thing flew away crowing.

Michael [*excitedly*]. Did you get it th' third time, did you
get it then ?

Sergeant. Wait till I tell yous : sthrange things an' unruly are happenin' in this holy land of ours this day ! Will I ever forget what happened th' third time I hot it ! Never, never. Isn't it a wondher an' a mercy of God that I'm left alive afther th' reverberatin' fright I got !

Michael [*eagerly*]. Well, what happened when you hot it then ?

Mahan [*eagerly*]. When you hot it for th' third time ?

Sergeant. Yous could never guess ?

Michael [*impatiently*]. Oh, we know we'd never guess ; no-one can go guessin' about demonological disturbances.

Mahan. Tell us, will you, without any more of your sthructural suggestions !

Sergeant. As sure as I'm standin' here ; as sure as sure as this gun is in me left hand [*he is holding it in his right one*] ; as sure as we're all poor, identified sinners ; when I hot him for th' third time, I seen him changin' into a——

Michael \
Mahan ∫ [*together*]. What ?

Sergeant [*whisperingly*]. What d'ye think ?

Mahan [*explosively*]. Oh, we're not thinkin' ; we can't think ; we're beyond thinkin' ! We're waitin' for you to tell us !

Sergeant. Th' soul well-nigh left me body when I seen th' unholy novelty happenin' : th' thing that couldn't be, yet th' thing that was. If I never prayed before, I prayed then — for hope ; for holy considheration in th' quandary ; for power to be usual an' spry again when th' thing was gone.

Michael. What thing, what thing, man ?

Mahan [*despairingly*]. Thry to tell us, Sergeant, what you said you said you seen.

Sergeant. I'm comin' to it ; since what I seen was seen by no man never before, it's not easy for a man to describe with evidential accuracy th' consequential thoughts fluttherin' through me amazed mind at what was, an' what couldn't be, demonstrated there, or there, or anywhere else, where mortals congregate in ones or twos or crowds astoundin'.

Michael [*imploringly*]. Looka, Sergeant, we're languishin' for th' information that may keep us from spendin' th' rest of our lives in constant consternation.

Sergeant. As I was tellin' you, there was th' crimson crest of th' Cock, enhancin' th' head lifted up to give a crow, an' when I riz th' gun to me shouldher, an' let bang, th' whole place went dead dark ; a flash of red lightning near blinded me ; an' when it got light again, a second afther, there was the demonised Cock changin' himself into a silken glossified tall-hat !

Michael [*horrified*]. A silken tall-hat !

Mahan. A glossified tall-hat !

Michael [*to Mahan — viciously*]. Now you'll quit undher-estimatin' what th' holy Missioner said last night about th' desperate an' deranging thrickeries of evil things loose an' loungin' among us ! Now can you see the significality of things ?

Mahan [*going away as far as he can from the tall-hat lying in the garden*]. Steer clear of it ; get as far away from it as we can ! Keep well abaft of it !

Sergeant [*puzzled*]. Keep clear from what ?

Mahan [*pointing to the hat*]. Th' hat, man, th' hat !

Sergeant [*seeing the hat beside him, and jumping away from it*]. I was near touchin' th' brim of it ! Jasus ! yous should have warned me !

Michael [*close to the Sergeant — in a whisper*]. Does it look anything like th' thing you shot ?

Sergeant [*laying a shaking hand on Michael's arm*]. It's th' dead spit of what I seen him changin' into durin' th' flash of lightning ! I just riz th' gun to me shouldher — like this [*he raises the gun to his shoulder*] to let bang.
   [*The garden is suddenly enveloped in darkness for a few moments. A fierce flash of lightning shoots through the darkness ; the hat has disappeared, and where it stood now stands the Cock. While the lightning flashes, the Cock crows lustily. Then the light as suddenly comes back to the garden, and shows that the Cock and the hat have gone. Michael and Mahan are seen to be lying on the ground, and the Sergeant is on his knees, as if in prayer.*

Sergeant. Holy St. Custodius, pathron of th' police, protect me !

Michael [*in a whisper*]. Are you there, Sailor Mahan ?

Mahan [*in a whisper*]. Are you there, Michael Marthraun ?

Michael. I'm done for.

Mahan. We're both done for.

Sergeant. We're all done for.

Mahan. Th' smell of th' sulphur an' brimstone's burnin'
me.

Michael. Now you'll give up mockin' Shanaar, if it's not
too late.   You seen how Marion's head was ornamented, an' it'll not be long till Lorna has them too.

Sergeant [*now sitting down, so that he is to the left of Michael,
while Mahan sits to the right of him, so frightened
that he must blame someone*]. We'll have to curtail th'
gallivantin' of th' women afther th' men.   Th' house
is their province, as th' clergy's tired tellin' them.
They'll have to realise that th' home's their only proper
place.

Michael. An' demolish th' minds that babble about
books.

Sergeant [*raising his voice*]. Th' biggest curse of all !
Books no decent mortal should touch, should never
even see th' cover of one !

Michael [*warningly*]. Hush !   Don't speak so loud, or th'
lesser boyo'll hear you !

Sergeant [*startled*]. Lesser boyo ?   What lesser boyo ?

Mahan [*whispering and pointing*]. Th' boyo in th' bottle
there.

Sergeant [*noticing it for the first time*]. Why, what's in it ?

Michael. Th' best of whiskey was in it till some evil spirit
put a spell on it, desthroyin' its legitimate use.

Sergeant [*unbelievingly*]. I don't believe it.   Nothin' could
translate good dhrink into anything but what it was
made to be.   We could do with a dhrink now.
                    [*He advances cautiously towards the table.*

Michael [*excitedly*]. Don't meddle with it, man ; don't stimulate him !

    [*The Sergeant tiptoes over to the table, stretches his hand out, and touches the bottle. He immediately lets out a yelp, and jumps back.*

Sergeant. Oh ! Be God, it's red-hot !

Mahan [*angrily*]. You were told not to touch it ! You're addin' to our dangers.

Michael [*shouting*]. Good God, man, couldn't you do what you're told ! Now you've added anger to its impositional qualities !

Sergeant [*nursing his hand*]. Aren't we in a nice quandary when an evil thing can insconce itself in a bottle !

Michael. Th' whole place's seethin' with them. You, Sergeant, watch th' road north ; you, Sailor Mahan, watch it south ; an' I'll keep an eye on th' house. [*Mahan goes to one end of the wall, the Sergeant to the other, and both stretch over it to look different ways along the road. During the next discussion, whenever they leave where they are, they move cautiously, crouching a little, as if they were afraid to be seen ; keeping as low as possible for security.*] One of us'll have to take th' risk, an' go for Father Domineer at once. [*He waits for a few moments, but no-one answers.*] Did yous hear me, or are yous lettin' on to be deaf ? I said one of us'll have to go for Father Domineer. [*There is no reply.*] Are you listenin' to me be any chance, Sailor Mahan ?

Mahan. I heard you, I heard you.

Michael. An' why don't you go, then ?

Mahan [*coming down towards Michael — crouching low*]. Nice thing if I met th' Cock barrin' me way ? Why don't you go yourself ?

Michael. What about th' possibility of me meetin' him ? I'm more conspicuous in this disthrict than you, an' th' thing would take immediate recognisance of me.

Sergeant [*coming down towards them — crouching too*]. Me an' Sailor Mahan'll go together.

Michael [*indignantly*]. An' leave me to grapple with *mysteriosa Daemones* alone ? [*He turns his face sky-wards*] Oh, in this disthrict there's not a sign of one willin' to do unto another what another would do to him !

Mahan [*fiercely*]. That's a lie : there isn't a one who isn't eager to do to others what others would do to him !
[*The Bellman, dressed as a fireman, comes in, and walks along on the path outside. He has a huge brass fireman's helmet on his head, and is wearing a red shirt and blue trousers. He has a bell in his hand which he rings loudly before he shouts his orders. The three men cease their discussion, and give him their full attention.*

Bellman [*shouting*]. Into your houses all ! Bar th' doors, shut th' windows ! Th' Cock's comin' ! In the shape of a woman ! Gallus, Le Coq, an' Kyleloch, th' Cock's comin' in th' shape of a woman ! Into your houses, shut to th' windows, bar th' doors !
[*He goes out in the opposite direction, shouting his orders and ringing his bell, leaving the three men agitated and more frightened than ever.*

Sergeant [*frantically*]. Into the house with us all — quick !

Michael [*hindering him — ferociously*]. Not in there, you
fool ! Th' house is full o' them. You seen what
happened to the whiskey ? If he or she comes, th'
thing to do is to take no notice ; if he or she talks,
not to answer ; and take no notice of whatever questionable shape it takes. Sit down, quiet, th' three of us.

 [*The three men sit down on the ground — Michael to the
 right, the Sergeant to the left, and Mahan in the centre.*

Michael [*trembling*]. Now, let th' two of yous pull yourselves together. An' you, Mahan, sing that favourite
of yours, quietly, as if we were passing th' time
pleasantly. [*As Mahan hesitates*] Go on, man, for God's
sake !

Mahan [*agitated*]. I can't see how I'll do it justice undher
these conditions. I'll thry. [*He sings, but his voice
quavers occasionally :*]

‘Long time ago when men was men
An' ships not ships that sail'd just to an' fro-o-o,
We hoisted sail an' sail'd, an' then sail'd on an' on
    to Jericho-o-o ;
With silks an' spice came back again because we'd
    nowhere else to go !

Michael ⎱[*together*]. Go, go !
Sergeant ⎰

Mahan [*singing*] :

Th' captain says, says he, we'll make
Th' pirates where th' palm trees wave an' grow-o-o,
Haul down their sable flag, an' pray, before we hang
    them all, heave yo-ho-ho ;
Then fling their bodies in th' sea to feed th' fishes
    down below !

Michael ⎫
Sergeant ⎰ [*together*]. Low, low !

 [*A golden shaft of light streams in from the left of the road,
 and, a moment afterwards, Loreleen appears in the midst
 of it. She stands in the gateway staring at the three men
 squatted on the ground.*

Loreleen [*puzzled*]. What th' hell's wrong here ?

Michael [*in a whisper — motioning Mahan to continue*]. Go
on, man.

Mahan [*singing — with more quavers in his voice*] :
 An' when we've swabb'd th' blood away,
 We'll take their hundhred-ton gunn'd ship in tow-o-o ;
 Their precious jewels'll go to deck th' breasts of women,
  white as snow-o-o ;
 So hoist all sail an' make for home through waves that
  lash an' winds that blow !

Michael ⎫
Sergeant ⎰ [*together*]. Blow, blow !

 [*Loreleen comes into the garden, and approaches the men.
 The golden light follows her, and partly shines on the
 three singers.*

Loreleen [*brightly*]. Singin' is it the three of you are ?
Practisin' for the fancy-dress ball tonight, eh ? Ye do
well to bring a spray of light, now and again, into a
dark place. The Sergeant's eyes, too, whenever Lorna
or me passes by, are lit with a light that never was on
sea or land. An' th' bould Sailor Mahan is smiling
too ; only dad is dour. [*She glances at the bottle on the
table.*] The song is heard, th' wine is seen, only th'
women wanting. [*She runs over to the porchway, and
shouts into the house*] Lorna, Marion, come on down,
come out here, an' join th' enthertainment !

[*Lorna and Marion come trotting out of the house into the garden. They are both clad in what would be called fancy dress. Lorna is supposed to be a gypsy, and is wearing a short black skirt, low-cut green bodice, with a gay sash round her waist, sparkling with sequins. Her fair arms are bare. Her head is bound with a silver and black ornament, similar in shape to that already worn by Marion. Her legs are encased in black stockings, and dark-red shoes cover her feet. Marion is dressed as a Nippy, a gay one. She has on a short, bright-green skirt, below which a black petticoat peeps ; a low-cut bodice of a darker green, and sports a tiny black apron to protect her costume. She wears light-brown silk stockings and brown shoes. Outside the white bandeau round her head she wears the ornament worn before. The two women stare at the three men.*]

Lorna [*vexatiously*]. Dhrunk is it ? To get in that state just when we were practisin' a few steps for tonight's fancy-dress dance ! [*She notices the bottle.*] Looka th' dhrink left out in th' sun an' air to dhry ! [*She whips up the bottle, and places it inside on the floor of the porch.*] An' even th' Sailor Mahan is moody too ! [*She goes over to the Sergeant, stands behind him, and lays a hand on his head. She is now in the golden light which shines down on the Sergeant too.*]

I saw a ship a-sailing, a-sailing on th' sea ;
An' among its spicy cargo was a bonny lad for me !

[*The Sergeant rises slowly, as if enchanted, with a foolish look of devotion on his face, till he stands upright beside Lorna, glancing at her face, now and again, very shy and uncertain. While this has been happening, Loreleen has gone to Sailor Mahan, and now stands behind him with a hand on his head.*

Loreleen [*down to Sailor Mahan*] :

I saw a man come running, come running o'er th' lea,
sir,
And, lo, he carried silken gowns
That couldn't hide a knee
That he had bought in saucy towns ;
An' jewels he'd bought beyond th' bounds
Of Asia's furthest sea.
And all were lovely, all were fine,
An' all were meant for me !

[*Sailor Mahan rises, as if enchanted, till he stands upright
beside Loreleen, slyly looking at her now and again.*

Marion. Aw, let's be sensible. [*She sees the gun.*] What's
th' gun doin' ? Who owns th' gun ?

Sergeant. It's mine. I'm on pathrol lookin' to shoot
down th' demon-bird loose among innocent people.

Marion. Demon-bird loose among innocent people !
Yous must be mad.

Sergeant [*indignantly*]. We're not mad ! It's only that we
were startled when th' darkness came, th' lightning
flashed, an' we saw Mr. Marthraun's tall-hat turnin'
itself into th' demon-bird !

Lorna [*mystified*]. Th' darkness came, th' lightning
flashed ? A tall-hat changin' into a demon-bird !

Michael [*springing to his feet*]. Ay, an' this isn't th' time for
gay disturbance ! So go in, an' sthrip off them gaudy
things, an' bend your mind to silent prayer an' long
fastin' ! Fall prostrate before God, admittin' your
dire disthress, an' you may be admitted to a new dis-
pensation !

Lorna [*to Michael*]. Nonsense ! Your new tall-hat was

delivered an hour ago, an' is upstairs now, waitin' for
you to put it on. [*To Marion*] Take that gun in, dear,
outa th' way, an' bring down th' tall-hat to show him
he's dhreamin'.

> [*Marion takes up the gun, and goes into the house with it,
> as Michael, in a great rage, shoves Mahan aside to face
> Lorna fiercely.*

Michael [*loudly*]. Who are you, you jade, to set yourself
up against th' inner sight an' outer sight of genuine
Christian men ? [*He shouts*] We seen this thing, I tell
you ! If you knew what you ought to know, you'd
acknowledge th' thrained tenacity of evil things.
Betther had I left you soakin' in poverty, with your rags
coverin' your thin legs, an' your cheeks hollow from
mean feedin'. Through our bulgin' eyes, didn't we see
th' horrification of me tall-hat turnin' into th' demonised cock ? Me tall-hat, you bitch, me own tall-hat is
roamin' round th' counthry, temptin' souls to desthroy
themselves with dancin' an' desultory pleasures !

Mahan [*gripping Michael's arm*]. Aw, draw it mild, Mick !

Michael [*flinging off Mahan's hold*]. Go in, an' take them
things, showy with sin, off you, an' dhress decent !
[*He points to Loreleen*] It's you who's brought this blast
from th' undherworld, England, with you ! It's easy
seen what you learned while you worked there — a
place where no God is ; where pride and lust an'
money are the brightest liveries of life ! [*He advances
as if to strike her, but Mahan bars his way.*] You painted
slug ! [*Marion comes from the house, carrying a fresh,
dignified tall-hat, noble in its silken glossiness. She offers it
to Michael who jumps away from it.*] No, no, take it
away ; don't let it touch me.

[*Marion puts the hat on the table, and the three men stare at it, as if expecting something to happen.*

Lorna [*darting into the porch, and returning with the bottle. It has gone back to its former colour*]. Let's have a dhrink to give us courage to fight our dangers. Fetch another glass, Marion.
   [*Marion goes in, and returns with a glass. Lorna uncorks the bottle, and takes up a glass to fill it.*

Michael [*warningly*]. Don't meddle with that dhrink, or harm may come to us all !

Lorna [*recklessly*]. If I can't wrap myself in th' arms of a man, I'll wrap myself in a cordial. [*She fills the glass, then she fills another one, and gives it to Loreleen ; then she fills a third, and gives it to Marion.*] Here, Loreleen. [*Loreleen takes the glass.*] Here, Marion.
                    [*Marion takes the glass from her.*

Mahan [*doubtfully, and with some fear*]. I wouldn't, Lorna, I wouldn't dhrink it — there's some kind of a spell on it.

Lorna. Is there, now ? I hope to God it's a strong one ! [*Raising her glass*] Th' Cock-a-doodle Dandy !

Marion ⎱ [*raising their glasses — together*]. Th' Cock-a-doodle
Loreleen ⎰ Dandy !
   [*The three women empty their glasses together. Lorna fills her glass again, and goes over to the Sergeant.*

Lorna [*offering the glass to the Sergeant*]. Dhrink, hearty man, an' praise th' good things life can give. [*As he hesitates*] Dhrink from th' glass touched by th' lips of a very fair lady !

Sergeant [*impulsively*]. Death an' bedamnit, ma'am, it's
a fair lady you are. [*He takes the glass from her*] I'm not
th' one to be short in salutin' loveliness !
  [*He drinks, and a look of delightful animation gradually
  comes on to his face.*

Loreleen [*who has filled her glass again — going over to Sailor
Mahan, and offering him the drink*]. Here, Sailor Mahan,
man of th' wider waters, an' th' seven seas, dhrink !
[*As he hesitates*] Dhrink from th' glass touched by th'
lips of a very fair lady !

Mahan [*taking the glass — impulsively*]. Here's a one who
always yelled ahoy to a lovely face an' charmin' figure
whenever they went sailin' by — *salud !*
  [*He drinks, and the look of animation gradually comes on to
  his face too.*

Marion [*who has filled her glass the second time — going over to
Michael and offering him the drink*]. Dark man, let th'
light come to you be dhrinkin' from a glass touched
be th' red lips of a fair young maiden !

Michael [*who has been watching the others enviously — taking
the glass from her*]. Gimme it ! I won't be one odd.
Yous can't best me ! [*He drinks it down greedily. A
reckless look steals over his face.*]
  [*During the last few moments, Lorna has been humming a
  tune, which has been taken up by an accordion, very
  softly. Then the Messenger appears on the pathway outside, and it can be seen that he is the player. He sits
  sideways on the wall, still playing softly a kind of a
  dance tune.*

Michael [*to Marion*]. In our heart of hearts, maid Marion,

we care nothin' about th' world of men. Do we now,
Sailor Mahan ?

Mahan [*cautiously — though a reckless gleam is appearing in
his eyes too*]. We all have to think about th' world o'
men at times.

Michael. Not with our hearts, Sailor Mahan ; oh, not
with our hearts. You're thinkin' now of th' exthra
money you want off me, Sailor Mahan. Take it,
man, an' welcome ! [*Enthusiastically*] An' more ! You
can have double what you're askin', without a whimper,
without a grudge !

Mahan [*enthusiastically*]. No, damnit, Michael, not a
penny from you ! We're as good as bein' brothers !
Looka th' lilies of th' field, an' ask yourself what th'
hell's money !

Michael [*excitedly*]. Dhross, be God ! Dhross, an' nothin'
else ! [*To Marion*] Gimme that hat there !
    [*She gives it to him. He puts it on, puts an arm round her
    waist, and they begin to move with the beat of the music.
    As Michael puts his arm around her waist, the ornament
    on her head rises into a graceful, curving horn, but he
    does not notice it.*
    [*At the same time, the Sergeant, having put an arm round
    Lorna, moves in the dance, too. As he does so, the orna-
    ment on her head, too, becomes a curving horn, but he
    does not notice it. Then Mahan goes over stealthily to
    Loreleen, who is watching the others, and stabs her shyly
    in the ribs with a finger. She turns, smiles, takes hold
    of his arm, and puts it round her waist. Then the two
    of them join the others in moving round to the beat of the
    music, the cock-like crest in Loreleen's hat rising higher
    as she begins to move in the dance.*

[*After a few moments, the dance quickens, the excitement grows, and the men stamp out the measure of the music fiercely, while the three women begin to whirl round them with ardour and abandon. While the excitement is at its height, a loud, long peal of thunder is heard, and in the midst of it, with a sliding, rushing pace, Father Domineer appears in the gateway, a green glow enveloping him as he glares down at the swinging dancers, and as a loud, lusty crow from the Cock rings out through the garden.*

[*The dancers, excepting Loreleen, suddenly stand stock still, then fall on one knee, facing the priest, their heads bent in shame and some dismay. Loreleen dances on for some few moments longer, the music becoming softer, then she slowly ends her dance to face forward towards the priest, the Messenger continuing to play the tune very softly, very faintly now.*

Father Domineer [*down to those in the garden — with vicious intensity*]. Stop that devil's dance ! How often have yous been warned that th' avowed enemies of Christianity are on th' march everywhere ! An' I find yous dancin' ! How often have yous been told that pagan poison is floodin' th' world, an' that Ireland is dhrinkin' in generous doses through films, plays, an' books ! An' yet I come here to find yous dancin' ! Dancin', an' with th' Kyleloch, Le Coq, Gallus, th' Cock rampant in th' disthrict, desthroyin' desire for prayer, desire for work, an' weakenin' th' authority of th' pastors an' masters of your souls ! Th' empire of Satan's pushin' out its foundations everywhere, an' I find yous dancin', *ubique ululanti cockalorum ochone, ululo !*

Messenger [*through his soft playing of the accordion*]. Th' devil was as often in th' street, an' as intimate in th' home when there was nor film nor play nor book.

Father Domineer. There was singin' then, an' there's
singin' now ; there was dancin' then, an' there's
dancin' now, leadin' innocent souls to perjure their
perfection. [*To Loreleen*] Kneel down, as th' others do,
you proud an' dartin' cheat, an' beg a pardon !

Loreleen [*obstinately*]. I seek no pardon for th' dance that's
done.

Father Domineer [*turning away from her*]. Seek for it then
when pardon hides away.

Michael. Oh, what have I done ! I've bethrayed meself
into a sudden misdoin' !

Mahan. Mea culpa, me, too, Father !

Father Domineer. Oh, Michael Marthraun, an' you, Sailor
Mahan, Knights of Columbanus, I come to help yous,
an' I catch yous in th' act of prancin' about with
shameless women, dhressed to stun th' virtue out of all
beholdhers !

Michael. It was them, right enough, Father, helped be
th' wine, that done poor me an' poor Sailor Mahan
in ! I should have remembered that a Columbanian
knight told me a brother Columbanian knight told him
another brother has said that St. Jerome told a brother
once that woman was th' gate of hell ! An' it's thrue
— they stab a man with a knife wreathed with roses !

Father Domineer. Get up, get up, an' stand away from
me ; an' let ye never be loungers again in th' fight for
good against evil. [*They all rise up humbly, the women to
one side, the men to the other, and go back some way, as the
Priest comes into the garden. Loreleen strolls defiantly over
to the table, and sits sideways upon it. To Mahan*] An' now,

Sailor Mahan, a special word for you. On my way here, I passed that man of yours who's livin' in sin with a lost an' wretched woman. He dodged down a lane to give me th' slip. I warned you, if he didn't leave her, to dismiss him — did you do so? [*Mahan is silent.*] I have asked you, Mahan, if you've dismissed him?

Mahan [*obstinately*]. I see no reason why I should dismiss me best lorry driver.

Father Domineer [*coldly*]. You don't see a reason? An' who are you to have any need of a reason in a question of this kind? [*Loudly*] I have a reason, an' that's enough for you!

Mahan [*defensively*]. He's a fine worker, Father, an' th' nation needs such as him.

Father Domineer [*loudly*]. We're above all nations. Nationality is mystical, maundering nonsense! It's a heresy! I'm the custodian of higher interests. [*Shouting*] Do as you're told — get rid of him!

Michael [*wheedling*]. It's all right, Father — he'll do what your reverence tells him. Sailor Mahan's a thrue Columbanian.

Mahan [*angrily — to Michael*]. He won't do what his reverence tells him!

[*Down the path outside comes the Lorry Driver, a man of thirty years of age. He doesn't look a giant, but there is an air of independence and sturdiness about him. He is wearing a leather jacket, a pair of soldier's khaki trousers, and an oily-looking peaked cap. His face is tanned by the weather, and his upper lip is hidden by a well-trimmed moustache. He hesitates for a moment when*

he sees Father Domineer; but, stiffening a little, he con-
tinues his walk to the gateway, into the garden.   He
stands a little way from Mahan, looking at him,
evidently having something to say to him.

Father Domineer [*sneeringly*]. Ah, the gentleman himself
has arrived. [*To the man*] We were just talking of you,
my man. I have told Mr. Mahan to dismiss you.
You know why. You're a scandal to th' whole place ;
you're a shame to us all. Either leave this woman
you're living with, or go to where that sort of thing's
permitted. [*Loudly*] You heard me ?

Lorry Driver [*surlily*]. I heard you.

Father Domineer [*impatiently*]. Well ?

Lorry Driver. I come to speak with Mr. Mahan, Father.

Mahan [*quickly*]. Me, Jack ! Oh, yes ; what's the
throuble now ?

Lorry Driver. Plenty, sir. The turf-workers have left th'
bog, an' we've no turf to load. Th' delegate says he
sent a telegram to Mr. Marthraun, sayin' th' men
would leave th' bog, if no answer came within an hour.

Messenger. He did, an' I delivered it.

Michael. Damnit, but I forgot about it ! The tension
here put it out of me mind !

Father Domineer [*catching the Lorry Driver by an arm*]. Never
mind turf or tension now. Are you going to go
from here ?

Lorry Driver [*obstinately*]. I'll go, if Mr. Mahan tells me
to go.

Father Domineer [*in a fury*]. Isn't it a wondher God doesn't strike you dead ! I tell you to give the wretched woman up, or go, an' that's enough for either Sailor Mahan or you. [*He shakes the Lorry Driver's arm.*] Will you give that wretched woman up ; will you send that woman of yours away ?

Lorry Driver [*resentfully*]. Eh, don't be pullin' th' arm outa me !

Father Domineer [*his fury growing*]. Did you send that woman away ; are you going to do it ?

Lorry Driver [*shaking his arm free, and stepping back*]. Aw, let go ! I didn't an' I won't !

Father Domineer [*in an ungovernable burst of fury*]. You wretch, would you dare to outface your priest ? Get out of me sight !
   [*He lunges forward, and strikes the Lorry Driver swiftly and savagely on the side of the head. The man falls heavily ; lies still for a moment ; tries feebly to rise ; falls down again, and lies quite still.*

Mahan [*frightened*]. He's hurted, Father ; you hot him far too hard.

Father Domineer [*frightened too — with a forced laugh*]. Nonsense ! I just touched him. [*He touches the fallen man with his foot.*] Get up, get up — you're not that much hurt.

Mahan [*bending over the Lorry Driver, and placing a hand on his breast*]. I'm afraid he's either dyin' or dead, Father !
   [*Father Domineer runs over agitatedly to the fallen man, kneels down beside him, and murmurs in his ear. Then he raises his head to face the others.*

Father Domineer [*to the others*]. Yous all saw what happened. I just touched him, an' he fell. I'd no intention of hurting him — only to administer a rebuke.

Sergeant [*consolingly*]. Sure, we know that, Father — it was a pure accident.

Father Domineer. I murmured an act of contrition into th' poor man's ear.

Messenger [*playing very softly*]. It would have been far fitther, Father, if you'd murmured one into your own.

END OF SCENE II

Scene III

It is towards dusk in the garden now. The sun is setting, and the sky shows it. The rich blue of the sky has given place to a rich yellow, slashed with green and purple. The flag-pole stands black against the green and yellow of the sky, and the flag, now, has the same sombre hue.

The big sunflowers against the wall have turned into a solemn black, too ; the house has a dark look, save where a falling shaft from the sun turns the window above the porch into a golden eye of light. Far away, in the depths of the sky, the evening star can be faintly seen.

In the distance, for some time, the sounds of drumming, occasionally pierced by the shrill notes of a fife, can be heard.

Mahan is sitting at the table, busy totting up figures on papers spread out before him, his face knotted into creases of anxiety and doubt.

Lorna and Marion are leaning against the wall, away from the gateway, and near the house. Their gay garments are covered with dark hooded cloaks to temper the coolness of the evening air.

Lorna. They all seem to be out on th' hunt — police an' soldiers, with th' bands to give them courage. Th' fools !

Marion. D'ye think they'll get him ? Th' place'll lose its brightness if th' Cock's killed.

Lorna. How can they desthroy a thing they say themselves is not of this world ? [*She goes over to Mahan, and stares at him for a moment.*] It's cooler. The sun's settin'.

190

Mahan [*hardly noticing*]. Is it ?   I didn't notice.   I'm busy.
Everything thrust through everything else, since that
damned Cock got loose.   Th' drouth now dhryin'
everything to dust ;   the turf-workers refusin' to work,
th' women thinkin' only of dancin' an' dhress.   But
we'll lay him low, an' bury him deep enough to forget
he ever came here !

Lorna. Th' men on th' bog work hard ;   they should get
all you've got to give them.

Mahan [*resentfully*]. An' why th' hell shouldn't they work
hard ?   Who'd keep th' fires of th' nation burning, if
they didn't ?

Lorna. They work for you, too ;   an' for Michael.   He's
got a pile in th' bank, an' rumour says you've got one
too.

Mahan [*whining*]. Michael may ;   I never had, an' I'm
losin' th' little I had since I lost me best lorry dhriver
— blast th' hand that hot him !   [*The Cock suddenly
glides in, weaving a way between Mahan at the table, and
Lorna, circling the garden, and finally disappearing round the
gable-end of the house ; the dance tune softly keeps time with
his movements.   Jumping to his feet*] What was that ?   I
thought I saw him prancin' by me !

Lorna [*startled too*]. What was what ?

Mahan. Th' Cock in his black plumage, yellow legs, an'
crimson crest !

Marion [*who has gone tense*]. You put th' heart across me !
I thought you meant th' poor dead man.
                              [*She turns to look along the road again.*

Lorna [*to Mahan*]. There's little use worryin' over figures till you settle with th' men.

Mahan [*irritably*]. That's Mick's business, that's Mick's business !

Marion [*running over to whisper excitedly to Lorna*]. Here they are — Father Domineer an' Mr. Marthraun comin' along th' road !

Mahan [*irascibly*]. Aw, what does that Father Domineer want comin' here when we've so much to think about ! Delayin' things ! I want to get away from here before it gets dark.

Lorna. Didn't you know they're goin' to purge th' poor house of its evil influences ?

Mahan [*irritably*]. Oh, can't they do first things first ?
  [*Along the pathway outside come Father Domineer and Michael, followed by a lad. The lad is One-eyed Larry. His face is one alternately showing stupidity or cunning, according to whomsoever may be speaking to him. Where his left eye was is a black cavity, giving him a somewhat sinister look. He is lanky and rather awkward-looking. He is wearing a black cassock or soutane, piped with red braid, and is bare-headed. He is carrying a small bell, a book, and an unlighted candle. He shuffles along after the two men, and follows them into the garden.*

Father Domineer. We'll banish them, never fear, Michael, before I have to leave th' parish because of that unhappy accident. I've faced worse. Be staunch. Th' bell is powerful, so is th' book, an' th' blessed candle, too. [*He glances at the women.*] Let yous women keep to th' farther end of th' garden. [*He glances at Mahan.*] We won't be long, Sailor Mahan. [*Suddenly, as he,*

Michael, and One-eyed Larry reach the porch] Where's that other one ?

Michael. Is it Loreleen, me daughter, Father ?

Father Domineer. She's no daughter of yours, Michael. [*Bending down to whisper warningly*] Get rid of her, get rid of her — she's dangerous !

Michael. How get rid of her, Father ?

Father Domineer. Pack her off to America !

Michael [*respectfully — as they are about to go into the house*]. I'll go first, Father.

Father Domineer [*setting him gently aside*]. No, no ; mine th' gap of danger.
        [*The three of them go in, the Priest first, then Michael, and, lastly, One-eyed Larry. Marion and Lorna move over to the farther side of the garden.*

Lorna. It's all damn nonsense, though Michael has me nerves in such a way that I'm near ready to believe in anything.

Mahan. Waste of time, too. It'll take a betther man than Father Domineer to dhrive evil things outa Eire.

Marion. Messenger says he's only addin' to their number, an' soon a noddin' daffodil, when it dies, 'll know its own way to hell. [*The roll of a drum is heard and a great boo-ing. Marion runs to the wall to look over it, and up the road. Excitedly*] A girl runnin' this way, hell for leather. My God, it's Loreleen !
        [*After a few moments, Loreleen runs along the pathway outside, and dashes in through the gateway to Lorna, who catches her in her arms. Clumps of grass and sods of*

turf, and a few stones follow Loreleen in her rush along the road.

Loreleen [*out of breath*]. God damn th' dastards of this vile disthrict ! They pelted me with whatever they could lay hands on — th' women because they couldn't stand beside me ; th' men because there was ne'er a hope of usin' me as they'd like to ! Is it any wondher that th' girls are fleein' in their tens of thousands from this bewildhered land ? Blast them ! I'll still be gay an' good-lookin'. Let them draw me as I am not, an' sketch in a devil where a maiden stands !

Lorna [*soothingly*]. Be calm, child ! We can't go in, for Father Domineer's inside puttin' things in ordher. [*Releasing Loreleen*] I'll run along th' road to them dis-turbers, an' give them a bit o' me mind ! [*She catches hold of Marion's arm*] Come on, Marion !
   [*She and Marion rush out along the road, and pass out of sight.*

Loreleen [*staring at the house*]. He's inside, is he ? That's not where th' evil is, th' gaum, if he wants to know.

Mahan [*seriously*]. Come here, Loreleen ; nearer, for I've something to say to you. [*As she does not stir, he grips her arm, and draws her farther from the house.*] We might be heard.

Loreleen [*suspiciously*]. What do you want, Sailor Mahan ? You're not of one mind with them who chased me ?

Mahan [*a little embarrassed*]. Aw, God, no ! Me sails of love are reefed at last, an' I lie quiet, restin' in a lonely harbour now. I'm too old to be flusthered with that kinda folly. I just want to warn you to get outa this disthrict.

Loreleen [*bitterly*]. Why must I go ? Is it because I'm
good-lookin' an' gay ?

> [*But the bold Mahan isn't indifferent to the charms of
> Loreleen. So he goes on to show Loreleen the youthfulness
> of his old age ; that his muscles are still strong, his
> fibres flexible. He becomes restless, and walks about,
> occasionally glancing at the house, nervous at what may
> be happening inside. When he comes to a chair, he non-
> chalantly swings a leg over the back of it, turning on the
> foot of the same leg to swing the other one back again.
> These actions, like the conversation, though not done in a
> hurry, are done quickly, as if he wanted to say all he had
> to say before any interruption.*

Mahan [*swinging a leg over a chair*]. Partly because you're
good-lookin' an' partly because of th' reckless way you
talk. Remember what happened to poor Jack. I'd
clear out if I were you.

> [*He vaults on to the table, swings round it on his backside,
> and vaults from it on the opposite side, a little stiffly.*

Loreleen. How'm I to clear out ? I've no money left.
Th' forty pounds I had, Dad put into his bank for me,
an' now won't give me a penny of it, because he says
if I got it, I'd go to England ; an' if I went to England,
I'd lose me soul, th' shaky, venomous lout ! An' I
keep quiet because of Lorna. [*Hurriedly, as Mahan is
stiffly climbing a few feet up the flag-pole*] Oh, don't be
doin' th' monkey on a stick ! Maybe you could help
me ? Could you, would you ?

Mahan [*sliddering from the pole, swinging a leg over a chair, and
coming closer to her*]. Now that's what I'd hoped you'd
say. This is th' first time I've caught you alone. I'll
give you what you need, an' you can weigh anchor,

an' be off outa this damned place.   Listen, darlin' :
you steal out tonight to th' Red Barn, west of th' Holy
Cross, an' I'll dhrive there with what'll get you as far
as you want to go.   [*He suddenly puts an arm round her in
a kind of clutch.*]   Jasus, you have lovely eyes !

Loreleen [*trying to pull his arm away*].   Oh, Sailor Mahan,
don't do that !   Let me go — someone may see us !

Mahan [*recklessly*].   You deserve to be ruffled a bit !   Well,
will you come to th' Red Barn, while th' rest are goin'
to th' dance, an' save yourself ?   Yes or no !

Loreleen.   Maybe, maybe ; yes, yes, I'll go.   Let go your
clutch !
    [*The house shakes ; a sound of things moving and crockery
    breaking comes from it ; several flashes of lightning spear
    out through the window over the porch ; and the flag-pole
    wags drunkenly from side to side.*
    [*Marion and Lorna appear on the pathway outside the wall,
    and hurry along into the garden just as One-eyed Larry
    comes running out of the house, his face beset with fear.
    His one eye takes in the picture of Loreleen breaking away
    from Mahan.   Loreleen turns aside from One-eyed Larry,
    while Mahan, embarrassed, turns to face him.*

One-eyed Larry [*excitedly*].   It's startin' in earnest !   There's
a death-sthruggle goin' on in there !   Poor Father
Domineer's got a bad black eye, an' Micky Marthraun's
coat is torn to tatthers !

Lorna [*hurrying into the garden*].   What's happened, what's
happenin' ?

Mahan [*with dignity — to One-eyed Larry*].   Misther Marthraun in your mouth, me lad.

Loreleen [*mischievously*]. Let th' lad tell his funny story.

One-eyed Larry [*turning on Loreleen*]. It's funny to you because you're in league with th' evil ones ! [*To the others*] One o' Father Domineer's feet is all burned be a touch from one o' them, an' one o' Micky's is frozen stiff be a touch from another. [*To Mahan*] Maybe you'd ha' liked me to have lost me other eye while you were warmin' yourself in that one's arms !

[*He points to Loreleen.*

Mahan [*furiously*]. You one-eyed gett, if you had two, I'd cyclonise you with a box !

Loreleen [*unmoved — a little mockingly*]. An' how did th' poor lamb lose his eye ?

Mahan [*indifferently*]. Oh, when he was a kid, he was hammerin' a bottle, an' a flyin' piece cut it out of his head.

One-eyed Larry [*venomously*]. You're a liar, that wasn't th' way ! It was th' Demon Cock who done it to me. Only certain eyes can see him, an' I had one that could. He caught me once when I was spyin' on him, put a claw over me left eye, askin' if I could see him then ; an' on me sayin' no, put th' claw over th' other one, an' when I said I could see him clear now, says he, that eye sees too well, an' on that, he pushed an' pushed till it was crushed into me head.

Loreleen [*mockingly*]. What a sad thing to happen !

[*The house shakes worse than before, and seems to lurch over to one side. The flag-pole wags from side to side merrily ; there is a rumble of thunder, and blue lightning flashes from the window. All, except Loreleen, cower together at*

*the far end of the garden. She stands over by the wall,
partly framed by the sable sunflowers.*

Marion [*full of fright*]. Sacred Heart ! Th' house'll fall
asundher !

Loreleen [*gleefully*]. Let it ! It's th' finest thing that could
happen to it !

One-eyed Larry [*trembling violently*]. It's now or never for
them an' for us. They're terrible powerful spirits.
Knocked th' bell outa me hand, blew out th' candle, an'
tore th' book to threads ! Thousands of them there are,
led be th' bigger ones — Kissalass, Velvethighs, Reeda-
buck, Dancesolong, an' Sameagain. Keep close. Don't
run. They might want help. [*Screeches like those of barn
owls are heard from the house, with the " too-whit too-whoo " of
other kinds, the cackling of hens, and the loud cawing of crows.
Frantically pushing his way to the back of the others*] Oooh !
Let me get back, get back !

> [*The house shakes again ; the flag-pole totters and falls flat ;
> blue and red lightning flashes from the window, and a great
> peal of thunder drums through the garden. Then all
> becomes suddenly silent. They all hang on to each other,
> shivering with fear, except Loreleen, who lights a cigarette,
> puts a foot on a chair, leans on its back, looks at the house,
> and smokes away serenely.*

Lorna [*tremulously*]. Why has th' house gone so silent
suddenly ?

One-eyed Larry [*from the rear*]. They've either killed th'
demons, or th' demons has killed them.

Marion. God save us, they must be dead !

Loreleen [*with quiet mockery*]. Welcome be th' will o' God.

Lorna [*suddenly — with great agitation*]. Get back, get back!
Run! There's something comin' out!

 [*She, Marion, and One-eyed Larry race for the gateway,
rush on to the sidewalk, and bend down, so that only their
heads can be seen peeping over the wall. Mahan shrinks
back to the far end of the garden, and Loreleen remains
where she is.*

 [*From the house, sideways, through the now lurching porch,
come Father Domineer and Michael. Both are limping,
Father Domineer on his left foot, Michael on his right one.
Domineer has a big black eye, his coat is awry on his
back, and his hair is widely tossed. Michael's coat hangs
in tatters on him. Father Domineer's face is begrimed
with the smudges of smoke, and both look tired, but
elated.*

 [*One-eyed Larry at once runs out, and takes his place
reverently behind them, standing with his hands folded
piously in front of his breast, his eyes bent towards the
ground. Mahan straightens up, and Lorna and Marion
return to the garden. Loreleen remains as she was.*

Father Domineer [*as he enters with Michael*]. Be assured, good
people, all's well, now. The house is safe for all. The
evil things have been banished from the dwelling.
Most of the myrmidons of Anticlericus, Secularius, an'
Odeonius have been destroyed. The Civic Guard and
the soldiers of Feehanna Fawl will see to the few who
escaped. We can think quietly again of our Irish
Sweep. Now I must get to my car to go home, and have
a wash an' brush up. [*To Marion and Lorna*] Off you go
into the house, good women. Th' place, th' proper
place, th' only place for th' woman. Straighten it out,
and take pride in doing it. [*He shoves Marion towards the
porch*] Go on, woman, when you're told! [*To Michael*]

You'll have to exert your authority more as head of the house.

Michael [*asserting it at once — to Lorna*]. You heard what Father Domineer said. Go on ; in you go, an' show yourself a decent, God-fearin' woman.

Father Domineer [*trying to be gracious — to Lorna*]. Th' queen of th' household as th' husband is th' king.
   [*Marion has gone into the house with a sour-looking face, and Lorna now follows her example, looking anything but charmed.*

Father Domineer [*turning to Loreleen*]. And you — aren't you going in to help ?

Loreleen [*quietly*]. No, thanks ; I prefer to stay on in the garden.

Father Domineer [*thunderously*]. Then learn to stand on the earth in a more modest and suitable way, woman ! [*Pointing to ornaments on crest of hat and breast of bodice*] An' do you mind that th' ornaments ye have on of brooch an' bangle were invented be th' fallen angels, now condemned to everlastin' death for worshippin' beauty that faded before it could be clearly seen ? [*Angrily*] Oh, woman, *de cultus feminarum malifico eradicum !*

Michael. That one's mind is always mustherin' dangerous thoughts plundered outa evil books !

Father Domineer [*startled*]. Books ? What kinda books ? Where are they ?

Michael. She has some o' them in th' house this minute.

Father Domineer [*roaring*]. Bring them out, bring them out ! How often have I to warn you against books ! Hell's

bells tolling people away from th' thruth! Bring
them out, *in annem fiat ecclesiam nonsensio*, before th'
demoneens we've banished flood back into th' house
again!

[*Michael and One-eyed Larry jostle together into the porch
and into the house to do Father Domineer's bidding.*

Loreleen [*taking her leg down from the chair, and striding over to
Father Domineer*]. You fool, d'ye know what you're
thryin' to do? You're thryin' to keep God from
talkin'!

Father Domineer. You're speakin' blasphemy, woman!

Mahan. What do people want with books? I don't
remember readin' a book in me life.

[*Michael comes back carrying a book, followed by One-eyed
Larry carrying another. Father Domineer takes the book
from Michael, and glances at the title-page.*

Father Domineer [*explosively*]. A book about Voltaire! [*To
Loreleen*] This book has been banned, woman.

Loreleen [*innocently*]. Has it now? If so, I must read it
over again.

Father Domineer [*to One-eyed Larry*]. What's th' name of
that one?

One-eyed Larry [*squinting at the title*]. Ullisississies, or something.

Father Domineer. Worse than th' other one. [*He hands his
to One-eyed Larry*] Bring th' two o' them down to th'
Presbytery, an' we'll desthroy them. [*Loreleen snatches
the two books from One-eyed Larry. One-eyed Larry tries to
prevent her, but a sharp push from her sends him toppling over.
Loreleen, with great speed, darts out of the gateway, runs along*

*the pathway, and disappears.   Standing as if stuck to the
ground]* Afther her, afther her !

Michael [astonished].   Me legs won't move !

Mahan
One-eyed Larry}*[together].* Nor mine, neither.

> [*As Loreleen disappears, the Cock suddenly springs over the
> wall, and pirouettes in and out between them as they
> stand stuck to the ground.*

> [*Cute ears may hear the quick tune, played softly, of an
> accordion, as the Cock weaves his way about.   The
> Sergeant appears running outside, stops when he sees the
> Cock, leans over the wall, and presents a gun at Michael.*

Michael [frantically — to Sergeant].   Not me, man, not me !
> [*Terribly excited, the Sergeant swings the gun till it is
> pointing at Mahan.*

Mahan [frantically]. Eh, not me, man !
> [*After the Cock has pirouetted round for some moments,
> while they all remain transfixed, the scene suddenly goes
> dark, though the music continues to sound through it.
> Then two squib-like shots are heard, followed by a clash of
> thunder, and, when the garden enjoys the light of early
> dusk again, which comes immediately after the clap of
> thunder, the music as suddenly ceases.*

> [*The returning light shows that Father Domineer is not
> there ; that Michael and Mahan are stretched out on the
> ground ; and that One-eyed Larry is half over the wall,
> his belly on it, his legs trailing into the garden, his head
> and shoulders protruding into the road.*

Michael [moaning].   Shot through the soft flesh an' th'
hard bone !

Mahan [*groaning*]. Shot through th' hard bone an' th' soft flesh !

One-eyed Larry [*shouting*]. Mrs. Marthraun, Marion, we're all killed be th' Cock an' th' Sergeant !
> [*Lorna and Marion come running out of the house over to the two prostrate men.*

Lorna. What's happened ? Where's th' Sergeant ?

One-eyed Larry [*sliddering over the wall, frantic with fear*]. I seen him runnin' off when he'd shot us all ! I'm goin' home, I'm goin' home ! Father Domineer's been carried off be th' Demon Cock — I'm off !
> [*He runs swiftly down the road, and disappears.*

Lorna [*bending over Michael*]. Where were you hit ? D'ye think there's a chance of you dyin' ?

Michael [*despairingly*]. I'm riddled !

Lorna [*feeling his body over*]. I can't see a speck of damage on you anywhere, you fool.

Marion [*who has been examining Mahan*]. No, nor on this fella either.

Michael. I tell you th' bullet careered through me breast an' came out be me back !

Mahan. An' then tore through me back an' came out be me breast !

Lorna. What darkness was One-eyed Larry talkin' about ? An' Father Domineer carried off be the Cock ! Me nerves are all gettin' shatthered. It's all very thryin'. [*She pokes Michael roughly with her foot.*] Here, get up, th' both of yous. There isn't a thing wrong with either of you.

Mahan [*sitting up cautiously, and feeling in his breast pocket*].
What th' hell's this ? [*He pulls out a bullet bigger than a
cigar.*] Looka, Michael Marthraun, th' size of th'
bullet that went tearin' through you an' then through
me ! [*Very devoutly*] Good angels musta gone along
with it, healin' all at th' same time that it tore our
vitals.

Michael [*as devoutly*]. Some higher an' special power musta
been watchin' over us, Sailor Mahan. Sharin' a
miracle, now, Sailor Mahan, we're more than brothers.

Mahan [*fervently*]. We are that, now ; we are indeed.
I'll keep this bullet till th' day I die as a momento of a
mementous occasion !

Lorna [*impatiently*]. Get up, get up. An' don't disturb
us again while we're practisin' for the fancy-dhress
dance tonight in th' hope of winning a spot prize.

Michael [*furiously to her*]. You'll win no spot prize, an'
there'll be no dance till that Demon Cock's laid low !
[*To Mahan — piously*] Thrue men we are, workin' in a
thruly brotherly way for th' good of th' entire community — aren't we, Sailor Mahan ? That's what
saved us !

Mahan [*as piously*]. We are that, Michael ; we are indeed ;
especially now that we've settled th' question finally
so long disputed between us.

Michael [*suspiciously, a note of sharpness in his voice*]. How
settled it ?

Mahan. Be you arrangin' to give me, not only what I was
askin', but twice as much.

Michael [*sarcastically*]. Oh, did I now ? That was damned

good of me ! [*Angrily*] No, nor what you were askin'
either. D'ye want me to ruin meself to glorify you ?
An' didn't I hear a certain man promisin', nearly on
his oath, he'd give his lorries for next to nothin' to
serve th' community ?

Mahan [*shouting*]. When I was undher a spell, fosthered on
me here ! I'm goin', I'm goin.' I'll argue no more !
[*He goes out by the gate and along the road, pausing as he is
about to disappear.*] For th' last time, Michael Marthraun,
are you goin' to do th' decent for th' sake of th' nation,
an' give me what I'm askin' ?

Michael [*with decision — quietly*]. No, Sailor Mahan, I'm
not. [*He shouts*] I'd see you in hell first !

Mahan [*as he goes*]. A sweet goodbye to you, an' take a
dhrug to keep from stayin' awake o' nights thinkin' of
the nation's needs !

Lorna [*persuasively*]. Be reasonable, Michael. You're
makin' enough now to be well able to give him all he
asks.

Michael [*savagely seizing her arm*]. Listen, you : even
though you keep th' accounts for me, it's a law of
nature an' a law of God that a wife must be silent
about her husband's secrets ! D'ye hear me, you
costumed slut ?

Lorna [*freeing herself with an effort*]. Don't tear th' arm
out of me ! If you want to embalm yourself in money,
you won't get me to do it !
    [*The sound of the wind rising is heard now — a long,
    sudden gust-like sound, causing Michael to do a sudden
    rush towards the gate, pressing himself back all the time,*

*and gripping the wall when he gets to it.   The two women
do not notice the wind.*

Michael. Jasus ! that was a sudden blast !

Lorna [*wondering*]. Blast ?   I felt no blast.

Marion [*shaking her head*]. He's undher a spell again.
   [*One-eyed Larry comes running along the road outside,
   excited and shouting.   He is holding on tensely to the
   waist-band of his trousers.*

One-eyed Larry [*without the wall*]. A miracle, a miracle !
Father Domineer, outa th' darkness, was snatched from
th' claws of the Demon Cock, an' carried home safe on
th' back of a white duck !

Lorna [*amazed*]. On th' back of a white duck ?   When
will wondhers cease !   They're all goin' mad !

Michael [*clapping his hands*]. Grand news !   Was it a wild
duck, now, or merely a domestic one ?

One-eyed Larry. Wild or tame, what does it matther ?   It
carried him cheerily through th' sky, an' deposited him
dacently down on his own doorstep !

Michael [*with deep thought*]. It might well have been one
of me own sensible ducks that done it.

One-eyed Larry [*coming to the gate*]. Wait till I tell yous.
Th' Demon Cock's furious at his escape, an' he's
causin' consthernation.   He's raised a fierce wind be
th' beat of his wings, an' it's tossin' cattle on to their
backs ; whippin' th' guns from th' hands of Civic
Guard an' soldier, so that th' guns go sailin' through
th' sky like cranes ; an' th' wind's tearin' at the clothes

of th' people.   It's only be hard holdin' that I can
keep me own trousers on !

Michael [*eagerly*]. Th' wind near whipped me on to th'
road a minute ago.
   [*The Bellman enters on the pathway outside, and meets One-
   eyed Larry at the gateway, so that the two of them stand
   there, the one on the left, the other to the right of it.*
   [*The collar and one arm are all that are left of the Bellman's
   coat, and his shirt has been blown outside of his trousers.
   He is still wearing the brass hat.   His right hand is
   gripping his waist-band, and his left carries the bell that
   he is ringing.*

Bellman [*shouting*]. Get out, get in !   Th' Demon Cock's
scourin' th' skies again, mettlesome, menacin', mol-
estifyin' monsther !   Fly to your houses, fall upon
your knees, shut th' doors, close th' windows !   In a
tearin' rage, he's rippin' th' clouds outa th' sky, because
Father Domineer was snatched away from him, an'
carried home, fit an' well, on th' back of a speckled
duck !

One-eyed Larry [*startled into anger*]. You're a liar, it wasn't
a speckled duck !   What are you sayin', fella ?   It was
a pure white duck that carried th' Father home !

Bellman [*angrily — to One-eyed Larry*]. Liar yourself, an'
you're wrong !   It was a speckled duck that done it ;
speckled in black, brown, an' green spots.   I seen it
with me own two eyes doin' th' thrick.

One-eyed Larry [*vehemently*]. I seen it with me one eye in
concentration, an' it was a duck white as th' dhriven
snow that brought him to his domiceel.

Lorna. I'd say white's a sensible colour, an' more apter for th' job.

Michael. I'd say a speckled duck would look more handsome landin' on a doorstep than a white fowl.

Marion [*thoughtfully*]. I wondher, now, could it have been Mr. McGilligan's tame barnacle goose ?

Michael [*explosively*]. No, it couldn't have been Mr. McGilligan's tame barnacle goose ! Don't be thryin' to scatther confusion over a miracle happenin' before our very eyes !

 [*The Sergeant comes rushing in along the pathway out-*
 side the wall, and runs into the garden through the gate-
 way, roughly shoving the Bellman and One-eyed Larry
 out of his way. His cap is gone, a piece of rope is tied
 round his chest to keep his coat on ; and, when he reaches
 the gate, all can see that he wears no trousers, leaving
 him in a long shirt over short pants. He is excited, and
 his face is almost convulsed with fear and shame.

Sergeant [*shoving One-eyed Larry and Bellman aside*]. Outa me way, you fools ! [*Rushing into the garden — to Michael*] Give me one of your oul' trousers, Mick, for th' love o' God ! Whipped off me be a blast of th' wind me own were. When I seen them goin', me entire nature was galvanised into alarmin' anxiety as to what might happen next.

Michael. A terrible experience ! What's to come of us, at all !

Sergeant [*tearfully*]. Why isn't Father Domineer here to help ? He doesn't care a damn now, since he was carried home, safe an' sound on th' back of a barnacle goose !

One-eyed Larry [*dumbfounded and angry*]. A barnacle goose ? What are you sayin', man ? It was a dazzlin' white duck that brought him home.

Bellman [*to One-eyed Larry*]. I'm tellin' you it was a specially speckled duck that done it.

Sergeant [*emphatically*]. It was a goose, I'm sayin'. Th' Inspector seen it through a field-glass, an' identified it as a goose, a goose !

Lorna [*amused — laying a hand on Marion's shoulder*]. Look at him, Marion. All dollied up for th' fancy-dhress dance !

Marion [*hilariously*]. It's lookin' like th' blue bonnets are over th' bordher !

Michael [*angrily — to the Sergeant*]. Get into th' house, man, an' don't be standin' there in that style of half-naked finality ! You'll find some oul' trousers upstairs. [*Turning on Lorna and Marion as the Sergeant trots timidly into the house*] You two hussies, have yous no semblance of sense of things past an' things to come ? Here's a sweet miracle only afther happenin', an' there yous are, gigglin' an' gloatin' at an aspect in a man that should send th' two of yous screamin' away ! Yous are as bad as that one possessed, th' people call me daughter. [*The sound of the wind now rises, swifter, shriller, and stronger, carrying in it an occasional moan, as in a gale, and with this stronger wind comes the Messenger, saunter-ing along outside the wall, sitting down on it when he reaches the end farthest from the house. Nothing in the garden is moved by the wind's whistling violence, except Michael, the Bellman, and One-eyed Larry (who have been suddenly hustled into the garden by the wind).*]

These three now grip their waist-bands, and begin to make sudden movements to and fro, as if dragged by an invisible force ; each of them trying to hold back as the wind pushes them forward. The Messenger is coaxing a soft tune from his accordion ; while Marion and Lorna are unaffected by the wind, and stand staring at the men, amused by their antics.

Michael [*a little frantic*]. Listen to th' risin' evil of th' wind ! Oh, th' beat of it, oh, th' beat of it ! We know where it comes from — red wind on our backs, black wind on our breasts, thryin' to blow us to hell !

Bellman [*gliding about, pushed by the wind ; holding on to his trousers with one hand, while he rings his bell with the other one*]. Fly into th' houses, close th' windows, shut th' doors !

One-eyed Larry [*gliding in opposite direction*]. We can't, we can't — we go where th' wind blows us !

Messenger. What ails yous ? I feel only th' brisk breeze carrying the smell of pinewoods, or th' softer one carryin' th' scent of th' ripenin' apples.

Michael [*to the women, while he holds fast to his waist-band*]. Get in, an' sthrip off them coloured deceits, smellin' of th' sly violet an' th' richer rose, sequestherin' a lure in every petal ! Off with them, I say, an' put on a cautious grey, or th' stated humbleness of a coal-black gown ! [*The Sergeant comes from the house wearing Michael's best black Sunday trousers. He comes from the porch shyly, but the moment he steps into the garden, his face flashes into a grim look, and he grabs hold of the waist-band, and glides about as the others do. Michael, seeing the trousers — with a squeal of indignation*] Me best Sunday black ones !

Couldn't your damned plundherin' paws pounce on something a little lowlier to wear ?

Bellman. Get into th' houses, shut to th' doors, close th' windows !

[*Father Domineer suddenly appears on the pathway outside, and stands at the gateway looking into the garden. A gust of wind, fierce and shrill, that preceded him, declines in a sad wail, and ceases altogether, leaving a sombre silence behind it. Father Domineer's hair is tossed about ; he has a wild look in his eyes, and he carries a walking-stick to help him surmount the limp from the hurt he got when warring with the evil spirits.*

Father Domineer [*stormily*]. Stop where yous are ! No hidin' from the enemy ! Back to hell with all bad books, bad plays, bad pictures, and bad thoughts ! Cock o' th' north, or cock o' th' south, we'll down derry doh down him yet. Shoulder to shoulder, an' step together against th' onward rush of paganism ! Boldly tread, firm each foot, erect each head !

One-eyed Larry
Michael
Bellman
Sergeant } [*together — very feebly*]. Hurraah !

Father Domineer. Fixed in front be every glance, forward at th' word advance !

One-eyed Larry
Michael
Bellman
Sergeant } [*together — very feebly*]. Advance !

Father Domineer. We know where we're goin', an' we know who's goin' with us.

Michael. The minsthrel boy with th' dear harp of his country, an' Brian O'Lynn.

Bellman. Danny Boy an' th' man who sthruck O'Hara.

One-eyed Larry. Not forgettin' Mick McGilligan's daughter, Maryann !
     [*Sounds of fifing and drumming are heard, mingled with the sound of boo-ing, a little distance away.*

Father Domineer [*jubilantly*]. Listen to th' band ! We're closin' in ; we're winnin' ! [*He puts a hand up to shade his eyes, and peers forward.*] They've collared one of them ! Aha, a woman again ! [*A pause.*] A fine, familiar one too. [*He shouts*] Lead th' slut here, Shanaar, right here in front of me !
     [*He goes through the gateway, and waits in the garden for things to come.*
     [*Shanaar appears on the pathway, followed by the two Rough Fellows dragging Loreleen along. She is in a sad way. Her hair is tumbled about ; her clothes are disarranged ; her bodice unbuttoned, and her skirt reefed half-way up, showing a slim leg, with the nylon stocking torn. One of the Rough Fellows is carrying her hat with its cock-like crest in his hand. A blood-stained streak stretches from a corner of an eye half-way down a cheek. Her face is very pale, and intense fright is vividly mirrored in it. She is dragged by the arms along the ground by the men, led by Shanaar, to where the Priest is standing. When she is nicely placed before him, she hangs her head, ashamed of her dishevelled state, and of the way she has been pulled before him. Other men and women follow them in, but are checked from crowding the pathway by an order from the Priest. The Messenger rises from his seat on the wall, and comes near to where the men are*

holding Loreleen. He has placed the carrying straps of his accordion over his shoulders, and now bears the instrument on his back. Michael, the Bellman, and One-eyed Larry stand some way behind the Priest. Marion and Lorna have started to come to Loreleen's assistance, but have been imperiously waved back by Father Domineer, and have retreated back towards the house, where they stand to stare at what happens. Shanaar stands at the gateway, gloating over the woeful condition of Loreleen.

Father Domineer [*to those following the men dragging in Loreleen*]. Go back; keep back there! Give th' honied harlot plenty of space to show herself off in.

Shanaar [*down to Father Domineer*]. Tell her off, Father; speak to her in th' name of holy Ireland!

Father Domineer [*to Sergeant*]. You go, Sergeant, an' keep them from coming too close; [*to Shanaar*] an' you, Shanaar, stand at the opposite end to keep any others from pressing in on us. [*To the men holding Loreleen*] Bring her a little closer.   [*The men drag her closer.*

Father Domineer. Now, jerk her to her feet. [*The men jerk her upright.*] Well, me painted paramour, you're not looking quite so gay now; your impudent confidence has left you to yourself. Your jest with heaven is over, me lass! [*To the men*] How did you ketch her?

1st Rough Fellow [*with pride*]. We've been on her tail, Father, for some time. We ketched her in a grand car with a married man; with a married man, Father, an' he thryin' to put an arm round her.

2nd Rough Fellow [*butting in to share the pride of capture*]. So we hauled her outa th' car, and hustled her here to you.

Lorna [*running over to the man nearest to her, and catching his arm*]. Let th' poor lass go, you cowardly lout ! I know you : your whole nature's a tuft of villainies ! Lust inflames your flimsy eyes whenever a skirt passes you by. If God had given you a tusk, you'd rend asundher every woman of th' disthrict !

Father Domineer [*angrily — to Lorna*]. Get back to your place, woman ! [*Shouting, as she hesitates*] Get back when I tell you !
　　[*Lorna moves slowly away from Loreleen's side and goes into the house.*

Marion [*as she follows Lorna into the house*]. Dastard Knights of Columbanus, do noble work, an' do it well !

Loreleen [*to Father Domineer — appealingly*]. Make them let me go, Father, an' let me get into th' house ! It was Sailor Mahan promised me enough to take me away from here that made me go to him. I shouldn't have gone, but I wanted to get away ; [*brokenly*] get away, away ! Five pounds he gave me, an' they took them off me, with th' last two pounds of me own I had left.

Father Domineer [*savagely*]. Sailor Mahan's a decent, honest soul, woman ! A man fresh for th' faith, full of good works for clergy an' his neighbours. [*He bends down to hiss in her ears*] An' this is th' man, you sinful slut, this is th' man you would pet an' probe into a scarlet sin !

Loreleen. I only wanted to get away. I wanted to get away from Sailor Mahan as much as I wanted to get away from all here.

Father Domineer [*to the two Rough Fellows*]. Where's Sailor Mahan ?

1st Rough Fellow. Th' people pelted him back to his home an' proper wife, Father, an' he's there now, in bed, an' sorry for what he thried to do.

Loreleen [*plaintively*]. Make them give me back th' last few pounds I had.

Father Domineer [*to the Rough Fellows*]. You shouldn't have handled Sailor Mahan so roughly. Where's the money ?

2nd Rough Fellow. We tore it up, Father, thinkin' it wasn't fit to be handled be anyone of decent discernment.

Loreleen [*emphatically*]. They didn't ; they kept it. [*Stifling a scream*] Oh, they're twisting me arms !

Father Domineer [*cynically*]. Don't be timid of a little twinge of pain, woman, for, afther th' life you've lived, you'll welther in it later. [*To the two Rough Fellows*] Yous should have kept th' money to be given to th' poor.

Messenger [*coming over to the Rough Fellow on Loreleen's right — calmly*]. Let that fair arm go, me man, for, if you don't, there's a live arm here'll twist your neck instead. [*With a shout*] Let it go ! [*After a nod from the Priest, the 1st Rough Fellow lets Loreleen's arm go. The Messenger goes quietly round to the 2nd Rough Fellow.*] Let that fair arm go, me man, or another arm may twist your own neck ! Let it go ! [*The 2nd Rough Fellow sullenly does so.*] Now stand a little away, an' give th' girl room to breathe. [*The two Rough Fellows move a little away from Loreleen.*] Thank you. [*To the Priest*] Now, Father, so full of pity an' loving-kindness, jet out your bitther blessin', an' let th' girl go. An' thry to mingle undherstandin' with your pride, so as to ease th' tangle God has suffered to be flung around us all.

Father Domineer [*fiercely — to the Messenger*]. Keep farther away, you, for th' crowd is angry and their arms are sthrong ! We know you — enemy to th' glow of tradition's thruth, enemy to righteous reprobation, whose rowdy livery is but dyed in rust from th' gates of hell ! [*To Loreleen*] An' you, you'd hook your unholy reputation to a decent man's life. A man, like Sailor Mahan, diligent in his duty, th' echo of whose last prayer can ever be heard when another worshipper enters th' church. You'd sentence him to stand beside you, you shuttle-cock of sin !

Loreleen [*roused to indignation*]. Oh, end it, will you ! You fail in honesty when you won't make them give me back what they robbed from me. When you condemn a fair face, you sneer at God's good handiwork. You are layin' your curse, sir, not upon a sin, but on a joy. Take care a divil doesn't climb up your own cassock into your own belfry !

Father Domineer [*furiously*]. You'll dhribble th' blackness of sin no longer over our virtuous bordhers ! [*He hisses the words out*] Stipendium peccati mors est ! Get away from here quicker than you came, or it's in your coffin you'll be — in your coffin, your coffin !

Shanaar [*from the gateway*]. A merciful sentence, an aysey one, for a one like her !

Loreleen [*half defiantly*]. How am I to go where I'd like to go, when they took all I had off me ? How am I to go for miles with me clothes near rent from me back, an' frail shoes on me feet ?

Father Domineer [*putting his face closer to hers*]. Thrudge it ; thrudge on your two feet ; an' when these burn an' blister, go on your knees ; an' when your knees are broken an' bruised, go on your belly ; crawl in th' dust, as did th' snake in th' Garden of Eden, for dust is th' right cushion for th' like of you ! [*He raises himself erect, and commands in a loud voice*] Go now !

    [*Loreleen turns away, goes slowly through the gateway, and along the road outside. As Loreleen reaches the gate, Lorna runs out of the house. She is wearing a dark-red cloak, and carries a green one over her arm. She has a fairly large rucksack strapped on her back.*

Lorna [*calling as she runs out of the house*]. Loreleen ! [*Loreleen halts but does not turn her head.*] Loreleen, I go with you ! [*Lorna shoves Father Domineer aside at the gateway, nearly knocks Shanaar over, and hurries to Loreleen. Draping the green cloak over Loreleen's shoulders*] I go with you, love. I've got a sthrong pair of shoes in the sack you can put on when we're free from th' Priest an' his rabble. Lift up your heart, lass : we go not towards an evil, but leave an evil behind us !

    [*They go out slowly together.*

Father Domineer [*taking the Sergeant by the arm*]. Let her go quietly to her own. We'll follow some of the way to prevent anyone from harming her. [*Down to Michael*] Be of good cheer, Michael ; th' demon is conquered — you can live peaceful an' happy in your own home now.

    [*He goes out with the Sergeant, followed by all who may be there, except Michael, the Messenger, and Shanaar.*

    [*The Messenger goes back to the wall, sits on it sideways, takes the accordion from his back, and begins to play, very softly, the air of " Oh, Woman Gracious ". Shanaar leans on the wall from the outside, looking down at*

Michael, who is now seated gloomily on a chair beside the table, an elbow resting on it, his head resting on the hand.

Shanaar [*down to Michael*]. His reverence never spoke a thruer word, Mick, than that of you'd have happiness an' peace now. You were a long time without them, but you have them now.

Michael [*doubtfully*]. Maybe I have, Shanaar, an', God knows, I need them. [*He pauses for a moment, thinking*] I wondher will Lorna come back ?

Shanaar [*emphatically*]. Oh, devil a come back ! You need have no fear o' that, man. An' fortunate you are, for a woman's always a menace to a man's soul. Woman is th' passionate path to hell !

Messenger [*playing softly on his accordion and singing*] :

> Oh, woman gracious, in golden garments,
> Through life's dark places, all glintin' go ;
> Bring man, in search of th' thruth tremendous,
> Th' joy that ev'ry young lad should know.

> Then come out, darlin', in reckless raiment,
> We'll dance along through Ireland gay,
> An' clip from life life's rich enjoyments,
> An' never want for a word to say.

[*Marion has come into the porch, and now stands at the door, watching the Messenger. She is covered to her knees by a bright-blue cloak.*

> Cling close to youth with your arms enthrancin',
> For youth is restless, an' loth to stay ;
> So take your share of th' kisses goin',
> Ere sly youth, tirin', can slink away !

[*Marion crosses the garden towards the gate, and is about to go through it when the Messenger catches her by the arm.*

Would you leave me here, alone, without a lass to love me ?

Marion [*gently removing the hold of his hand on her arm*]. Your voice is dear to me ; your arm around me near seals me to you ; an' I'd love to have——

Messenger [*quickly*]. Your lips on mine !

Marion. But not here, Robin Adair, oh, not here ; for a whisper of love in this place bites away some of th' soul ! [*She goes out by the gateway, and along the road taken by Lorna and Loreleen. The Messenger stays where he is, wistful and still. Just before she goes*] Come, if you want to, Robin Adair ; stay, if you will.

Shanaar [*to the Messenger*]. Stay, Messenger. Take a warnin' from a wise oul' man, a very wise oul' one, too. [*He turns his head to look peeringly to the left along the road*] What's this I see comin' ? If it isn't Julia, back from Lourdes, an' she on her stretcher still ! I'd best be off, for I've no inclination to thry a chatter with a one who's come back as bad as she was when she went.

   [*He bends down nearly double, so as not to be seen, and slyly and quietly steals away.*

   [*After a pause, Julia comes in on her stretcher, carried by the two Rough Fellows as before, her father, silent and stony-faced, walking beside her. The stretcher is laid down in the garden just inside the gate. Julia is covered with a rug, black as a winter's sky, and its sombre hue is enlivened only by the chalk-white face of the dying girl. The Messenger has gone from the gateway, and now stands in a half-to-attention, military way, a little distance from the stretcher, looking down at Julia. Julia's father stands, as before, behind her head. Michael sits, un-noticing, elbow on table, his head resting on his hand.*

Julia [*in a toneless voice — to no-one in particular*]. Lorna, I want Lorna.

Messenger [*gently*]. She's gone, Julia.

Julia. Gone ? Gone where ?

Messenger. To a place where life resembles life more than it does here.

Julia. She's a long way to go, then. It's th' same every-where. In Lourdes as here, with all its crowds an' all its candles. I want Loreleen.

Messenger. She's gone with Lorna, an' Marion's followed them both.

Julia. Then there's no voice left to offer even th' taunting comfort of asking if I feel better.

Messenger. There's Michael Marthraun there.

Julia [*after a long look at Michael*]. He, poor man, is dyin' too. No-one left, an' th' stir there was when I was goin' — th' Mayor there, with all his accouthered helpers ; th' band playin' ; Father Domineer spoutin' his blessin' ; an' oul' Shanaar busy sayin' somersaultin' prayers ; because they all thought I would bring a sweet miracle back. [*She pauses.*] There was no miracle, Robin ; she didn't cure me, she didn't cure me, Robin. I've come back, without even a gloamin' thought of hope. [*She pauses again ; with a wan smile*] I can see your whole soul wishin' you could cure me. Touch me with your questionable blessin' before I go.

Messenger [*very softly*]. Be brave.

Julia. Nothin' else, Robin Adair ?

Messenger. Evermore be brave.

Julia [*after a pause*]. Dad, take me home.
   [*The Rough Fellows take up the stretcher and carry it out,
   the stony-faced father following in the rear without a
   word.*

Michael [*raising his head from his hand to look at the Messenger*].
   Maybe Lorna might come back.   Maybe I mightn't have
   been so down on her fancy dhressin'.

Messenger [*tonelessly*].   Maybe she will ;   maybe you
   mightn't.

Michael [*tonelessly too*].   It'll be very lonely for me now.
   All have left me. [*He takes a set of rosary beads from his
   pocket, and fingers them.*]   I've no one left to me but
   th' Son o' God. [*He notices the Messenger settling the
   accordion comfortably on his back, and watches him going to the
   gate.*]   Are you goin' too ?

Messenger [*shortly*].   Ay.

Michael.   Where ?

Messenger. To a place where life resembles life more than
   it does here.

Michael [*after a pause*].   What, Messenger, would you
   advise me to do ?

Messenger [*turning at the gate to reply*].   Die.   There is little
   else left useful for the likes of you to do.
   [*He swings his accordion comfortably before him, and plays
   a few preliminary notes.   Then he starts to sing softly as
   he goes away along the pathway outside ;   while Michael*

leans forward on to the table, and buries his head in his arms.

Messenger [*singing and accompanying himself on the accordion— as he is going off*] :

She's just like a young star out taking the air —
Let others be good or be clever —

With Marion gay, a gay flower in her hair,
Life becomes but a pleasant endeavour.

When building a city or making the hay,
I'll follow her close as night follows day,

Or lads follow lasses out nutting in May,
For ever and ever and ever !

THE END

STAR OF THE SEA

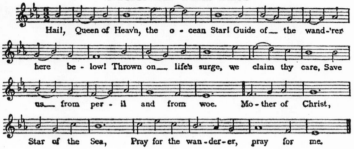

Hail, Queen of Heav'n, the o-cean Star! Guide of__ the wand-'rer here be-low! Thrown on__ life's surge, we claim thy care, Save us__ from per-il and from woe. Mo-ther of Christ, Star of the Sea, Pray for the wan-der-er, pray for me.

WHEN MEN WAS MEN

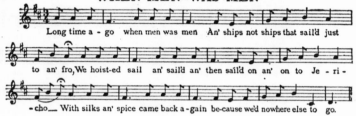

Long time a-go when men was men An' ships not ships that sail'd just to an' fro, We hoist-ed sail an' sail'd an' then sail'd on an' on to Je-ri--cho__ With silks an' spice came back a-gain be-cause we'd nowhere else to go.

LORELEEN'S SHANTY

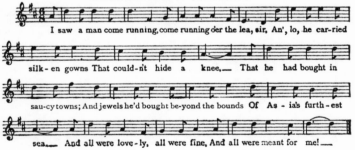

I saw a man come running, come running o'er the lea, sir, An', lo, he car-ried silk-en gowns That could-n't hide a knee,__ That he had bought in sau-cy towns; And jewels he'd bought be-yond the bounds Of As-ia's furth-est sea.__ And all were love-ly, all were fine, And all were meant for me!__

MUSIC FOR COCK'S DANCE

OH, WOMAN GRACIOUS

Oh wo - man gra - cious, in gold - en gar - ments, Through life's dark plac - es, all glint - in' go; Bring man, in search of the truth tre - mend - ous, The joy that ev - 'ry young lad should know.

MARION

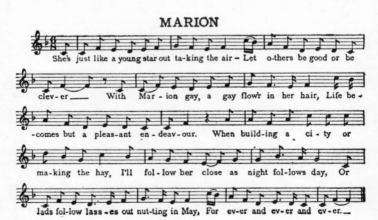

She's just like a young star out ta - king the air — Let o - thers be good or be clev - er___ With Mar - ion gay, a gay flow'r in her hair, Life be - comes but a pleas - ant en - deav - our. When build - ing a ci - ty or ma - king the hay, I'll fol - low her close as night fol - lows day, Or lads fol - low lass - es out nut - ting in May, For ev - er and ev - er and ev - er.__

BEDTIME STORY

An Anatole Burlesque in One Act

CHARACTERS IN THE PLAY

JOHN JO MULLIGAN, *a clerk*
ANGELA NIGHTINGALE, *a gay lass*
DANIEL HALIBUT, *a clerk — friend to Mulligan*
MISS MOSSIE, *a very respectable lodging-house keeper*
A POLICEMAN
A DOCTOR
A NURSE

———

SCENE

A bachelor-flat in Dublin.

TIME.—The present.

The sitting-room of the bachelor-flat rented by John Jo Mulligan from Miss Mossie, owner of one of the old houses of Dublin, decayed a little, but still sternly respectable, and kept presentable by her rigid attention to it. She has divided it into lodgings for respectable young gentlemen. A rather dull though lofty room. To the right is an ordinary gas fire ; over it a mantelpiece on which is a clock, flanked on either side by a coloured vase ; over these, on the wall, a square, gilt-framed mirror. Further up, towards back, is a door leading to Mulligan's bedroom. By the back wall, near this door, is a small bookcase with a few books sprawled out on its shelves ; and on top is a pale-green vase holding a bunch of white pampas grass. To the left of this is a window, now heavily curtained with dull, brown hangings. In the window's centre is a stand holding a coloured flower-pot containing some kind of a palm plant. Further on is a picture of a whitewashed cottage, well thatched with straw, a brown pathway before the door, with purple heather growing in tufts on its edges, and, in the distance, the dark-blue peaks of hills, all surmounted by a bright blue sky. In the side wall on the left is the door leading to the rest of the house. On this door several overcoats are hanging. To the left of it is an umbrella-stand in which are a walking-stick and two umbrellas, one newer than the other. Close to the fireplace is an armchair clad in dark-green leather, and further away, at an angle, is a settee to hold two, clad in the same colour. In the room's centre is a round table covered with a red table-cloth. On the table are a photograph or two, a vase of chrysanthemums, and a book, open, with its face turned down, so that the place might not be lost when the reader left it aside. The room is lighted from a bulb hanging from the centre of the ceiling ; the light is softened by being covered with a yellow parchment shade. A standard lamp

stands on the floor a little way from the sitting-room door,
towards the window, its light mollified by a deeply-fringed red
silk shade. A key is sticking in the keyhole of the sitting-room
door. A pair of Mulligan's tan shoes are beside the fireplace.
It is three or four of a cold, sleety January morning.

The fire is unlit, the room in darkness, when, presently, the
bedroom door opens, and Mulligan comes into the sitting-room,
showing the way to himself by the light of an electric torch. He
is but half dressed, in blue shirt, bright-checked, baggy plus-fours,
and coloured-top stockings. He is a young man of twenty-four
or -five; tall, but not thin. His hair is almost blond, and he
wears it brushed back from his forehead, which is too high for the
rather stolid face, giving him, at times, the look of a clown
having a holiday. His upper lip has a close-cropped moustache.
He is a constitutionally frightened chap, never able to take the
gayer needs of life in his stride — though he would be glad to
do it, if he could ; but he can never become convalescent from a
futile sense of sin. His clean-shaven face shows a very worried
look. He comes into the room cautiously, waving the light over
the floor, the table, the chairs, as if looking for something — as
a matter of fact, he is ; then returns to the door to peep into the
bedroom.

Mulligan [*sticking his head into the room — in a cautious*
    whisper]. I can't see the thing anywhere. Sure you
    left it out here ? [*There is no reply to the question.*] I
    say I can't find it anywhere out here. [*There is no reply.*
    He mutters to himself as if half in prayer] I shouldn't have
    done it ; I shouldn't have done it ! I musta been
    mad. Oh, forgive me ! [*He clicks his tongue, and peeps*
    into the room again.] Dtch dtch ! Gone asleep again !
    [*Whispering*] Angela ! Angela ! [*In a louder whisper*]
    Are you awake ? Eh, Angela ?

Angela [*within the room — sleepily*]. Wha' ?

Mulligan [*echoing her*]. Wha', wha' ! [*To himself*] Oh, it was a mad thing to do. Miserere mei. [*Speaking into room with irritation*] Have you forgotten what you sent me out to get ? [*Appealingly*] Please try to arouse yourself, Angela !

Angela [*within*]. Wha' ?
   [*Silence again for a few moments while Mulligan flashes the light on to the clock.*

Mulligan. It's going to four o'clock in the morning, Angela.

Angela [*within*]. Didja get the lipstick ?

Mulligan [*testily*]. I've told you I can't see it anywhere.

Angela [*sleepily*]. Have another look — there's a dear. I know I left it out there somewhere.

Mulligan [*shivering a little*]. It's nothing like a tropical climate out here, you know.

Angela [*sleepily*]. It's easy to li' the fire, isn't it ?
   [*Mulligan crosses to the fireplace, turns the gas tap, and sees that the meter wants another shilling. He irritatedly turns the tap off, and, crossing quickly back to the bedroom, knocks over the vase of flowers on the table, sending the water spilling over the table and on to the floor.*

Mulligan [*half to himself and half to Angela — with annoyance*]. There's the vase down ! Wather into me shoes and all over the floor ! [*Putting his head into the bedroom again*] I've knocked the vase down now ! The place is flooded ! And I can't light the fire — the meter needs another shilling.

Angela [*sleepily*]. Look in me han'bag, somewhere about. Maybe there's a bob in it.

> [*In desperation, Mulligan goes to the cupboard, opens it, takes out a wallet from which he takes a shilling, goes back to fireplace, puts it in the slot, and lights the fire. Then he returns to the bedroom door.*]

Mulligan [*putting his head into the bedroom again*]. Angela, are you up yet? The whole place is flooded. [*He gets no answer.*] You're not going asleep again, are you? Angela!

Angela [*within — sleepily*]. What time is it?

Mulligan [*in a loud and impatient whisper*]. I told you long ago. It's going to four o'clock in the morning. That friend of mine I told you of, will be back any minute from his all-night dance, before you slip away, if you don't hurry.

Angela [*from within*]. And what if he is? If he knew what had been going on in here, he'd be sorry he ever went to the dance.

Mulligan. Looka, Angela, I don't feel a bit funny about it. We should never have done it. Please get up, and face the situation. Remember your solemn promise to slip off when things were still.

> [*Angela appears at the door. She is a girl of twenty-five to twenty-seven, tall, trimly-formed, and not without dignity. Her hair is auburn, inclining towards redness. She is something of a pagan.*
>
> [*At present, she is dressed in her cami-knickers, covered by Mulligan's brown dressing-gown, and her bare feet are thrust into Mulligan's slippers. Far and away too good a companion of an hour, a year, or a life, for a fellow like Mulligan.*

Angela [*from the doorway*]. D'ye like the dark because your deeds are evil, or what? Switch on the light for God's sake, man, and let's have a look at each other before you banish your poor Eve from her Mulligan paradise.

Mulligan [*as he switches on the light*]. I was afraid someone outside might see it, stay to look, might hear our voices, and wonder.

Angela. Wonder at what?

Mulligan. At hearing a girl's voice in my room at this time of night or morning.

Angela [*mockingly*]. And isn't it a sweet thing for a girl's voice to be heard in a man's room at this time o' the night or morning?

Mulligan [*almost tearfully*]. You know it's not; not as we're situated. You know you did wrong to practise on a body who didn't know enough. Situated as we are, without divine warrant, it's not proper. We're in the midst of a violent sin, and you should be ashamed and sorry, instead of feeling sinfully gay about it. It's necessary to feel sorry for a sin of this kind.

Angela. You were quite gay when we were coming in, boy, weren't you? You've had your few bright moments, and you've given a sparkle to your life, so don't spoil it all. It may well be more serious for me than it is for you. [*She shivers.*] Burrr! It's cold here! I'll come back when the room's warmer, and make myself ready to meet the respectable world.
   [*She goes back into the bedroom, while he stands at the bedroom door for a few moments, not knowing what to do.*

Mulligan [*eyes raised appealing to the ceiling*]. Oh, that one'll

be well punished for her gaiety and carelessness in sin !
Oh, when will I forget this night's doings ?   Shattering
fall !   The very next day after me Novena too !   [*He
peeps into the bedroom.*]   Don't get too cosy there, or you
won't want to move.   Move we must, and soon.   [*He
goes to the cupboard, relocks it, and puts the key in his pocket ;
then he goes to the armchair, sits down in it, and starts to
put on his shoes.   Putting on a shoe — in a half-prayer*]
Sweet Saint Panteemalaria, get me outa this without
exposure.   [*He clicks his tongue*] Dtch dtch !   Soaking
wet !   and I'll be a cautious goer from this out — I
promise.   [*He goes over to bedroom door again with but one
shoe on, and peeps in.*]   Angela, room's warm now ;
quite warm.   The time's flying, mind you.   [*There is
no reply.*]   Aw, God, have you gone to sleep again !
Please, Miss Nightingale, please have some regard for
others !

Angela [*from within — sleepily*]. Did you find it ?

Mulligan. Find what, find what ?

Angela. Me lipstick you were looking for ?

Mulligan. No, no, I didn't ;   must be in there somewhere.

Angela. I remember I had it when you had me perched
on your lap.   Remember ?

Mulligan [*as if to someone in sitting-room*]. Oh, don't be
reminding me of things !   [*Into the bedroom*] No, I
don't remember.   Oh, for goodness' sake, get up !

Angela. All right, all right.   Put out a glass of wine, and
I'll be out in a minute.

   [*Mulligan goes to the cupboard, unlocks it, and takes out a
      bottle of wine and a glass.   He locks the cupboard again,
      leaving the key in the keyhole.   He goes to the table, fills*

out a glass of wine, and leaves it, with the bottle, on the
table, in readiness for Angela.

[He sits down in the armchair, puts on the other shoe, then
winds a woollen muffler round his neck, puts on a
pullover and coat that have been hanging over the back
of a chair, and finally places a trilby hat on his head.
As he does these things, he occasionally mutters to himself.

Mulligan [busy with the wine for Angela]. Not a single
thought has she for what might happen to me if
discovery came.   Utterly abandoned to her own
intherests.   [As he sits in chair putting on the second shoe —
in a full-blown prayer] Oh, gentle Saint Camisolinus,
guardianess of all good young people, get between me
and this petticoated demonsthrator of sinful delusion,
and I'll be O.K. for evermore.   I will, I promise !

[Angela comes into the room at last, and makes quick for
the fire.   She has put on her stockings — silk ones — and
skirt, a short, well-tailored one of darkish green, with
broad belt of dark red and black buckle.   She carries a
brown jersey over her arm, and her shoes in her hand.

Angela [throwing her shoes on to the armchair, and stretching
her hands to the fire]. Burrr !   It's cold out here still !
I thought you said the room was warm ?   [She notices
how he's dressed.]   All ready for the journey, eh ?   Soon
we'll be skiing down the stairs, wha' ?   Praying to all
the saints you know to see me out, eh ?

[She puts the jersey on over her head before the mirror over
the fireplace, and pats it down smoothly over her breast
and shoulders.

Angela.   We have to face the hard, cold facts now, haven't
we, dear ?

Mulligan.   We've got to think now of what would become
of me if you were discovered here.

Angela [*mockingly*]. Really ?   Of course, when one thinks of it, that becomes the one important problem.

Mulligan [*not noticing the mockery*]. It is, actually.   You see, Angela, the head of my department's a grand Knight of Columbanus, an uncompromising Catholic, strict in his thought of life, and if he heard of anything like this, I'd — I'd be out in the bleaker air, quick ; the little gilt I have on life would be gone ; I'd run to ruin ! God help me !

Angela [*prompting him*]. And then there's Father Demsey ?

Mulligan. Then there's Father Demsey whose right-hand man I am in the Confraternity and at all Saint Vincent de Paul meetings, with his " We can safely leave that matter with Mr. Mulligan ", or " John Jo will do this for us ".   You see, it's a matter of importance to more than me.   So, come on — we better get off at once.

Angela [*rising from the chair, and drinking the glass of wine*]. Angela's bright eyes, her scarlet lip, fine foot, straight leg, and quivering thigh have lost their charm for Mr. Mulligan.   He's all for go-ahead godliness now ! [*She pours out another glass of wine and drinks it.*]   And what is to become of me ? You don't care, and I don't care either.
   [*She moves about the room in a slow, semi-reckless rhythm as she lilts — Mulligan following her trying to get her quiet again.*

Angela [*lilting and moving about*] :
        I don't care what becomes of me,
        I don't care what becomes of me.

Mulligan [*shuffling after her as she moves as well as he can — in a low, anguished voice*]. Angela, please ! Sit down, do !

Angela [*lilting*] :
>   I don't care if I'm out till two,
>   I don't care for the man in blue.

Mulligan [*following her*]. Please, Miss Nightingale, be
serious ! The landlady'll hear you, and then we'll be
done !

Angela [*lilting*] :
>   I don't care what the people say,
>   Here, there, and everywhere ;

Mulligan [*appealing to the ceiling*]. Saint Curberisco, help
me !

Angela [*in a final burst*] :
>   For I'm going to be married in the morning,
>   So tonight, boys, I don't care !
[*Facing towards Mulligan.*] Sometime or other, we have
to face out of all we get into : face out of getting into
bed with a woman no less than face out into silence
from the glamour of prayer ; face out of summer into
winter ; face out of life into death !

Mulligan [*crossing himself*]. Your talk's near blasphemy,
Angela ! Now you're going where you shouldn't
venture. You'll bring a curse down on me, if you're
not careful ! Please be more discreet.

Angela. They're facts.

Mulligan. We're not fit for facts now.

Angela [*facing him fiercely*]. You stand there mustering up
moans for yourself, and never once realise that you've
ruined me ! Yes, ruined me !

Mulligan [*startled*]. Oh, God, d'ye hear her ! Ruined
you ? Oh, come, now, don't thry to act the innocent.

Angela. It's you who's acting the innocent, but it won't work. I was only an innocent kid till I met you. You led me on and destroyed all confidence in the goodness of me own nature ! You never, never ceased from persuasion till you got me here. I wasn't even to take off my hat, if I was the least bit suspicious. We were just to sit quiet discussing Yeats's poems. You were to sit ice-bound in your chair.

Mulligan [*indignantly*]. I led you on ! Angela Nightingale, you're inventing things. It was you insisted on coming, because you didn't like restaurants. A sorry thing for me I ever listened to you !

Angela [*ignoring his remarks*]. It's me's the sorry soul for listening to you. You promised a quiet hour of poetry, but we were hardly here when you began to move. Yeats's poems soon flew out of your head and hand. You got as far as "I will arise and go now, and go to Innisfree" ; then before the echo of the line was hushed, you had me clapped down on your knee. [*She becomes tearful.*] That was the start of my undoing. What am I going to do !

Mulligan [*lifting his eyes to the ceiling*]. There's lies ! [*Facing her*] Astounded I was, when without a word of warning, I found you fitting into me lap ! [*Coming closer to her — fervently*] The thruth is, if you want to know, that all the way to here, I was silently praying to a bevy of saints that you'd stay torpid in any and every emergency of look or motion !

Angela. You took care to leave your saints out on the doorstep ; ay, and shut the door in their faces, too. You gave your solemn word, before I'd take one step to this place, that you'd be as harmless as an image in

a looking-glass. I trusted you. I had heard you were
a good boy. I thought you were a gentleman.

Mulligan. What about your uplifting can-can round the
table while I was reading Yeats's poem ?

Angela [*going her own way*]. You made me believe you'd
keep the width of a world between us while we were
together, so's to avoid accidents. You said anyone
who knew you would tell me you had a profound
respect for girls ; that you were slow in love-making.

Mulligan [*with insistence*]. The can-can ; what about the
can-can around the table ?

Angela [*with a great wail in her voice*]. And then you
stunned me with your speed !

Mulligan [*with greater insistence*]. I'm asking you what
about the can-can you danced around the table while
I was thrying to read " I will arise and go now, and
go to Innisfree " ?

Angela [*acting the innocent*]. What can-can ? What are you
talking about ? I don't know what you mean by
can-can.

Mulligan. I mean the dance that uplifted your skirt out
of the way of your movements and juggled a vision
of spiritual desolation into a mirage of palpitating
enjoyments.

Angela [*appealing to the world at large*]. Oh, d'ye hear the
like o' that ! Meanness is most of you to try to put the
cloak of your own dark way round my poor shoulders !
The dance I did could be done by an innocent figure
in a nursery rhyme. You were bent on this awful
mischief from the first. I sensed it when I walked

with you — something evil hovering near. Oh, why didn't I follow me intuition ! [*She begins to be hysterical.*] And I thought you such a nice man ; and now, after fencing me in with shame, you're making out I gave you the stuff to make the fence around me. Oh, the infamy of it ! [*She moves rapidly up and down the room, clasping and unclasping her hands.*] Oh, what shall I do, where shall I go, what shall I say !

Mulligan [*getting very frightened*]. Angela, calm yourself. Speak lower, or you'll wake Miss Mossie, and we'll be ruined. Sit down ; do, please !

Angela [*fluttering about and staggering a little*]. I'm undone, undone completely. I won't be able to look any honest woman in the face ; I won't be able to shake the hand of any honest man I meet ; my future's devastated ! [*She presses a hand to her heart.*] I'm not feeling well ; not at all well ; you'd better get Miss Mossie.

Mulligan [*horrified and very agitated*]. Angela !

Angela [*staggering towards the chair*]. Not well at all. I feel I'm going to faint ! No, no ; yes, yes — I am going to faint !

  [*She sinks down on the chair, stretches out, and closes her eyes.*

Mulligan [*falling on a knee before her — well frightened now*]. Angela, don't ! Angela, dear, wake up ! [*Lifting his eyes to the ceiling.*] Saint Correlliolanus, come on, and deliver us from utther desthruction !

Angela [*plaintively and faintly*]. Wather !

Mulligan [*panic-stricken*]. No, wine ! [*He rises from his knee, pours out a glass of wine, and brings it to her.*] Oh,

Angela, why did you let yourself get into such a state ? Here, take it quietly in sips. [*As she drinks it*] Sip, sip, sip. That should do you good. Hope no one heard you. Miss Mossie sleeps with one ear cocked. [*He strokes her hand.*] You'll soon be all right, and able to slip away in a few minutes.

Angela [*noticing the ring on the hand stroking hers*]. Pretty ring ; garnet set in gold ; precious garnet didn't you say ?

Mulligan [*none too sure of what he should say*]. Yep. Not much value though.

Angela. Why's it on the little finger ?

Mulligan. Knuckle's too big on the right one ; won't go over it.

Angela [*fingering it*]. Let me see it in me hand. [*He hesitates, then takes it off, and gives it to her with reluctance. Putting it on the engagement finger*] Fits me to a nicety. How did you come by it ?

Mulligan. An uncle left it in my care when he went on a job to Hong Kong. He never came back, and as no one asked about it, I made it my own.

Angela. Oh ? Lucky one. [*She looks up into his face, smiling archly, displaying the finger with the ring on it*] Looks like we were an engaged couple, John Jo, dear, wha' ?

Mulligan. An engaged couple ? [*With an uneasy and constrained laugh*] Yis ! Funny thought, that ; quite. Feeling betther ?

Angela. Seem to ; hope it won't come over me again.

Mulligan [*fervently*]. God forbid ! What about taking off our shoes, and making a start ?   [*He takes off his.*]

Angela [*taking off her shoes*]. I suppose we must go sometime.

Mulligan [*trying to speak carelessly*]. Let's have the ring back, dear.

Angela [*as if she'd forgotten it*]. The ring? Oh, yes; I near forgot. [*She fiddles with it ; then suddenly straightens herself to listen.*] Is that the sound of someone at the door below?

Mulligan [*agitated again*]. Oh God, if it's Halibut home from the dance we'll have to wait till he settles down! I wish you'd gone when the going was good!

Angela [*who has taken off her shoes — rising from the chair*]. Come on, we'll chance it!

Mulligan [*pushing her back*]. Chance it! We can't afford to chance it. [*Going over to the door leading to rest of the house*] I'll reconnoitre down, and make sure the way's clear, before we chance it.

    [*He goes out of the room, is absent for a few moments, while Angela swallows another glass of wine ; then he returns hastily, a hand held up warningly for silence.*

Mulligan [*in a frightened whisper*]. Near ran into him on the stairs. Thank God it was so dark. Just had time to turn back. We'll have to wait now till he settles in. [*He listens at the door, shuts it suddenly, and glides over to Angela.*] Quick! He's gone by his own place, and is coming up here! [*He catches her by the arm, hurries her across the room, and shoves her into the bedroom.*] Get in, and keep silent for God's sake!

    [*As he shoves her in, a knock is heard at the sitting-room door. Mulligan shuts the bedroom door, slides over to the chair, sits down, takes the book from the table, and pretends to be reading.*

[*An'other knock is heard at the door, then it opens, and Mr.
Daniel Halibut is seen standing there. He is a man of
twenty-five, a little below medium height, inclining to
be plump. His hair is reddish, and a thick moustache
flowing from his upper lip hides his mouth. Sometimes
his hand tries to brush it aside, but the moment the hand
is removed, it falls back into its old place at once. A
fawn-coloured overcoat covers an informal evening-suit —
dinner-jacket and black tie. A black homburg hat is on
his head. He comes in as one who is full of himself as
if he had done himself well at the dance, and as one who
feels himself a man of the world above the cautious and
timorous Mulligan. His hat and coat are damp.*]

Halibut [*coming into the room*]. Ha, there you are, me son,
rotten night out ; sleet. Coming up, I could have
sworn I seen you coming down the stairs.

Mulligan [*in pretended surprise*]. Me coming down the
stairs ? At this time of the morning ? What would I
be doing on the stairs at this hour ?

Halibut. Well, what are you doing up at this time of
the morning ?

Mulligan. I found it impossible to sleep, so got up to see
if a bit of Yeats's poetry would make me drowsy.

Halibut. Is it Yeats, is it ? God, man, he wouldn't let
you sleep ; drive you nuts ! All people liking Yeats
are all queer. He's all questions. What am I ? Why
am I ? What is it ? How did it come ? Where will
it go ? All bubbles. Stuck up in the top of his ould
tower, he sent the bubbles sailing out through a little
loophole to attract the world outside. And all the
little writers copied them, and blew bubbles of their
own, till you could see them glistening among the

things of the althar, or shining in the hair of the girl
you were courting.

Mulligan [*with an obvious yawn*]. Well, Yeats has made me
sleepy, anyway. [*He flings the book on the table, and goes
to get out of the chair.*] I'll be off to bed again.

Halibut [*shoving him back into the chair*]. Wait till I tell
you. You should ha' been at the dance. There never
was a grander occasion ; divel a grander ever ! The
place was fair gushing with girls. And only a few
who'd make you shut your eyes if they were sitting
on your knee. A hilariously hopeful whirlwind of
skirt and petticoat, John Jo, when a waltz was on !

Mulligan [*getting up and edging Halibut towards the sitting-
room door*]. Go to bed, now, like a good fellow. I'm
tired. We'll talk about it tomorrow. Goodnight.

Halibut [*edging Mulligan back towards the fireplace*]. Wait till
I tell you. You are a boyo. You'd never guess who
was there ? Your old flame of a week — Jessie ! She
told me things ! When will you wake up ? When
he asked me out for the first time, says she, I expected
a hilarious night at a dance or a music-hall, says she ;
I near fainted, says she, when, instead, he asked me
to go with him to Benediction ! Mulligan's manage-
ment of maidens ! Oh, John Jo, when will you wake
up ?

Mulligan [*annoyed, pushing Halibut towards the door*]. If I
elect to keep from danger, that's my affair. Looka,
Dan, I've got to get up early to go to Mass on my way
to the office, so be a good fellow, and go. I'm not
concerned with girls.

Halibut. Betther if you were. [*He pushes Mulligan back*

toward the fireplace again.] You'd sleep betther at night for one thing. [*He puts an arm around Mulligan, and forces him into being a partner.*] Roamin' in th' gloamin', eh? Oh, boy! [*Lilting*] With a lassie by yeer side. Oh, it's lovely to go roamin' in th' gloamin'!

Mulligan [*angrily — struggling from Halibut's hold, and rather roughly forcing him to the door*]. Aw, lay off it, damn it, Dan! I'm in no mood for a Highland fling! Please go to your own room, and leave me in peace — I'm done in! [*He shoves him out and closes the sitting-room door.*

Halibut [*as he's being shoved out*]. All right, if that's the way you feel. It'd be a good thing to put your hand on a girl's knee, and chance it.
[*Mulligan listens at the door for a few moments. Then he gets down on his knees, and puts an ear to the floor. He rises, goes to the bedroom door, opens it, and calls Angela out.*

Mulligan. Now, Angela; now's our time. No delay, please.

Angela [*going behind the curtains on the windows*]. What kind of a night or morning is it? [*From behind the curtains*] Christ! It's snowing or something! [*She comes from behind them, goes to the door, and takes one of Mulligan's coats hanging there.*] I must have a coat.

[*Angela puts the coat on.*

Mulligan [*in a faint protest*]. Eh, Angela, that's me best one.

Angela [*taking an umbrella from the stand*]. And an umbrella, too.

Mulligan. That's me best umbrella.

Angela. Never mind, dear. I'll let you have it back when you hand me into the taxi on the all-night rank. Let's hurry now, boy. [*Mulligan opens the door cautiously, listens a moment ; takes a torch from a pocket, and shines it forth, then leads the way from the room, shutting the door gently behind him. Both of them are in their stockinged feet. After a few moments have passed, the door suddenly flies open, and Angela hurries in, followed by Mulligan wearing a look of agony on his face. They carry their shoes under their arms. As she comes in*] You louser, you'd have let me go off without it ! Didn't care a damn once you were rid of me. And all I have for another fortnight is in that handbag !

Mulligan [*appealingly*]. Speak lower, Angela, or you'll have the Mossie one down on top of us ! I just can't remember you having a handbag when you first came in.

Angela [*angrily*]. You can't remember ! Well, I had one, and a good one, too, and I've got to get it — see ! D'ye mean to hint I'm making it up ?

Mulligan [*in agony*]. No, no ; but for God's sake, speak easy ; please, Angela !

Angela [*leaving her shoes down, and pulling the cushions off the settee and throwing them on the floor*]. Well, then, find it for me. Mind you, had I been down the street when I missed it, I'd have banged the door down to get in to get it !

Mulligan [*leaving his shoes down, and pulling the table about, pulling the chairs from the wall, and pulling the umbrella-stand away, to look behind them*]. This is terrible ! I'll be ruined if I'm discovered. What colour was it ?

Where had you it last ?   Where d'ye think you could have put it ?

Angela. I don't know, fool.   It was a dark-green one I bought last week, and gave five pounds for.   I got confused and forgot about everything when you started to pull me on to your knee.

Mulligan. But we can't stay to look for it.   Miss Mossie'll soon be going about with her candle in her hand.

Angela. I'm not going without it !   I think I remember you snatching it outa me hand when you started to pull me on to your lap.

Mulligan. Oh, give over about me pulling you on to me lap, and give us a hand to look for it !   [*He runs into the bedroom, and starts to search there, flinging the bedclothes about.   In bedroom*] I can't see it anywhere here, so I can't.

Angela [*tearfully*]. And I was to come here only for a quiet glass of wine and a biscuit.   That's what you said, and kept repeating ;   and I believed you, oh, I believed you !

Mulligan [*coming out of bedroom*]. No sign of it there.

Angela [*marching up and down the room, clasping and unclasping her hands*]. Oh, isn't this a nice end to a quiet glass of wine and a biscuit !

Mulligan. Get a hold of yourself.   What sort was it ?

Angela. A pure morocco leather one, dark green, with initials on it filigreed in mother o' pearl.

Mulligan [*impatiently*]. Yis, yis ;   [*anxiously*] but how much was in it altogether ?

Angela. Fifteen pounds odd.

Mulligan [*aghast*]. Good Lord !

Angela. And the lipstick you couldn't find musta been in it too ; silver-cased and all ; and a lovely bracelet watch waiting to be mended. Oh, what will I do ! Oh; yes, and a silver brooch I wanted to get a pin for. What will I do, what will I do ?

Mulligan. You slip off, and when I come back, I'll search high and low for it.

Angela [*with rising nervous tension*]. And how am I to fare till you find it ? You wouldn't turn a hair if I was willing to go in my shift ! John Jo Mulligan, you're a dasthard ! It would be the price of you to let Miss Mossie and the whole house know the sort you are !

Mulligan. For God's sake, Angela ! What d'ye want me to do ; only tell me what you want me to do ?

Angela [*moving about distracted*]. And to think I thought I was safe with you ! [*Her glance falls on the cupboard, and she makes a bee-line for it.*] Could it have got in here ?

Mulligan [*hastily*]. No, no ; it couldn't have got in there.

Angela [*drawing out a leather wallet*]. What's this ?

Mulligan [*going over to take wallet from her*]. Nothing there but a few private letters, and a lot of bills.

[*But before he can reach her to get it away, she has whisked a bundle of notes from it.*

Angela [*giggling — a little hysterical*]. John Jo's hidden treasure. [*She counts them rapidly.*] Eighteen pounds ten. All fresh ones too. Nice to handle.

Mulligan. They're not mine. I'm minding them for a friend. You can put them back.

Angela [*mockingly*]. At once, dear. I'll mind them for you, dear. [*She takes a cheque-book out of the wallet.*] A cheque-book, too. [*As he comes closer*] Keep your distance, keep your distance, or I'll claw the gob off you !

Mulligan. I was only going to give you a few of them to tide you over, dear.

Angela [*fiercely*]. You were? How sweet of you ! I'll have them all, you primly-born yahoo. And more. [*She raises her voice*] And more !

Mulligan [*whisperingly*]. All right, all right, only keep calm ; keep quiet.

Angela [*indicating the cheque-book*]. Make me out a cheque for five pounds like a decent, honest man.

Mulligan [*taking a fountain pen from his pocket, and settling down to write*]. All right ; anything to pacify you.

Angela [*patronisingly patting his head*]. You're not the worst, John Jo. You're really a pleasant chap when you get going. Make a cheque out for ten, darling, to compensate for the goods in the handbag. Ten, dear ; that's all now. Well, we've had a right good time together. Pity I can't stay longer. See you again soon, when you're feeling frisky, eh? Naughty boy ! [*She has taken the cheque from the dazed Mulligan, put it in his wallet, and now straightens herself to go, taking her shoes off the floor, and putting them under an arm. At the door*] I know my way down, so don't you stir. I'll steal away like a maid of Araby. I'll be seeing you. Be good.
[*Dazed and stunned, Mulligan sits still for a few seconds ; then he gets up from the chair to look around him.*

Mulligan [*rising from the chair*]. Fully-fledged for hell, that one, and you never noticed it ! Oh, John Jo, John Jo !

[*He suddenly stiffens.*]   She had no handbag !   She never had a handbag !   Oh, Christ, she's codded me !   [*He looks in the cupboard, then looks over the table.*]   She's taken away me wallet, too !   Me umbrella !

[*He runs out of the room to follow her, so agitated that he leaves door wide open behind him.   There are a few moments of silence ;   then Miss Mossie appears at the open door with a lighted candle in a candlestick in her hand.   She is a short, stout woman of thirty-five or so. She is dressed in a brown skirt reaching to her ankles, and we get a glimpse of black stockings sinking into a pair of stout black shoes.   Her dark hair is gathered into a knob, and made to lie quiet on the nape of her neck.   She wears a yellow jumper, and a brown Jaeger topcoat is flung over her shoulders.   She wears spectacles. She looks into the room for a moment, a look of perplexed anxiety on her face, then turns aside to call to Halibut.*]

Miss Mossie. Mr. Halibut, Mr. Halibut, come up, come up quick !   [*Halibut appears at the door.   He is now wearing a pair of blue pyjamas, covered by a dressing-gown of dark red, and his bare feet are slippered.*]   Oh, Mr. Halibut, what can the matter be ?   Oh, dear, what can the matter be ?

Halibut [*agog with excitement*]. What's up, Miss Mossie ?

Miss Mossie [*coming into the sitting-room, followed by Halibut*]. Looka the state of the room ;   and Mr. Mulligan's just run out into the street in his stockinged feet !

Halibut [*astonished*]. No ?   How d'ye know he went out into the street ?

Miss Mossie. I seen him go.   I heard something stirring when I was putting on me jumper, so I looked out,

and there was Mr. Mulligan scuttling down the stairs.
Walking in his sleep, he musta been. He had an air
on him as if he was enraptured within himself ; a
look as if he was measuring life and death together to
see which was tallest.

Halibut. Is that right ? Coming back from the dance, I
thought I saw him on the stairs, too, but when I
came up, he was sitting reading Yeats's poems. Said
he couldn't sleep. I warned him against the poems.

Miss Mossie [*coming over to the bedroom door, and opening it*].
Oh, looka the state of this room, too ! Everything
flung about.

Halibut [*awed*]. Looks like he had a wild fit, or something !

Miss Mossie. Something terrific ! This isn't just disarray,
Mr. Halibut — it's an upheaval ! You don't think it
could be that something suddenly went wrong in him ?

Halibut [*startled by a thought*]. Wrong in him, Miss
Mossie ? What could go wrong in him ?

Miss Mossie. A quietly-disposed man like Mr. Mulligan
doesn't do this [*indicating disorder of rooms*] without
something whizzing within him.

Halibut [*frightened*]. You mean in his mind ?

Miss Mossie [*firmly*]. We must act. We can't let him
roam the streets or do any harm here. I'll phone the
police and a doctor, and I'll slip out for the constable
that usually stands at the street corner. [*They move to
the sitting-room door.*] I'll go now. You stay on the
lobby here in the dark, and watch over him if he
comes back.

Halibut [*dubiously*]. I'm not a strong man, Miss Mossie.

Miss Mossie. After all, Mr. Halibut, we don't want to be murdhered in our beds.

Halibut [*crossing himself*]. God forbid, Miss Mossie !

Miss Mossie. And the odd thing is, he'd be doing it with the best intentions. If he comes back, he may still be asleep, so don't shout at him and wake him too suddenly. Just humour him, unless he gets violent.

Halibut [*picturing in his mind all that might happen*]. Ay, violent — that's the danger !

Miss Mossie. Then you'll just have to close with him, and hold him till the constable comes.

Halibut [*panic-stricken*]. Close with him ? Hold him till the constable comes ? But, woman alive, I'm not gifted that way !

Miss Mossie. You'll do your best, I know ; if he overcomes you, it won't be your fault.

Halibut. Don't you think it would be only prudent to have a poker handy ?

Miss Mossie. Too violent-looking. [*Indicating a corner of the lobby*] There's the bit of curtain-pole I use to push the window up — you can keep that handy ; but don't let him guess why you have it. [*She takes the key from the inside and puts it in the keyhole on the outside of the door.*] There now, if the worst comes, you can fly out and lock him safely within the room.

Halibut. It sounds easy, but it's really a desperate situation.

Miss Mossie. Don't let him see you're frightened. Keep him under command. That's what me sisther did with me when I used to walk in my sleep a few years ago.

Halibut [*stricken with confused anxiety*]. What, you used to sleep-walk, too?

Miss Mossie. That's why I dhread the habit coming back to me, for then you never know whether you're always asleep and never awake, or always awake and never asleep. I'll be off now. You'll be quite safe if you only keep your wits about you.

[*She goes off with her candle, leaving a world of darkness to poor Halibut. There is a silence for a few moments, then the watcher in the darkness, and any who are listening, hear a patter of feet on stairs outside, and the voice of Mulligan calling out loudly the name of Miss Mossie several times. Then a great bang of a closing door; dead silence for a moment, till Mulligan is heard calling again.*

Mulligan [*outside*]. Dan, Dan, are you awake? Dan Halibut, are you awake, man? [*Mulligan appears on the lobby just outside the sitting-room door. He is talking to himself, a haggard, lost, and anxious look on his face, and he is a little out of breath. His coat and hat are damped by the falling sleet outside; his feet wet. He pauses on the lobby, and waves his electric torch about till its beam falls on the silent and semi-crouching Halibut.*] Oh, it's here you are? Thought you were in bed fast asleep. Called you, but got no answer. What a nig't! Twenty-eight pounds ten gone with the wind! [*He lifts a cushion from the floor to look under it.*] It's not there! [*He flings it viciously away. To Halibut*] What has you here in the dark and the cold?

Halibut. Just shutting the window to keep it from rattling.

Mulligan [*going into the sitting-room*]. We must do something. Miss Mossie's gone rushing hatless out into the darkness and the sleet. Hatless, mind you ! Looked as if she was sleep-walking again. A one-time habit of hers, did you know ? You'll have to go after her.

Halibut [*coming a little way into the room, but staying close to the door, holding the sprig of curtain-pole behind his back*]. I know, I know ; but what were you doing out in the sleet and the darkness *yourself* ? And in your stockinged feet, too, look at them !

Mulligan. Me ? Couldn't sleep ; felt stifled ; went out for some fresh air. Didn't think of shoes. Something whizzing in me mind. [*A little impatiently*] But you dress and go after Mossie. See what's wrong with her. Several times, before you came, she came into my room, fast asleep, at dead of the night, with a loving look on her face. We can't afford to let ourselves be murdhered in our sleep, Dan. [*He flops into chair.*] Saint Fairdooshius, succour me this night.

Halibut [*bewildered with anxiety, eyes lifted to ceiling in a low appeal*]. Oh, sweet Saint Slumbersnorius, come to me help now ! [*To Mulligan*] All right ; yes. I'll settle you in first. You go to bed, John Jo, quiet. Go to bed, go to bed, and go asleep, and go asleep !

Mulligan [*looking at Halibut curiously — a little impatiently*]. I've told you I can't sleep. Twenty-eight pounds ten, and my fine leather wallet gone forever !

Halibut [*in a commandingly sing-song way*]. Never mind. Put them out of your thoughts, and go to bed, go to bed, and go to sleep, and go to sleep — I command !

Mulligan [*half rising from his chair so that Halibut backs*

towards the door — staring at Halibut in wonderment].
What's wrong with you, Halibut ? [*He sinks back into
the chair again, and Halibut returns into the room.*]   Me
best coat and best umbrella, too !   Gone.

   [*His glance happens to fall on his hand, and he springs out
    of the chair with a jump, sending Halibut backing swiftly
    from the room again.*

Mulligan. Me ring !   I never got it back !

Halibut [*straying cautiously back into the room again*]. Money,
best coat, best umbrella, wallet, and ring !   When did
you lose all these things, man ?

Mulligan. A minute or so ago ; no, no, an hour ago ; two
hours ago ; more. [*He leans his arms dejectedly on the
table, and buries his head on them.*]   I di'n't lost them, Dan ;
I gave them away, flung them all away !

Halibut. In an excess of charity of having too many
possessions, or what ?   You know, I've warned you,
John Jo ; often warned you.

Mulligan [*raising his head from his arms — resentfully and
suspiciously*]. Warned me ?   How warned me ?

Halibut. I warned you that running out to devotions
morning and night, and too much valuable time spent
on your knees, would upset you one day or another.
And, now, you'll have to admit that these things
couldn't have happened to you if you had had a girl
with you tonight.

Mulligan [*with a wail of resentment*]. Oooh !   Don't be a
blasted fool ! [*He notices that Halibut has something behind
his back.*]   What's that you have behind you ?

Halibut [*trying to be carelessly funny*]. Me tail.   Didn't you know ? I'm a wild animal. [*He wags the piece of curtain-pole.*] Now, the wild animal says you're to go to bed, go to bed, and go to sleep, and go to sleep. Obey the wild animal at once !

Mulligan [*slowly rising from the chair, staring anxiously and suspiciously at Halibut*]. What's amiss with you, Halibut? Are you sleep-walking, too ? Leave down that curtain-pole. Don't be acting the goat, man. [*Coaxingly — as Halibut brings the piece of curtain-pole to his front*] Go on, Dan, oul' son, leave the thing down !

Halibut. As soon as you're safely settled in bed, John Jo. Then I'll pop out after Mossie. To bed ; to bed ; and go to sleep, go to sleep — I command !

Mulligan [*fear having come on him — suddenly seizes the wine-bottle by the neck, and holds it as a club, running to window, swinging back the curtains, and trying to open it*]. God Almighty, I'm alone with a lunatic ! [*Shouting — as he tries to open the window*] Help !

Halibut. I'll not let you destroy yourself — come away from that window, or I'll flatten you !

Mulligan [*wheeling round, still holding bottle by the neck to use it as a club, and facing towards Halibut*]. Looka, Halibut, leave that club down. [*Coaxingly*] Now, be sensible, Dan, like a good chap, and drop that club.

Halibut. Drop that bottle first, I say ; drop that bottle first !

Mulligan. Drop that club, I tell you. [*Fiercely*] Drop that club !

Halibut [*dancing up and down — panic-stricken*]. Put that bottle down !   Put it down, and go to bed, I tell you !

Mulligan [*dodging about*]. Drop that club at once, Halibut !

Halibut. Put that bottle down immediately !

Mulligan. I command you !

Halibut. I command you !
[*They have been dodging about without coming near to each other ;   Halibut swinging the piece of curtain-pole to and fro in front of him for protection.   In one of the blind swings, the pole slips from his hand, and sails out through the window, causing a great sound of falling glass.   They both stare at the window — dumbfounded for a few moments.*

Mulligan [*exultingly*]. Aha, I've got you now !
[*But Halibut has fled from the room, banged the door after him, and locked it from the outside.   Mulligan hurries to the door and presses his back to it.   Then Miss Mossie's voice is heard outside.*

Miss Mossie [*outside*]. Oh, what's happened ?   I feared it would end in violence !   Mr. Halibut, Mr. Halibut, are you much hurted ?

Mulligan [*shouting through the door to Miss Mossie*]. Miss Mossie ;   here, Miss Mossie !

Miss Mossie [*from outside*]. Oh, Mr. Mulligan, what have you done to poor, innocent Mr. Halibut ?   We've found him lying in a dead faint out here on the lobby.

Mulligan [*indignantly — shouting outwards*]. Poor, innocent Mr. Halibut !   What has he not tried to do to me !

He rushed in here, lunacy looking out of his eyes, and tried to shatther me with a club, with a club ; tried to murdher me ! Now he's locked me in.

Miss Mossie [soothingly]. Now isn't that a shame ! What a naughty man he is ! Never mind now. You go to your chair and sit down by the fire, and I'll get the key to open your door. Everything will be all right, Mr. Mulligan.

Mulligan [indignantly]. Everything isn't all right now ! I'll live no longer in the same house with Halibut !

Miss Mossie [coaxingly]. Do go and sit down by the fire, Mr. Mulligan, there's a dear. I'll bring you a hot drink, and we'll talk about things ; do, now, like a good man. [*Mulligan goes to the fireplace, and sits down in the armchair. He lights a cigarette and puffs it indignantly. After a few moments, the door opens, and Miss Mossie lets into the room a big, topcoated and helmeted policeman, the doctor with his case, wearing an anxious look on his face, and a nurse, enveloped with a dark-blue cloak on the left side of which is a white circle surrounding a large red cross. She carries the usual nursing-suitcase in her hand. Miss Mossie is in the midst of them, and Halibut, in the rear, with a ghastly pale face, rises on his tiptoes to gaze over their shoulders. All but Halibut form a semicircle round Mulligan's back, who puffs away, unconscious of the entrance of the crowd. Bending sidewise from behind the policeman to speak to the sitting Mulligan*] Now, Mr. Mulligan, we'll see what all this little disturbance was about, and what was the cause of it, and then we'll be all — er — O.K., eh ? And I've brought in a few kind friends to help me.

Mulligan [rising from his chair in blank surprise, and almost echoing Miss Mossie]. A few friends to help you ? [*He turns around to face Miss Mossie, but is confronted by the big, helmeted policeman, the doctor, and the nurse. He slides back into the chair almost in a dead faint. Falling back into the chair*] Good God !

CURTAIN

I DON'T CARE WHAT BECOMES OF ME

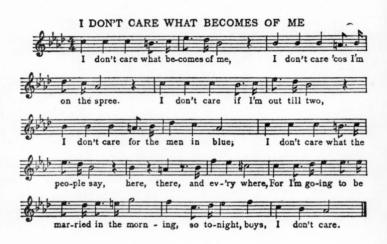

I don't care what be-comes of me, I don't care 'cos I'm on the spree. I don't care if I'm out till two, I don't care for the men in blue; I don't care what the peo-ple say, here, there, and ev-'ry where, For I'm go-ing to be mar-ried in the morn - ing, so to-night, boys, I don't care.

ROAMIN' IN THE GLOAMIN'

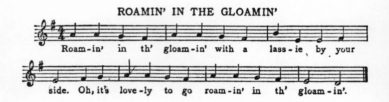

Roam-in' in th' gloam-in' with a lass-ie by your side. Oh, it's love-ly to go roam-in' in th' gloam-in'.

TIME TO GO

A Morality Comedy in One Act

CHARACTERS IN THE PLAY

MICHAEL FLAGONSON, *proprietor of a tavern*
BULL FARRELL, *proprietor of a general stores*
MRS. FLAGONSON, *Flagonson's wife*
BARNEY O'HAY, *farmer owner of five acres*
COUSINS, *farmer owner of twenty acres*
CONROY, *farmer owner of a hundred and fifty acres*
SERGEANT KILLDOOEY, *of the Civic Guards*
1ST CIVIC GUARD
2ND CIVIC GUARD
WIDDA MACHREE, *who has asked too much for a cow*
KELLY FROM THE ISLE OF MANANAUN, *who has given too little for it*
A YOUNG MAN
A YOUNG WOMAN

SCENE

Outside of Flagonson's Tavern and Bull Farrell's General Stores on the edge of an Irish country town, a day or so after a fair.

TIME.—The present.

The scene is the butt-end of an Irish town, small and untidy. To the left, part of Flagonson's Tavern façade can be seen. There are the door and a window to the right of it ; the roof is of slate, and a smoke-grimed chimney is sending out a little trickle of smoke. Over the doorway is a notice declaring that BEER AND SPIRITS FOR ALL can be had there ; between the window and the door is a larger notice holding the printed announcement on it of LUNCHES, DINNERS, AND TEAS — AD LIB ; the Latin phrase done out in larger letters. The front wall is brickwork half-way up, the rest is covered with a patchy rough-cast. A little way from the door are a rough wooden bench and a few kitchen chairs ; and a few tankards stand on the table.

Opposite to the Tavern stands the General Stores of Mr. Bull Farrell, jutting out far enough to show the wide doorway, a window, and part of the front wall. Along the wall is a board having on it the words BULL FARRELL. GENERAL STORES. FROM A NEEDLE TO AN ANCHOR. Arranged along the wall, leaning against it, are a new hoe, a dung-fork, a spade ; in front of them a new wheelbarrow, a dust-bin, a large box, and an eight-stone sack of phosphate. On the slated roof is a smoke-begrimed chimney from which ascends a little trickle of smoke.

Beyond these two establishments is a road going across, and smaller ways lead past in front of the Tavern and the General Stores. In the background is a scrubby field with a vista of a few cottages, thatched, in the distance. On the edge of the field, close to the edge of the road, are the remains of two trees, one near the Tavern and the other near the General Stores. Their branches are withered, and they look as if they had been blasted by lightning. A string of various-coloured bunting, triangular

*in shape, connects Tavern and Stores, and a tiny string of the
same bunting hangs over the Tavern door and over the door of
the General Stores. Each has a small Papal flag, perpendicular
stripes of white and yellow, stuck out from the upper part of the
windows.*

*Over all is a lovely magenta-coloured sky, fleeced here and
there by clouds, rosily-silver wherever the sun touches them.*

*Flagonson is standing by the edge of the table, his arse leaning
against it. He is a man of fifty-five, big-headed, and strongly
built. His hair, once a brilliant red, is now badly chaffed with
grey. Although his belly is beginning to advance too far into
the world, he is a well-formed, upstanding man. He is
mechanically wiping a tankard with a cloth.*

*Bull Farrell, owner of the General Stores, is very different
from Michael Flagonson. He is a wisp of a man, looking as
if a shove would send him with speed flying out of the world.
Although but forty years of age, he is quite bald, but his upper
lip clings on to a thick, dark, truculent moustache. He is
dressed in tweeds, and has a high, stiff, white collar round his
neck, encircled with a black tie. A dark-blue apron protects
his trousers from dust damage. Flagonson too wears a collar,
not quite so high as that worn by Farrell ; a low-necked dark
waistcoat, with white front, and a black bow nestling under the
stuck-out wings of the collar. His apron is a white one. Bull
Farrell is standing in his doorway looking towards Flagonson.*

Flagonson [*with a glance at the decorations*]. How lonesome
  an' woebegone the decorations look now the crowd's
  gone.

Bull [*glancing at them, too*]. Ay, with the coloured booths,
  the shoutin' of buyin' and sellin', the swearin' an'
  fightin' gone with th' crowd too, it's a bit lonely like.
  [*He glances at the decorations again.*] I dunno why you put
  them up. Waste of time ; waste of money.

Flagonson [*indicating those over Bull's door*]. You've a token hangin' there yourself.

Bull. Me great-grandfather bought them for some meetin' in honour of Dan O'Connell. They cost me nothin'.

Flagonson. An' what about the Papal flag?

Bull [*gloatingly*]. I nailed that off a kid bangin' the window with it to th' point of breakin'; and when I threatened the police on him, he was damned glad to get away without it.

Flagonson. The polis is the only ones to put th' fear o' God in them.

Bull. Only for them, they wouldn't leave a thing standin' in th' town. Durin' th' Fair, they had me plagued. I daren't ha' left a thing standin' outside; or it would have been gone while I was winkin'.

Flagonson. Well, it's all cold an' calm now, anyhow. Nothin' left of all the burly business but big farmer Conroy an' little farmer Cousins still arguin'. Cousins wants to sell an' Conroy says he wants to buy, though, afther twelve hours of talkin', they're no nearer to an agreement yet.

Bull [*coming from the door, and leaning towards Flagonson — confidentially*]. Conroy sees somethin' in them cattle, though no-one else can. Conroy's a cute one. He says he wants only to do a good turn to poor Cousins. [*He throws back his head, and gives a loud guffaw.*] Conroy doin' a good turn! He's takin' a helluva time to do it. Slow, but sure!

Flagonson. I dunno. Maybe he has a soft spot in him somewhere.

Bull [*with surprised indignation*]. Soft spot? Why, man alive, Conroy ud take the gold from a holy saint's halo an' shove it in th' bank !

Flagonson [*after a pause*]. I wondher what happened to that fine-lookin' woman in th' black dhress and the bright blue cloak thryin' to sell her cow to th' upstandin' chap in the saffron kilt an' th' gay, green shawl ?

Bull. She sold it all right to him, Barney O'Hay was tellin' me ; an' then she went east an' he went west, leadin' th' cow home.

Flagonson. It wasn't what you'd call a bulky Fair. I've seen betther, an' I've seen worse.

Bull. So've I ; but you musta made a bundle, seein' the house was packed all th' day an' half-way into th' night.

Flagonson [*a little sharply, touched with envy*]. An' isn't the sufferin' road out there worn away with the constant caravan of donkey-cars, pony-cars, an' motor-cars, loaded to th' brims, carryin' off stuff from your stores, so that you musta been ladlin' money into your positive possessions !

Bull [*placatingly*]. Don't grudge me mine, Mick, an' I won't grudge you yours.

Flagonson [*cheerily*]. God forbid I did, Bull, for it wouldn't be a Christian thing to do. Though me own takin's timidly topped last year's, I'd say I never seen a quieter Fair : all noise, a noise of bargainin', with a little laughter an' gaiety lost in th' commotion.

Bull. An' why was that ? Because the young are goin' who aren't already gone. Because there's ne'er a one, lad or lass, in th' disthrict between seventeen an' thirty. An' why are they gone ?

Flagonson. To bwetther themselves, God help them ! Even me own Judy an' Jack, up in Dublin, want me to settle them in London, where there's a bwetther openin', they say, God help them. Ay, an openin' into th' world that shuts them out from God !

Bull [*contemptuously*]. Ay, so our clergy say. [*He throws back his head, and laughs contemptuously.*] Th' clergy ! Ireland's a bird sanctuary for them. Priest-puffin island !

Flagonson [*with some remonstrance in his voice*]. Now, Bull, now, Bull, dhraw it mild about th' clergy ; not but I'd agree that it's hard to have an aysey mind with th' clergy pullin' out of us from all quarthers.

Bull. An' why th' hell haven't you got the spunk to fight some of their pirate pinchin' ? What with their blue sisthers of th' poor, the white nuns of th' needy, th' brown sisthers of our crippled companions, we're rooked in th' mornin's, an' rooked at night, if our doors aren't bolted !

Flagonson [*loosing his thoughts*]. With church collectors runnin' along every road an' passable path, an' hoppin' over every stile, pattherin' at your doors like hailstones in a storm ! With their " Th' collector from Bona Mors, Mr. Farrell " ; " th' collector, Mr. Farrell, for th' new presbytery be the new church " ; " Mr. Farrell, th' collector for the Foreign Missions " ; till a body's lightened of a lot he had to put away for a rainy day !

Bull [*remonstratively indignant*]. Then why don't you fight it, man ? [*He goes forward, and assumes a semi-fighting pose.*] Why don't you sthruggle against it, man? What ails you that you won't stand firm?

Flagonson [half hesitatingly]. I will, I will, Bull ; you'll see.

Bull [scornfully]. You will, you will ; I'll see, I'll see ! When will I see ? You've been sayin' that for years ! Abnegate, I say, then, if you're a man, man.

Flagonson [trying to be positive]. I will ; I must. This pinchin' be th' priests of th' little we have is gettin' unconthrollable !

Bull. Isn't that what I'm afther tellin' you ! Priest-puffin island. An' it's not a shillin' they want, or even half-a-crown ; oh, no ; th' mineemus now asked from a poor thrader is a pound, if you please. And if a pound's given, they'll say with a blisterin' glance, " If you're only givin' a pound, Mr. Farrell, you might as well make it one pound one ". Am I to be the one lone figure left standin', like a pillar without any support, to fight against this convulsion of givin' against our will ? Is there ne'er a man but meself left in th' land ? Are we to become only a scared an' scatthered crowd ? Are you goin' to do anything, or are you not ?

Flagonson [with heated resolution]. I am ! [*He bangs a tankard on the table.*] I will, I will ; I must !

Bull [with scornful impatience]. You must, you will ! There's no surety in your tankard-dhrummin'. [*Savagely*] But will you, man ; will you, will you ?
  [*Two cyclists, a Young Man and a Young Woman, have come in from around the Tavern, pushing their bicycles along the road. He is simply dressed in tweeds and wears a tweed cap ; his trouser-ends are thrust into his socks.*

She wears a dark jersey and green slacks. When they speak, they do so quickly, as if in a somewhat excited hurry. To Bull :

Young Man [*in quick excitement*]. How far from here, sir, is the remains of the Abbey of Ballyrellig ?

Bull. Th' oul' graveyard with th' ruins in it is it you mean ?

Young Man. It must be : th' one with the chapel of Saint Kurrakawn in it.

Young Woman [*rapidly*]. A lovely crypt with groined arches, supported by lovely semi-columns, decorated with lovely foliage an' faces.

Bull. D'ye tell me that, now ? Well, if what it is is what yous want, it's more'n fifteen miles farther on. But th' whole thing's lost, man, in thickets, brambles, an' briars.

Young Man [*still speaking quickly*]. There's still a pathway to it, I'm told.

Bull. D'ye tell me that, now ?

Young Woman. We simply must see it before we go away. It's just a dhream !

Bull. D'ye tell me that, now ?

Young Man [*to Young Woman*]. We'll want a meal first, dear. [*To Flagonson*] Can we have a fairly substantial one, sir ?

Flagonson [*with quiet assurance*]. Indeed, yous can ; anything in reason ; we're here to enthertain.

[*He indicates the notice on the wall.*

[*The Young Man and Young Woman wheel their bicycles towards the General Stores, and leave them leaning against the back wall.*

Young Man [*glancing inquiringly at the Young Woman*]. A nice chop would make a good start ?

Flagonson. A right royal start, if the chops were to be had, sir.

Young Woman [*after a pause — to the Young Man*]. A few nice, lean rashers, Ned, would do just as well.

Flagonson. Ay, miss, an' fat ones, either, if there was any to be had. You don't expect us to kill a pig to provide yous with rashers, do yous ?

Young Man [*annoyed and disappointed*]. Well, what have you, then ?

Flagonson. What about a boiled egg, a powerful cup o' tay, an' as much bread as you like to get down yous ?

Young Woman [*with a glance at the Young Man*]. That'll have to do, Ned.

Flagonson [*indicating the Tavern door*]. In with yous, then, an' th' lady inside'll give yous all yous can conveniently want. [*The Young Man and Young Woman go rather slowly into the Tavern. To Bull*] Shockin' th' way the young demand things nowadays !

Bull. Their effervesacatin' spirits nowadays is incontrollable !

[*Widda Machree appears around the back of the General Stores, walking along the road. She is a young woman of thirty. Her face is pale, well chiselled, and pure-looking. She wears a coloured scarf over her head,*

*peasant-wise, so that the round of her face only is seen.
A bright blue cloak draped from her shoulders half covers
a black skirt and blouse. She wears black stockings and
shoes. She is straightly built and slim, and has a
semi-plaintive air, though this is occasionally changed into
a humorous, half-cynical manner. She looks about her
for a moment, and then speaks to the two men.*

Widda Machree [plaintively]. I'm Widda Machree : me
sweetheart died the day we were to wed, an' neighbours
gave me the name I go by now. I'm in great throuble,
gentlemen. I can't stay aysey by the big turf fire an'
th' hearth swept clean. I have to thravel now along
th' big bog road, because of a sin, gentlemen ; an
ugly, mortal sin, an' a mean one, too. Ochone, oh,
ochone !

Flagonson. A bad burden to have on a conscience, ma'am.

Widda Machree. Ay ; I'm but a wandherin' cloud o'
conscience. There's ne'er a green glen left in Erin
for me now. Never on Lady Day agin will I wear me
dhress of speckled velvet, or sew the silver buckles on
me shining shoon. O ochone, ochone !

Bull. No good'll come be dwellin' on it, ma'am.

Flagonson. You're th' lady was bargainin' with th' kilted
gentleman over th' sale of your cow, aren't you ?

Widda Machree. That thransaction was me undoin',
gentlemen. I thought I could rise above th' temptation, but I sank below it. I'll sit down a second.
[*She sits down on the bench.*] I'm tired searchin' for th'
kilted gentleman. If he happens to pass by here, hold
him till I call again. Kelly's th' name. [*She gets up
and swings round on her toes in a kind of dance, chanting :*]

Has anybody here seen Kelly ?
K ee double ell y ;
Has anybody here seen Kelly,
Kelly from the Isle of Man-an-aun !

I must settle accounts with him. Oh, ochone, I did
a mean sin as well as a mortal one.

Bull. You looked sensible enough when I seen you
bargainin' away with th' kilted man, opposite Trinity
Church.

Widda Machree. At Trinity Church I met me doom,
gentlemen. Givin' so much of me peace of mind to
gain so little. Oh, miserere mei ! I'll never go near
th' church again till th' wrong's righted an' me soul
feels free. But who am I tellin' ? Sure you two musta
often felt th' same way yourselves, for yous musta shot
a gay lot o' rogueries into th' world in your time.

[*The quiet, matter-of-fact way that the last remark is
made seems to stun the two men for a few moments, and
they stand, silent, staring at her.*

Bull [*after a rather long pause*]. I can tell you, ma'am, that
the last remark you made is an entirely disilushunnary
designation ! There's ne'er a wisp of dishonesty to be
found in either of our two firms !

Widda Machree. Don't crown your rogueries with a lie
on top of them, good man. Didn't every soul I met
comin' along here tell me yous were th' two most
meritorious rogues in th' disthrict, an' that Canon
Bullero commends all yous do because of the whack
he gets out of it ?

Flagonson [*indignantly*]. Looka here, ma'am, I'm not
anxious to have mortal sins any way adjacent to me

respectable house ; an' th' bench you're occupyin' is meant for customers only.

Widda Machree. Your hint is tellin' me it's time to go, sir.

Bull [*coming nearer, and bending towards her till his face is close to hers — fiercely*]. An' with me fond farewell, let you tell all you meet that Bull Farrell hides no roguery undher the registered comfort of any priest's connivance, havin' refused to sanction th' givin' of ad libeetitum donations for th' period of sinny quaw non !
  [*Widda Machree rises from her seat, bows to the two men, and walks with slow dignity to the road. As she reaches it, the Young Man and the Young Woman come hurrying from the Tavern, both, evidently, in a deep state of indignation. They make for where their bicycles are. Mrs. Flagonson comes to the door to watch their departure. She is thirty-five, and not at all bad-looking. She is dressed neatly in a brown skirt and black bodice. A coloured cotton apron protects the skirt and the breast of the bodice.*

Young Man [*holding his bicycle ready to go — angrily*]. A nest of daylight robbers ! Five shillin's each for a crumb of bread, a cup of tea, and an egg wouldn't sit tight in a thimble ! Daylight robbery !

Mrs. Flagonson [*going over to Flagonson, and prodding him in the back with her forefinger*]. Not a word, mind you, Michael.
      [*She returns to the Tavern, and disappears within it.*

Young Man [*sadly*]. Times have changed ! When Brian Boru reigned, jewels an' costly garments could be left on the hedges without a soul thinkin' of touchin' them. But now !

Young Woman. I wondher what would Brian Boru think of it if he was alive today !

Young Man [*passionately*]. Or the Fenians before him, who set honour an' thruth before comfort or safety. High hangin' to ye on a windy night, yeh bunch of in-candescent thieves !

[*The Young Man and his companion go out indignantly, neither of the two men responding in any way. Widda Machree gazes fixedly at the two men for some moments during a short silence following the departure of the two young people. During the silence, the sound of coins jingling together is heard coming from Tavern and General Stores.*

Widda Machree [*thoughtfully*]. A dangerous sound ; a sound not to be mingled with the gentle jingle of the Mass bell. Take warnin' from me, gentlemen, who lost her virtue for a few lousy coins. Yous may go smilin' through th' world, gentlemen, but yous won't go smilin' through heaven. Let yous put more value into what yous give an' less into what yous get, before it's too late.

Bull [*determinedly*]. Looka, you ; go where you're goin' with less blather. We're not in th' same category, ma'am.

Widda Machree [*after a slight pause*]. Looka, you ; if sins were written on people's foreheads, th' two of yous would pull your caps well down over your eyes !

Flagonson. Please go, ma'am ; we're reticent people, an' not interested in th' bouncing uttherance of things meant for the veiled ear of a priest.

Widda Machree. I'm goin', me lad. [*She starts on her way.*]

I've warned yous. [*The sound of clinking coins, coming from the General Stores and the Tavern, which had faded, becomes clear again.*] Aha, there's th' dangerous sound again, boys !

[*She begins to sing, and again weaves herself into a dancing movement, wheeling round on her feet, and ending the chant just as she disappears around the Tavern.*]

Widda Machree [*singing*] :
Jingle coins, jingle coins, jingle all the day.
Count them all an' wrap them up an' tuck them safe
     away.
Jingle coins, jingle on till life has pass'd away,
Then change to foolish cries of woe upon th' judgement
     day !

Flagonson. Sounds a bit suspicious to me, Bull.

Bull. Suspicious ? Didn't she tell her own story herself ? A brazen bitch, Mick, an' a desiduous one, too !

Flagonson. Committin' mortal sin, mind you, with a go-boy in a sumptuous saffron kilt an' a gay green shawl.

Bull [*solemnly*]. I always had me doubts about them laddos goin' about in kilts, Mick. On occasions of this kind, a kilt's an unpredictable garment for any man to be wearin'. [*He comes closer.*] She'll excite th' neighbours against us if she's not conthrolled. I shouldn't wondher if she was a Red !

Flagonson [*shocked*]. No, no, God forbid ! We must let the clergy know at once !

Bull [*throwing back his head for a guffaw*]. Th' clergy ! Priest-puffin island again. Not th' clergy, man, but th' polis !

[*Barney O'Hay appears round the gable-end of the General Stores, and comes down from the road to Bull. He is a man of forty-five, thin and stringy. The evidence of continual toil and ever-present anxiety shows in the lines of his face which is seamed like a man of seventy. He is dressed in an old pair of khaki trousers, a shabby tweed coat, a little too short for him, and a well-worn waistcoat. A faded bowler hat covers his head, and his boots are patched. The one bright thing about him is a white, tall collar and brown tie which are symbols connecting him with the better-off farmers. He carries a blackthorn stick. He tries to walk briskly, but his steps are stiff ; and his effort to smile cheerily but fills his face with a deeper gloom.*]

Barney [*as he comes in*]. God save th' two men !

Flagonson ⎫
Bull   ⎬ [*together — very coldly*]. You, too, O'Hay.

Barney [*coming down to Bull as briskly as he can*]. Morra, Mr. Farrell — I've great news for you, so I have.

Bull [*doubtfully*]. Huh, have you ?

Barney [*breezily*]. Ay have I ; news'll cock y'up with pride an' pleasure.
    [*Flagonson has cocked his ears, though pretending to be indifferent.*

Bull [*irritably*]. Well, out with it, if it's good news.

Barney [*almost smacking his lips because of having something to say sure to please Farrell*]. Canon Whizzer's spreadin' it all over th' disthrict about you givin' him twenty pound this mornin'. Outa modesty, says he, Misther Farrell asked me to keep it secret ; but, says he, such

devotion is a thing to be told as an example to others.
[*There is a dead silence. Seeing Bull glaring at him angrily,
Barney looks at Flagonson, only to see him glaring angrily at
Farrell. Haltingly*] I hope there's nothin' wrong.

Flagonson [*to the world in general*]. God Almighty, a man
never knows what he's shakin' hands with nowadays !
What a quare sthress I'd have been in had I gone all
out to provoke th' clergy ! You'd think deception
would have lessened its dimensions in this year of our
anno domino !
[*Mrs. Flagonson comes from the Tavern and goes over to
Flagonson.*

Mrs. Flagonson [*prodding Flagonson with her forefinger in the
back*]. Come, Michael, help feed th' chickens.
[*She returns to the Tavern, and Flagonson follows her
meekly.*

Flagonson [*half to himself and half to the world — as he goes
into the Tavern*]. An' he only afther condemnin' a poor,
decent woman for simply makin' a mistake ! [*He
throws his head backwards, and gives a loud, mocking
guffaw.*] Priest-puffin island ! D'ye get me, Mr. Bull
Farrell !

Bull [*roughly and loudly to Barney*]. Well, what d'ye want,
blatherer ?

Barney [*frightened*]. I just came to get th' bag o' phosphates
from you.

Bull. When you plank down a tenner of what you owe,
you'll get it.

Barney [*half wailing*]. I couldn't, I couldn't, Misther
Farrell.

Bull. You couldn't, you couldn't ! You sold your pigs, didn't you ?

Barney [*plaintively*]. Ah, sir, for next to nothin'. Th' kitchen leavin's I collected didn't make them prime. Th' slovenly bitches round here put tea-leaves, cabbage stalks, an' orange peel into it. How could any animal fatten itself on that stuff ?

Bull. Gimme th' ten pounds you got for them, an' I'll let you have th' phosphate.

Barney. It was th' same with me acre o' hay — th' drouth banished all th' good out of it ; an' th' acre o' spuds was mostly smalleens. I can't give th' tenner at once, sir.

Bull [*almost shouting*]. Then get to hell outa here, then, if you can't !

    [*He turns away, goes into Stores, comes back to the door, where he stands, sourly smoking his pipe.*

    [*Barney goes back, abashed, to lean against the wall of the Stores, disconsolate.*

    [*Conroy and Cousins come in from the Tavern end ; Conroy briskly, Cousins more slowly, a harassed look on his face. Conroy is middle-aged, Cousins about thirty years old. Conroy a man of a hundred and fifty acres, Cousins a man of twenty acres. Conroy wears cord breeches, Cousins corduroy ones ; Conroy brown leggings, Cousins black ones, soiled with cow-dung ; Conroy wears a sparkling bowler hat, Cousins a rumpled tweed hat. Both wear coats of dark-coloured cloth, and both carry sticks : Conroy's a fine, thick malacca cane, Cousins' a blackthorn. They come to the table.*

Cousins [*following Conroy in*]. I just couldn't, Misther Conroy ; I've taken fifteen pounds off already.

They're fine beasts either for milkin' or beef; all-round animals, an' worth every penny of me first askin'.

Conroy [*turning to look at Cousins pitifully*]. None o' them would win a fourth prize at a thin-stock show, man. I know a beast when I see one. It'll take an age of feedin' before them beasts is the kinda cattle you're dhreamin' they are.

> [*Bull, becoming interested in the bargaining, comes out from the door, and listens intently. Barney O'Hay gradually straightens up from the wall, and becomes interested too.*

Cousins. You prodded them with your stick till your arm ached, an' couldn't make a dint. A healthy herd they come from. There's growin' goodness in them beasts, I'm tellin' you.

Conroy [*laying a caressing hand on Cousins' arm*]. Looka here, Cousins, I'm only thryin' to do a neighbour a good turn. I really don't want your beasts; they'll only be in th' way. Don't be too graspin', man! Here, take off another five pounds, an' I'll allow them to be mine.

Cousins [*shaking off Conroy's arm — indignantly*]. Five pounds, is it? I'll dhrive them home first! [*He makes to go off, and reaches the road, where he pauses.*] Is that your final offer, Misther Conroy?

Conroy [*up to him*]. Here, then — four pounds off: that, or nothin'!

Cousins [*coming back again*]. Here, I'll split that as a favour — two off, an' that's me final word.

Conroy. Three, then. Is it a bargain? If not, I'm done. [*He holds a hand out to Cousins.*] Come on, man; put your hand there!

Cousins. Two ten, or nothin'. Here, two fifteen, then. Nothin' fairer. [*He holds a hand out.*] Before I go!

Conroy [*bringing his hand down on Cousins' with a loud smack*]. Done! A dhrink for th' two of us. [*He raps on the table with his stick.*] Flagonson! Two whiskies!
　　[*Flagonson brings out the drinks and leaves them on the table. Conroy and Cousins take them up to drink when Kelly from the Isle of Mananaun comes round by way of the Tavern. He is tall and straight. He wears a saffron kilt and a green shawl is draped from a shoulder. A black balmoral hat, with a green feather sticking up from it, covers his head. A silver pin-brooch shines in his shawl. His face is pale and grave-looking, though occasionally showing a satirical line in it. He halts on the road, and looks towards the men.*]

Kelly [*down to the men*]. Did any of yous, by any chance, see a fine lady pass by? A lady with a fair face, gathered in a little with grief, but with ne'er a hint o' guile in it?

Flagonson [*with a wave of the hand — to Kelly*]. Go away, go away, we're busy people here.

Kelly [*musingly, as if to himself*]. A mortal sin torments my coming in and my going out; a mortal sin and a mean one. [*To the men*] Gentlemen, I must find the lady, and get back my good name.

Flagonson [*impatiently — with an angrier wave of his hand*]. Go away, man; we're busy people here, I'm tellin' you!

Kelly. So I see; all bent down over the thought of gain. [*A pause.*] Yous are all very close to hell now, gentlemen. Take warnin' be me who gave too little for what I got.

Cousins [*quickly*]. You bet th' poor lady's price down too low ?

Kelly. No, no ; I gave her what she asked, but she asked too little for what she gave.

Cousins [*excited*]. Didja hear that, Misther Conroy ? He didn't give th' lady a fair price. A mortal sin — there's sense in that, now.

Conroy [*fiercely* — *to Cousins*]. Sense in it, you fool, because it suits yourself.

Cousins. Th' gentleman's right — I didn't get half o' what I gave was worth.

Kelly. It's a curse on us all, brother : givin' too little for what we get.

Conroy [*angrily* — *to Kelly*]. You must be th' boyo who th' Sergeant told me was spreadin' ideas about incitin' to discontentation everywhere. I can tell you, th' polis'll soon be on your tail !

Flagonson [*to Kelly*]. Who are you, anyway ? No-one even knows your name.

Kelly [*doing the dance the Widda did, but turning round the reverse way — lilting*] :

> Th' name I'm called is Kelly,
> K ee double ell y ;
> Th' name I'm called is Kelly,
> Kelly from the Isle of Mananaun !

Go on, gentlemen, with your gettin' of gain while the great big world keeps turnin'.

Conroy [*jeeringly*]. G'wan, you, an' find your lady, an' cuddle her into agreein' with your curious theologicality.

Bull [*maliciously*]. Lady is it ? Seems like she's a one would settle down in a ditch with a donor.

Kelly [*calmly*]. Aha, so you've bad minds along with th' love of gain. You thry to pin on others th' dirty decorations that may be hangin' on your own coats. [*He points, one after the other at Conroy, Bull, and Flagonson. Lilting :*]
Who were you with last night ?
Who were you with last night ?
Will you tell your missus when you go home
Who you were with last night ?

Flagonson [*in anguished indignation*]. This is more than a hurt to us : this hits at the decency of the whole nation !

Kelly [*pointing his forefinger straight at Conroy*]. Do you go to Mass ?

Conroy [*spluttering*]. Do I go to Mass ? Of course I go to Mass, sir !

Kelly. An' don't you feel odd an' outa place there, thinking of gains in the week gone, and th' gains of th' week to come ?

Conroy. Me outa place there ! What th' hell d'ye mean, man ?

Barney [*bursting out from his somewhat obscure corner, and standing forth to confront Kelly*]. I'll not stand here to hear Misther Conroy insulted ! I'll have you know Misther Conroy's chairman of the Catholic Young Men's Society ; that Misther Conroy's name's down for th' medal of St. Silvesther ; that Misther Conroy's a Grand Knight of St. Columbanus ; an' that Misther

Conroy's a particular friend of Monsignor Moymelligan's !

Kelly. Aha, but is Misther Conroy a particular friend of th' saints ?

Conroy [*furiously*]. I'm not goin' to stand here an' see th' saints insulted ; an' I'll not stand here, either, to listen to your unannounceable mystheries that would shear all companionable manners from our business consortations !

Cousins [*soothingly*]. Aysey, Misther Conroy ; aysey !

Conroy [*raging*]. Good God, what are we payin' the Civic Guards for ! Where are th' loafers hidin' ? Is a man like me to be hunted into an indetermination rage by th' unsponsored, pseudo religiosity of a kilted bum ! I'll soon put th' law on his heels ! [*He rushes on to the road past Kelly, then turns to face him.*] You musta come from some quare place, I'm thinkin', to be makin' a mock of all the things we hold so sacred. I'll settle you !

   [*He makes to rush off behind the Tavern. Kelly points a
     forefinger towards his back, and emits a sharp, short
     whistle, and Conroy suddenly stops dead in his rush,
     and stands stiff, one leg stretched out before the other,
     having stopped in the act of finishing a step forward. The
     others look on with amazement and some alarm.*]

Kelly [*down to the surprised men — somewhat humorously*]. See ? A pointing finger can stop him in his stride. As long as it points, he stays put. But a stretched arm would soon grow tired, so I'll send him off on his errand of mercy.

   [*He again emits a short, sharp whistle, lowers his arm, and
     Conroy resumes his rush, apparently unaware of what*

has happened.   The others, a little frightened, draw
gradually away from Kelly, towards the protection of the
houses — Flagonson and Cousins to the Tavern, and
Bull and Barney towards the General Stores, till they
are half hidden standing in the entrance to each.

Kelly. Don't be slinkin' off like as if yous had murdhered
Nellie O'Flaherty's beautiful dhrake.   [*The clink of
coins is heard again in Tavern and Stores.*]   Aha, that's
how th' harp o' Tara sounds today !   What's it
playin' ?   [*The tune of " Jingle Bells " is softly heard.*]
I am in my sleep, an' don't waken me.   A signature
song !   [*Going slowly away behind the General Stores,
lilting as he crosses :*]
Jingle coins, jingle coins, jingle all th' day,
Jingle them at night again, for coins have come to stay.
Jingle coins till silent Death comes in his frozen sleigh
To gather yous an' all your coins, an' jingle yous away !
   [*He disappears around the back of the General Stores.   The
   rest, by this time, are hidden within Tavern and Stores,
   their heads only peeping out around the jambs of the
   doorways.*

Flagonson [*peeping out from behind the door*].   Is he gone ?

Cousins [*coming out a little way from the Tavern door*].   Yis.
No sign of him now.

Bull [*coming out of the Stores*].   We should have faced him
out ;   should've stood up to him ;   defied him.   We're
not worums !

Flagonson [*decisively*].   No, Bull, no.   There was magic in
that figure, man.   When he pointed at me and asked
me who I was with last night, I felt it slippin' up an'
down me spine.

Cousins [*timidly*]. All th' same, he said one thing worth thinkin' of when he told us it was a mortal sin to give too little for a thing you're buyin'.

Barney [*assertively*]. Misther Conroy was right ; he musta come from some quare place, for to bring in th' topic of religion outa hours shows a quare mind. [*He suddenly listens.*] I hear a step. Someone's comin' again.

> [*They all make for Tavern and Stores, and try to peep round the doorways towards the road. The Sergeant comes stealthily in along the road, looking fearfully to right and left. He comes down till he is close to the Tavern.*

Sergeant [*in towards the Tavern — in a loud whisper*]. Misther Farrell, are yous there ? [*He hurries across to the Stores, and whispers towards the door.*] Misther Flagonson, are yous there ?

> [*The four men, affected by the stealthiness of the Sergeant, become stealthy too. They come out of Tavern and Stores to gather round him, heads bent inwards towards each other, and shoulders crouched low.*

Flagonson. What is it, Sergeant ? What has you goin' about gathered up like a cod in a pot ?

Sergeant [*warningly*]. Hush ! Thry to feel unconscious of all wrong-doin'. Thry to look, not like the gaums yous are, but like innocent ones.

Bull [*impatiently*]. What sorta talk's this, Sergeant ?

Sergeant. Hush, I'm sayin'. Not so loud. Th' west's asleep. Th' Inspector says to me, Killdooey, he says, find out th' antecedents of th' person.

Flagonson. Ah, the antecedents.

Sergeant. An' no names mentioned, Sergeant, says he, for identification might prove dangerous. [*He suddenly looks down at each arm.*] Now which is me right arm an' which is me left one ?

Bull [*indicating it*]. That's your right one. Godamit, man, don't you know one arm from t'other yet ?

Sergeant [*not noticing Bull's remark*]. Folly it up to Carlow, he says.

Barney. Folly what up to Carlow, man ?

Sergeant [*whispering low*]. Th' person, sir. Folly th' person, says th' Inspector, even if th' person goes up to Carlow.

Cousins. We don't get th' dhrift of what you're dhrivin' at, Sergeant.

Sergeant [*seizing Flagonson by the arm*]. Looka, Bull Farrell, I love a lassie. D'ye know ?

Flagonson [*bewildered*]. Yis, yis, I know.

Sergeant [*lilting*] :
        A bonnie Hielan' lassie :
    [*In a loud and positive burst of song :*]
        She's as pure as th' lily in th' dell !

Flagonson. Yis, yis, you can tell us about that again. What's throublin' us is what's throublin' you ?

Sergeant [*dreamily*]. Ay, ay ; it's th' person who's goin' about dividin' th' people into fightin' over what th' person says.

Cousins [*impatiently*]. An' what, in God's name, is th' person actually sayin', Sergeant ?

Sergeant [*dreamily*]. Th' person's in th' throes of a mortal sin for sellin' a cow to someone, an' askin' too much for it, so th' person's sayin' ask less than you'd like to get for a thing you're sellin'.

Cousins [*indignantly*]. No, no ; that's against all law an' livability ! Where's th' freedom our poor boys died to get, if a body daren't ask for what he wants for a thing he's sellin' ? You're mixin' things up, Sergeant ; th' kilted person passin' here said th' very opposite !

Sergeant. Th' skirted person, you mean ?

Cousins. Th' kilted person, I'm sayin'.

Flagonson [*excitedly*]. We forgot th' first one !

Sergeant. Which first one, what first one ?

Flagonson. A person opposin' in appearance th' person we have in mind now.

Sergeant [*putting a hand to his brow to help in very deep thought*]. Then th' person has two presenceses. [*He pauses, then stretches out his right arm in front of him.*] We'll get to th' bottom of it, sure's this is me left arm !

Barney [*in a whisper — to Bull*]. Is he dhrunk or what ? [*Barney has been watching the Sergeant for some time with intensity, and now moves very gradually away from the group, keeping still a watch on the Sergeant.*

Sergeant [*dreamily*]. Comin' through th' rye to here, I felt shaky. I thried to whistle, but no sound came to me assistance. I sucked in an' I blew out, but ne'er a single sound came to me assistance. [*He puts his face close to Bull's, and whispers*] Looka, Inspector, I feel like — what do I feel like ? I feel like th' man who

sthruck O'Hara ! [*He takes his face away from Bull's,
and begins to sing, accompanying, at first, with so sudden a
sway that the others (except Barney) catch hold of him and
are forced to join in the movement. The Sergeant goes on
accompanying the words with the movements which the words
seem to suggest (at times, somewhat violent), and those
clinging to him are forced to move with him. Singing and
carrying on mime movements :*]

First we mopp'd th' floor with him,
Dragg'd him up an' down th' stairs ;

Then we had another go, undher tables, over chairs.
Such a sight you never saw —
Before he'd time to say his prayers,

Rags an' bones were all we left
Of th' man who sthruck O'Hara !

Barney [*shrinking back towards the Stores*]. God Almighty, th'
fella's touched !

Flagonson [*agonised*]. Aw, pull yourself together, Sergeant !
[*The Sergeant, with an effort, straightens himself as if
for parade. Outside, the voice of Widda Machree is
heard lilting quietly the chorus of " I Know Where I'm
Goin' ".*]

Widda Machree [*lilting, outside*] :
              I know where I'm goin',
              And I know who's goin' with me ;
              I know who I love,
              But th' dear knows who I'll marry !
       [*Widda Machree comes in from the back of the General
       Stores. The men sense her presence, and stand tense in a
       semicircle together, their backs to the road along which
       the Widda is walking. She looks down towards them.*

Just as she comes in, the Sergeant wilts away again, crouching and tense as the rest are.

Bull [*in a whisper — to the Sergeant*]. Now or never, Sergeant, thry to pull yourself together !

Widda Machree. God save yous all. I feel me journey's endin'. [*She lilts and wheels around in a kind of dance :*]
             Has anybody here seen Kelly ?
             Kay ee double ell y ;
             Has anybody here seen Kelly ?
             Kelly from th' Isle of Mananaun !
[*Down to the men*] Have yous seen a spirit, or what, yous are so silent ?   Have yous no music in yous save the din of the market-place ?

Bull [*whispering passionately to the Sergeant*]. Now, Sergeant, up, an' answer her !

Widda Machree. No picture in your minds but a warrant for an arrest, or a bill demandin' pay for goods delivered ?

Sergeant [*in a whisper to Bull*]. I have to wait for reinforce-ments !

Widda Machree. You is neither fit for heaven nor to take th' floor at Phil the Fluther's Ball ! [*From around the back of the Stores, opposite to where the Widda Machree stands, Kelly comes. He halts when he sees her, and both gaze silently at each other for some moments. Then each holds out arms to the other as they come close.*] My brother !

Kelly. My sisther ! [*Offering her a purse*] Take all I kept from you ; and take th' cow back, too, for I gave less than I should when I was buying.

Widda Machree [*offering him a purse*]. Take back all you

gave, an' keep th' cow, for I asked more than I should
when I was sellin'.

Kelly
Widda Machree } [*together*]. Forgive !

[*They enter into each other's arms.*

Kelly. More than sisther !

Widda Machree. More than brother !
     [*A blast from a police whistle is heard ; the Sergeant leaps
     to life, and Conroy, followed by two Civic Guards,
     rushes in, the 1st Civic Guard still blowing his whistle.
     They halt for a second when they see the two embracing,
     and look on for a second.*

Conroy [*excitedly*]. There they are — the ruffians !   Sur-
round them ; hold them tight !

1st C. Guard [*waving papers in the air*]. We've got th'
warrants indictin' them for breaches of th' peace.

2nd C. Guard [*waving papers in the air*]. An' a full-blown
certificate from Doctor Simples showin' neither of
them non compos mentis.

Flagonson }   Handcuff them !

Bull   } [*in unison*] Put them behind bars at once.

Barney   }   Solitary confinement for th' pair o' them.

Cousins   }   Yis, yis ; th' sight of them unsettles us.
     [*Widda Machree and Kelly are handcuffed, the Sergeant and
     the 1st Civic Guard placing themselves beside Kelly,
     while the 2nd Civic Guard takes charge of Widda
     Machree.*

Conroy. Go on, Sergeant, dhrag them off before we hear

more of their lies, one sayin' " Give more when you're buyin' ' ", an' th' other sayin' " Ask less when you're sellin' ' ".

Kelly [*to Conroy*]. Th' sayin's, sir, are but two sides of the same thruth.

Conroy [*angrily*]. Will you take away th' deludherin' louser, Sergeant, an' not be lettin' him go on talkin' !

Kelly [*pointing to the blasted trees*]. Soon yous'll all be no more than are these two barren, deadened trees. Then when yous are silent stiffs, others will count your coins.

Sergeant [*laying a hand on Kelly's shoulder*]. Come on, me man, to where you'll be cured into seein' things as we all see them.

2nd C. Guard [*laying a hand on Widda Machree's shoulder*]. An' you, me woman, come along to where your poor mind'll be mended.

Kelly [*to Widda Machree*]. It is time to go, sisther.

Widda Machree [*to Kelly*]. It is time to go, brother.

Kelly [*embracing and kissing her*]. Goodbye, fair sweetheart.

Widda Machree [*kissing him*]. Goodbye, my love.
  [*The Sergeant, followed by the 1st Civic Guard, leads out Kelly by way of the Stores ; the 2nd Civic Guard leads out Widda Machree by way of the Tavern. As they go, Kelly and the Widda Machree perform their wheeling dance they did before, while Kelly says his last farewell, and Widda Machree says hers.*

Kelly [*wheeling quietly in his semi-dance, as he goes out*] :
        Goodbye to holy souls left here,
        Goodbye to man an' fairy ;

Widda Machree [*wheeling quietly in her semi-dance as she goes out*] :

> Goodbye to all of Leicester Square,
> An' th' long way to Tipperary.

Conroy [*taking off his hat and mopping his head with a big handkerchief*]. What a dispicable pair ! Thank th' holy saints that that danger's past. [*To Cousins*] Now let us settle up in peace.

> [*He takes a wallet from his pocket, is about to open it, when he cocks an ear to listen.*
>
> [*The tune of " Jingle Coins ", accompanied by voices singing the words, is heard, sung and played softly, as if coming from a great distance.*

Voices [*with accompaniment*] :

Jingle coins, jingle coins, jingle all the day,
Jingle them at night again, for coins have come to stay.
Jingle them till silent Death comes in his frozen sleigh
To gather you and all your coins, and jingle yous away !

Conroy. Is that th' sound of singin' somewhere I hear ?

Cousins. Yis ; seems to be something familiar.

Bull. The Civic Guards cod-actin' in th' barracks down th' road.

> [*Conroy opens his wallet as he stands by the table, and is about to count out notes, when the Sergeant and 1st Civic Guard rush in from behind the Stores. They are in a great state of excitement.*

Sergeant [*to the others — breathless*]. Did he go this way ? We seen him flash by here. Are yous dumb ? Answer !

Conroy. Who, who, man ?

Sergeant. Kelly from th' Isle of Mananaun. Just slid out o' th' handcuffs, out of our hold, an' was gone !
[*The 2nd Civic Guard rushes in, panic-stricken, from around the Tavern.*

2nd C. Guard [*hysterically*]. Did she go this way ? I seen her flashin' by. Goddamnit, answer !

Conroy. Who, who, man ?

2nd C. Guard. Th' lady, th' hussy. Just slid outa me grip, an' was gone !

Conroy [*with a furious shout*]. Then go afther them an' get them, you blasted fools !
[*The Sergeant and the 1st Civic Guard rush out in one direction, the 2nd Civic Guard in the other.*
[*The tune of "Jingle Coins" played on trumpet and drum becomes loud and clear now, and all stand tensely to listen. The two barren trees in the background suddenly flush with blossom, foliage, and illuminated fruit.*

Bull [*listening*]. They're mockin' us in some place or another ; in some place unknown.

Cousins [*excitedly pointing to the trees*]. Look, looka th' threes !

Barney [*falling on his knees*]. Jayayus, a miracle !

Cousins [*falling on his knees*]. They musta been saints !
[*Bull and Flagonson now fall on their knees, too, and all face towards the glowing trees.*
[*After a few moments, Mrs. Flagonson appears at the Tavern door, goes over to Flagonson, taking no notice of what has happened, and prods her husband in the back with her forefinger.*
[*The glowing trees begin to fade as soon as Mrs. Flagonson prods her husband in the back.*

Mrs. Flagonson [*prodding her husband*]. Come in, Michael, an' help me tot up th' takin's.

> [*Without a word, Flagonson gets up and follows his wife into the Tavern, and the glowing trees fade away utterly, becoming dead and barren again. The others rise a few moments afterwards, stand still for a second or so, then look sheepishly at each other.*

Conroy [*roughly to Cousins*]. Come on in, an' let's settle up in quietness for th' scrawls o' cattle I was a fool to buy.   [*He goes into the Tavern.*

Bull [*to Barney*]. No use o' you stayin' here. Bring me th' tenner, or you'll get no phosphate from me.

> [*He goes into the Stores.*

> [*Barney turns slowly away and makes for the road to go home, and on the way out Cousins stops him with a question.*

Cousins [*to the dejected Barney*]. Didja see anything, Mr. O'Hay ? I wondher what was it I seen ?

Barney. If I seen anything, an' if you seen anything, what was seen was only an halleelucination !

> [*He goes dejectedly on his way, and Cousins goes slowly into the Tavern.*

END OF THE PLAY

HAS ANYBODY HERE SEEN KELLY?

Has an-y-bo-dy here seen Kel - ly?

Kay ee dou-ble ell y; has an-y-bo-dy here seen

Kel - ly? Kel-ly from the Isle of Man - an - aun.

JINGLE COINS, JINGLE COINS

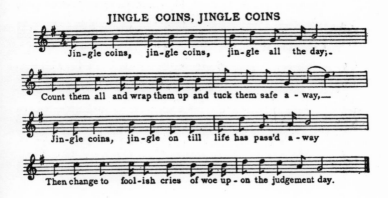

Jin-gle coins, jin-gle coins, jin-gle all the day;.

Count them all and wrap them up and tuck them safe a - way,—

Jin-gle coins, jin-gle on till life has pass'd a-way

Then change to fool-ish cries of woe up - on the judgement day.

WHO WERE YOU WITH LAST NIGHT

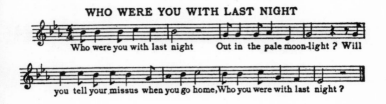

Who were you with last night Out in the pale moon-light ? Will

you tell your missus when you go home, Who you were with last night ?

I LOVE A LASSIE

I love a lass-ie, a bon-nie Hie-lan' las-sie, she's as
pure. as the li - ly in the dell.

THE MAN WHO STRUCK O'HARA

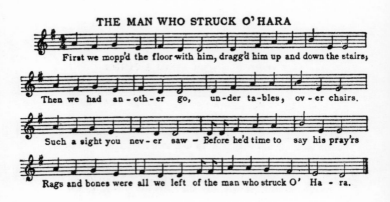

First we mopp'd the floor with him, dragg'd him up and down the stairs;
Then we had an - oth - er go, un-der ta-bles, ov - er chairs.
Such a sight you nev - er saw — Before he'd time to say his pray'rs
Rags and bones were all we left of the man who struck O' Ha - ra.

I KNOW WHERE I'M GOING

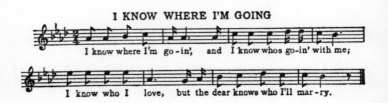

I know where I'm go - in', and I know whos go-in' with me;
I know who I love, but the dear knows who I'll mar - ry.

THE END